FROM NURSERY
RHYMES TO
NATIONHOOD

Children's Literature and Culture
Jack Zipes, Series Editor

Children's Literature Comes of Age
Toward a New Aesthetic
by Maria Nikolajeva

Sparing the Child
Grief and the Unspeakable in Youth
Literature
About Nazism and the Holocaust
by Hamida Bosmajian

Rediscoveries in Children's Literature
by Suzanne Rahn

Inventing the Child
Culture, Ideology, and the Story of Childhood
by Joseph L. Zornado

Regendering the School Story
Sassy Sissies and Tattling Tomboys
by Beverly Lyon Clark

A Necessary Fantasy?
The Heroic Figure in Children's Popular
Culture
edited by Dudley Jones and Tony Watkins

White Supremacy in Children's Literature
Characterizations of African Americans,
1830–1900
by Donnarae MacCann

Ways of Being Male
Representing Masculinities in Children's
Literature and Film
by John Stephens

Retelling Stories, Framing Culture
Traditional Story and Metanarratives in
Children's Literature
by John Stephens and Robyn McCallum

Pinocchio Goes Postmodern
Perils of a Puppet in the United States
by Richard Wunderlich and Thomas J.
Morrissey

Little Women and the Feminist Imagination
Criticism, Controversy, Personal Essays
edited by Janice M. Alberghene and Beverly
Lyon Clark

The Presence of the Past
Memory, Heritage, and Childhood in Postwar
Britain
by Valerie Krips

The Case of Peter Rabbit
Changing Conditions of Literature for
Children
by Margaret Mackey

The Feminine Subject in Children's
Literature
by Christine Wilkie-Stibbs

Ideologies of Identity in Adolescent Fiction
by Robyn McCallum

Recycling Red Riding Hood
by Sandra Beckett

The Poetics of Childhood
by Roni Natov

Voices of the Other
Children's Literature and the Postcolonial
Context
edited by Roderick McGillis

Narrating Africa
George Henty and the Fiction of Empire
by Mawuena Kossi Logan

Reimagining Shakespeare for Children and
Young Adults
edited by Naomi J. Miller

Representing the Holocaust in Youth
Literature
by Lydia Kokkola

Translating for Children
by Riitta Oittinen

Beatrix Potter
Writing in Code
by M. Daphne Kutzer

Children's Films
History, Ideology, Pedagogy, Theory
by Ian Wojcik-Andrews

Utopian and Dystopian Writing for
Children and Young Adults
edited by Carrie Hintz and Elaine Ostry

Transcending Boundaries
Writing for a Dual Audience of Children and
Adults
edited by Sandra L. Beckett

The Making of the Modern Child
Children's Literature and Childhood in the
Late Eighteenth Century
by Andrew O'Malley

How Picturebooks Work
by Maria Nikolajeva and Carole Scott

Brown Gold
Milestones of African American Children's Picture Books, 1845–2002
by Michelle H. Martin

Russell Hoban/Forty Years
Essays on His Writing for Children
by Alida Allison

Apartheid and Racism in South African Children's Literature
by Donnarae MacCann and Amadu Maddy

Empire's Children
Empire and Imperialism in Classic British Children's Books
by M. Daphne Kutzer

Constructing the Canon of Children's Literature
Beyond Library Walls and Ivory Towers
by Anne Lundin

Youth of Darkest England
Working Class Children at the Heart of Victorian Empire
by Troy Boone

Ursula K. Le Guin Beyond Genre
Literature for Children and Adults
by Mike Cadden

Twice-Told Children's Tales
edited by Betty Greenway

Diana Wynne Jones
The Fantastic Tradition and Children's Literature
by Farah Mendlesohn

Childhood and Children's Books in Early Modern Europe, 1550–1800
edited by Andrea Immel and Michael Witmore

Voracious Children
Who Eats Whom in Children's Literature
by Carolyn Daniel

National Character in South African Children's Literature
by Elwyn Jenkins

Myth, Symbol, and Meaning in *Mary Poppins*
The Governess as Provocateur
by Georgia Grilli

A Critical History of French Children's Literature
by Penny Brown

The Gothic in Children's Literature
Haunting the Borders
Edited by Anna Jackson, Karen Coats, and Roderick McGillis

Reading Victorian Schoolrooms
Childhood and Education in Nineteenth-Century Fiction
by Elizabeth Gargano

Soon Come Home to This Island
West Indians in British Children's Literature
by Karen Sands-O'Connor

Boys in Children's Literature and Popular Culture
Masculinity, Abjection, and the Fictional Child
by Annette Wannamaker

Into the Closet
Cross-dressing and the Gendered Body in Children's Literature
by Victoria Flanagan

Russian Children's Literature and Culture
edited by Marina Balina and Larissa Rudova

The Outside Child In and Out of the Book
by Christine Wilkie-Stibbs

Representing Africa in Children's Literature
Old and New Ways of Seeing
by Vivian Yenika-Agbaw

The Fantasy of Family
Nineteenth-Century Children's Literature and the Myth of the Domestic Ideal
by Liz Thiel

From Nursery Rhymes to Nationhood
Children's Literature and the Construction of Canadian Identity
by Elizabeth A. Galway

FROM NURSERY RHYMES TO
NATIONHOOD

Children's Literature and the
Construction of Canadian Identity

E L I Z A B E T H A . G A L W A Y

Routledge
Taylor & Francis Group

NEW YORK AND LONDON

First published 2008
by Routledge
270 Madison Ave, New York, NY 10016

Simultaneously published in the UK
by Routledge
2 Park Square, Milton Park, Abingdon, Oxon OX14 4RN

Routledge is an imprint of the Taylor & Francis Group, an informa business

© 2008 Taylor & Francis

Typeset in Minion by
Swales & Willis Ltd, Exeter, Devon

Printed and bound in the United States of America on acid-free paper by
Sheridan Books, Inc.

Library of Congress Cataloging in Publication Data
Galway, Elizabeth A., 1974–
 From nursery rhymes to nationhood : children's literature and the
construction of Canadian identity / by Elizabeth A. Galway.
  p. cm. — (Children's literature and culture ; 52)
  Includes bibliographical references and index.
 1. Children's literature, Canadian—History and criticism. 2. National
characteristics, Canadian, in literature. 3. Literature and society—Canada—
History. 4. Group identity—Canada. I. Title.
PR9193.9.G35 2008
810.9′92820971—dc22   2007038242

ISBN10: 0–415–95848–2 (hbk)
ISBN10: 0–203–92927–6 (ebk)

ISBN13: 978–0–415–95848–6 (hbk)
ISBN13: 978–0–203–92927–8 (ebk)

AUGUST, 1902

THE
CANADIAN
BOY

A MAGAZINE
FOR
Young Canada

BRIGHT

PATRIOTIC

HELPFUL

ENTERTAINING

The Canadian Boy Pub. Co.,
Shallow Lake, Ont.

10 cents a Copy. $1.00 Per Year.

Contents

Series Editor's Foreword   xi

Acknowledgments   xiii

Introduction: From Nursery Rhymes to Nationhood   1

Chapter 1   The View from Afar: British and American Perspectives   13

Chapter 2   Forest, Prairie, Sea, and Mountain: Canadian Regionalism   33

Chapter 3   A Question of Loyalties: Britain and Canada   43

Chapter 4   Due South: America and Canada   65

Chapter 5   Sleeping with the Enemy?: The Figure of the French
Canadian   79

Chapter 6   Flint and Feather: The Figure of the Indian   95

Chapter 7   Fact or Fiction?: The Making of Canadian History   115

Chapter 8   "The True North Strong and Free": Landscape and
Environment   145

Conclusion   173

Notes   179

Selected Bibliography   185

Index   193

Series Editor's Foreword

Dedicated to furthering original research in children's literature and culture, the Children's Literature and Culture series includes monographs on individual authors and illustrators, historical examinations of different periods, literary analyses of genres, and comparative studies on literature and the mass media. The series is international in scope and is intended to encourage innovative research in children's literature with a focus on interdisciplinary methodology.

Children's literature and culture are understood in the broadest sense of the term 'children' to encompass the period of childhood up through adolescence. Owing to the fact that the notion of childhood has changed so much since the origination of children's literature, this Routledge series is particularly concerned with transformations in children's culture and how they have affected the representation and socialisation of children. While the emphasis of the series is on children's literature, all types of studies that deal with children's radio, film, television, and art are included in an endeavor to grasp the aesthetics and values of children's culture. Not only have there been momentous changes in children's culture in the last fifty years, but there have been radical shifts in the scholarship that deals with these changes. In this regard, the goal of the Children's Literature and Culture series is to enhance research in this field and, at the same time, point to new directions that bring together the best scholarly work throughout the world.

Jack Zipes

Acknowledgments

I would like to thank the following people for their support and assistance in the production of this book: the late Chris Brooks, Regenia Gagnier, Philippa Gates, Kevin Howey, Eileen Margerum, Kevin McGeough, Roderick McGillis, and Tony Simoes Da Silva. Thanks are also due to the Department of English at the University of Exeter for providing me with funding that enabled me to undertake much of the research necessary for this study. I would also like to thank the staff at the Lillian H. Smith branch of the Toronto Public Library for always being so helpful and generous with their time. Acknowledgement must also be made of the resources provided by the British Library, the University of Toronto Libraries, the Canadian Institute for Historical Microreproductions, and the Metropolitan Toronto Reference Library. I would also like to acknowledge that I have used some of the material in this book by permission of the *Victorians Institute Journal*, *Short Story*, and *Canadian Children's Literature*.

Special thanks are due to Angelique Richardson at the University of Exeter. I greatly appreciate her advice, guidance, and enthusiasm for this project, along with her generosity of time and spirit. I would also like to give thanks to everyone at Routledge who has helped with the production of this manuscript, including Max Novick, Erica Wetter, Jack Zipes, Liz Levine, and Frederick Veith. I would also like to express my appreciation for the work done by Ellie Rivers and Swales and Willis Ltd. I must also acknowledge the support I have received from my family, including Fred D'Onofrio, and express my heartfelt thanks to my sisters, and to my parents, for their unfailing love and support. Their encouragement and unparalleled generosity have made this work possible.

Introduction
From Nursery Rhymes to Nationhood

On July 1, 1867, England's parliament passed the British North America Act, marking the official birth of Canadian Confederation. Canada has subsequently undergone changes in size, population, and political leadership. Yet many of the country's identifying features and concerns that were prominent at the time of Confederation remain of importance nearly a century and a half later. It was in the decades following the initial union of the first provinces that the concepts of Canadian nationhood and national identity began to flourish. Between the time of Confederation and the first decade of the twentieth century Canadians were coming to terms with their country's new role as an independent nation, and striving to reconcile the lingering demands of imperial union with the increasingly unique needs and aspirations of Canada itself. While these struggles and challenges were apparent in the political debates and economic policies of the time, the various ideological tensions that operated within Canada following Confederation also influenced the country's cultural expressions through art, music, and literature.

The Development of Canadian Literature

Following Confederation, literature became an important tool by which to secure loyalty to the new nation. The influence literature could have on the "national spirit" was apprehended, if imperfectly, by politicians and writers alike (Bailey 1972: 59). As Carole Gerson has observed: "The motives underpinning the position that English Canada required an indigenous literature could be political or moral or both; taken for granted was the notion that one of the primary purposes of a national literature was the fostering of patriotism" (36). There is evidence of this in the literature from nineteenth-century Canada, which frequently demonstrates that many writers were keenly aware of the relationship between literature and nation building.

1

In spite of this fact, critics have tended to overlook evidence of a distinctly Canadian sense of identity and independence that was finding expression from the late-nineteenth century onwards. This is partly a result of the fact that much of the literature produced in Canada between 1867 and 1914 clearly reflects the importance of the lingering ties to Britain, and is overtly imperialistic. Consequently, critics have tended to view the arrival of a truly national literature as a phenomenon of the twentieth century that flowered after the First World War. The literature written prior to this is often dismissed as inconsequential and derivative, or, at the very least, early works that are distinctly Canadian are considered to have been few and far between. Furthermore, because critics have been primarily concerned with identifying when a national literature of *quality* emerged in Canada—a highly subjective exercise—many have overlooked the significance of much of the nation's early writing.

In the face of nineteenth-century imperial fervour many works of distinctly Canadian tone and content have gone unobserved by those concerned with the country's literary history. T.D. MacLulich argues that in nineteenth-century Canada, "writers did not show the urge towards national self-definition that is so evident in their American counterparts" (1988: 20). Despite such claims, the fact remains that there are many works of Canadian literature from the nineteenth century that demonstrate an early effort to articulate the nation's individuality through the written word. While one cannot ignore the imperialistic tone that characterises a great deal of early Anglophone Canadian writing, at the same time, much of this literature contains expressions of various notions of Canadian nationhood, independence, and national identity.

As historian Hans Kohn has observed, "Nationalities are the products of the living forces of history, and therefore are fluctuating and never rigid. They are groups of the utmost complexity and defy exact definition" (1955: 9). This complexity is evident in Canada's early expressions of national identity. While there are a few key elements that early writers identified with Canada, many works from the post-Confederation period offer competing definitions and visions of the Canadian national identity. In spite of these sometimes contradictory views, however, what is evident is the feeling on the part of many writers that Canada is a distinct nation with its own unique needs, achievements, and aspirations.

Writers and literary critics of this era, and even some savvy politicians, regarded Canadian literature as a powerful tool to be used to help build the nation. In 1887, for example, Hunter, Rose and Co. published Thomas Frederick Young's collection of poetry *Canada, and Other Poems*. The work's preface outlines the value that writers and publishers placed on fostering Canadian literature at this time:

> The literature of this country is in its infancy. It must not always remain
> so, or the expectations we have in regard to making it a great nation, will

never be fulfilled. Literature gives life to a nation, or rather it is the reflection of a nation's life and thought, in a mirror, which cheers, strengthens and ennobles those who look into it, and study what is there displayed. Literature must grow with our nation, and, when growing, it will aid the latter's progress in no small degree. (iii)

Similarly, nineteenth-century literary critics such as David Chisholme, editor of the *Montreal Herald*, and A.J. Christie, editor of the *Canadian Magazine and Literary Repository*, advocated the creation of a literature "which would take inventory of a new country, to begin the process of naming and familiarizing" (Ballstadt 1975: xvii). In essence, these writers were encouraging "Literary nationalism . . . the companion, advocate, and often forerunner of political nationalism" (Tausky 2002: 795). Efforts to create a distinctly Canadian literary voice were apparent in the literature for adults and children alike, and many nineteenth-century authors recognised the connection between literature and patriotic propaganda.

At the end of the nineteenth century, writers, educators, journalists, and those concerned with Canada's position in the world measured the country and its progress by its cultural output and emphasised the importance of literary production. They calculated the nation's success as a whole in terms of both the quantity and the quality of its cultural outpourings, and often determined the value of Canadian literature by comparing it to that of other countries; namely, Britain and the United States. Literary critics of the time tended to either view with pessimism what they considered a relative lack of literary production in Canada, or attempted to bolster pride in Canadian literature and to emphasise the extent to which Canadians were writing. In 1871 for example, W.A. Foster (1840–1888) published *Canada First; or, Our New Nationality; An Address*. Foster was a Toronto barrister whose concern for the future of Canada and the far-reaching impact of Confederation led to his involvement in the Canada First Movement.[1] The title page of this address bears an introductory note by the publishers that endorses the view that the birth of a great national literature is at hand:

There is an intellectual vivification, at last, in Canada, and there are indications that the native mind is at present awakening from the lethargy which has hitherto shrouded and dwarfed it. This is expressed in many ways, and is most observable . . . in the recognized necessity for a Canadian magazine—a vehicle of native thought and culture. (Foster 1871: title page)

Foster writes that while the body of Canadian literature in 1871 is small, all the necessary ingredients for a rich national literature are ready and waiting to be employed:

We may have no native ballad for the nursery, or home-born epic for the study; no tourney feats to rhapsodise over, or mock heroics to emblazon on our escutcheon; we may have no prismatic fables to illumine and adorn the preface of our existence, or curious myths to obscure and soften the sharp outline of our early history; yet woven into the tapestry of our past, are whole volumes of touching poetry and great tomes of glowing prose that rival fiction in eagerness of incident, and in marvellous climax put fable to the blush. We need not ransack foreign romance for valorous deeds, nor are we compelled to go abroad for sad tales of privation and suffering. The most chivalrous we can match; the most tried we can parallel. (Foster 1871: 5)

While Foster recognises that there are a relatively small number of native ballads and home-born epics in 1871 Canada, he does not see this as a reflection of a lack of national history or character. Rather, he optimistically implies that the time for Canadian literature to flourish and to do justice to the nation's unique story is near.

As an article by Sir John George Bourinot in *The Anglo-American Magazine* of 1900 indicates, people frequently tied this concern with the improvement of Canadian literature to the issue of the nation's growth:

The five and a quarter millions of people who own Canada from the Atlantic to the Pacific, are displaying a mental activity commensurate with the expansion of territory and accumulation of wealth. . . . In fact, all the scientific, historical, and political contributions of three decades, whether good, bad, or indifferent in character, make up quite a pretentious library, which shows the growth of what may be called Canadian literature, since it deals chiefly with subjects essentially of Canadian interest. The attention that is now particularly devoted to the study and writing of history and the collection of historical documents relating to the Dominion proves clearly the national or thoroughly Canadian spirit that is already animating the educated and cultured class of its people. (Bourinot 1900: 99)

Bourinot, who was an expert on Canadian parliamentary procedure, a government adviser on constitutional issues, and a supporter both of Confederation and Imperial Federation, conceives of Canada as being "owned" by its inhabitants, and the creation of a national literature is one means of proving such ownership. Canada's early writers were in fact laying claim to a new national culture, and were writing the nation in accordance with their own vision of it. This is in keeping with Benedict Anderson's definition of the nation as "an imagined political community" and his argument that "Communities are to be distinguished, not by their falsity/genuineness, but by the style in which they are imagined" (6). The style in which Canadian writers of the nineteenth century "imagined" the nation says much about the sense of national identity that was developing at this time.

The Special Role of Children's Literature

The question of national identity has long been a subject of interest in Canada. Literary critics have argued that our age of post-colonial discourse requires a new approach to Canadian literary study including "a restoration of context, a rereading of texts, a reinterpretation of codes, and opening of textual containment" (Turner 1995: 14–15). One new and necessary approach is to examine a large body of Canadian literature—namely, that intended specifically for children—that has remained largely ignored by scholars. By neglecting to study early Canadian children's literature, critics have failed to fully acknowledge the degree to which writers intended to foster feelings of national identity, independence, pride, and unity following Confederation. The study of this previously overlooked genre of Anglophone Canadian literature contributes to a new understanding of the country's literary history and the role of literature in the development of concepts of Canadian national identity following 1867.

While scholars have been slow to examine the important impact that children's literature had on this process, nineteenth-century writers and educators were themselves keenly aware that such writing might help foster national pride and loyalty. They saw the power of literature to influence national progress and growth as a particular strength of the literature consumed by young readers, at whose formative age such materials could have an even greater influence.

Children's literature, while written for a young audience, can reveal much about the concerns of the adult society that is responsible for the writing, publication, and distribution of such material. There is an intimate and inextricable relationship between the adult writer and the child reader, and the adult has an enormous impact on all aspects of children's literature. If children's literature is an arena for adults to play out what Jacqueline Rose calls their "fantasy of childhood" (1994: 138), it can certainly be a means by which adults can express other concerns. The children's literature popular in Canada following Confederation did not simply reflect fantasies of childhood; it served as a means by which idealised fantasies of Canadian nationhood and identity could be played out. Writers were using the genre as a means of promoting and constructing specific ideologies of national identity and as a means of strengthening national unity by fostering knowledge of, pride in, and loyalty to Canada in the nation's youth.

The proliferation of critics and scholars in fields such as education and child psychology who are concerned with what is "good" and acceptable reading for children demonstrates the generally held view that children's literature is influential in nature. More than any other genre of writing, children's literature is scrutinised and judged according to the effect it may have on its readers and its "suitability" for its intended audience. Paradoxically, scholars have often dismissed and overlooked children's literature, considering it trivial precisely because of its young audience. Yet those involved in the teaching profession have long used literature as an important tool of enlightenment and instruction. The influential nature of children's literature is evident from the important role it has played in the educational process, and as such it is a genre that can act as a valuable means of understanding many aspects of social and cultural history.

Nineteenth- and early twentieth-century Canadian children's literature functioned in a similar manner to the imperial tales written on the other side of the Atlantic, where much of the work of writers such as Rudyard Kipling and Rider Haggard expressed a desire to instil imperial attitudes in a young readership. In Canada, children's literature served as a means of fostering pride in the new country, strengthening national unity, and forming national identity.

However, there are few in-depth examinations of the significance that early Canadian children's literature holds for a full understanding of the nation's literary and cultural traditions. In the preface to his bibliography of Canadiana in children's periodicals from 1870–1950, Gordon Moyles notes the failure to take accurate account of this genre:

> The history of early Canadian children's literature—from the late-nineteenth century to the mid-twentieth century—has been summed up, by the few who have bothered to discuss it, in a few paragraphs and largely dismissed as being inconsequential. . . . One generally concludes from such sparse commentary that there is little to comment on or discuss. (1955: 7)

As Moyles' bibliography demonstrates, it is in exploring "the vast wealth" of material featured not simply in novels but in periodicals that "the true state" of early Canadian children's literature is revealed (Moyles 1955: 7). The more than 1,000 citations in Moyles' bibliography shed new light on the true wealth of early children's literature written either by Canadians or about Canada.

The importance placed on the role Canadian children could play in their nation's future is also reflected in the interest shown in public education in the last two decades of the nineteenth century, including the efforts to create an accessible public school system. Children were considered vital to the nation's progress and their education and literature were seen to play an influential role in this process. It is frequently within the ranks of children's literature that one finds the clearest expressions of Canadian nationalism. As the genre has developed it has aimed increasingly to entertain, but this has not caused it to lose the didactic overtones that characterised the genre's earliest forms. The majority of texts maintain the goal of educating readers, and the fact that adults commonly hold children to be impressionable and receptive to new ideas makes the literature written for them a vehicle for guidance and instruction. Because the adult plays an enormous role in the process of providing reading material for children, the lessons inherent in this literature act as a barometer of the ideology and principles of the society that produces and consumes such works. Given this privileged status, children's literature can provide an exceptional means by which to explore the influences at work in shaping and defining national culture and character. It is through examining this influential body of literature that one can make a true assessment of the early development of national identity in Canada.

The Young Audience

Between Confederation and the first decade of the twentieth century the literature made available to Canada's children in English—written not only by Canadians but by Americans and Europeans as well—played a vital role in identifying central elements of the Canadian national identity as it was expressed in Anglophone Canada. The majority of these works are long out of print but remain a vital means of illuminating the events and concerns at play in the nation's formative years.[2] Although many early Canadian works and authors may have been forgotten, their influence resonates in Canada to this day. This material was part of an important stage in Canada's development, helping to determine today's notions of what Canada represents, and it provides insight into the efforts undertaken to help the country achieve a sense of identity and unity following Confederation.

The young people who were reading these works in the late-nineteenth century represented Canada's urban and rural populations, its wealthy and poor, and its male and female constituents. Primarily, however, there was a large middle class to whom writers addressed the bulk of children's literature. Canadian writers of the time tended to be educated and middle class and they repeatedly draw their protagonists and events from the world of these so-called average Canadians.

Be they struggling pioneers, Christian missionaries, or young schoolboys, the majority of the characters in this literature reflect an image of Canadian society as a place where citizens unite in an effort to forge a life in a new land. Much of this material also includes an emphasis on education for all classes, reflecting the egalitarian ideal that in Canada, class distinctions would not preclude opportunities for basic education and advancement for poorer members of society. Nevertheless, the question of educational rights certainly sparked controversies over issues of language and religion in late nineteenth-century Canada, evidenced by the Manitoba School Crisis of 1890. And while writers may downplay them, class distinctions are not entirely absent from this literature, and evidence of some social inequality is apparent.

In particular, gender differences are decidedly pronounced. While both boys and girls would have read much of this literature, which was written by both men and women, these works tend to address either a young female or a young male readership. Periodicals with titles like *The Canadian Boy*, for example, are clearly intended for a male audience. Indeed, the majority of the works that survive from this period are addressed to a young male readership. Nevertheless, it is probable that girls made up a portion of the audience for this material. Boys and girls alike would have read texts included in the school curriculum, or those awarded as school prizes, while siblings of both sexes would likely have shared a variety of books and magazines.

Yet even when the readership of these works may have consisted of both males and females, much of the children's literature produced in Canada in the nineteenth century centres on tales of young boys and their adventures. Perhaps the physical challenges posed by Canada's natural environment were partly responsible for this proliferation of "masculine" tales of outdoor escapades and the raw elements of nation-building. Or perhaps the existing European models of children's literature did not allow for young Canadian women to have their reality portrayed in a world of fiction dominated by the adventure story. J.S. Bratton argues that the nineteenth century had "established the norm of the domestic tale" for young girls, and that "no model which could be utilised for the representation of the sterner face of pioneering and imperialist motherhood had yet been established" (1989: 197). This could explain why the majority of the early Canadian children's stories in this study centre on male protagonists, even when the authors are women. Tales of the wilds of Canada invited stories of hunting and exploration, pursuits undertaken predominately by boys and men.

One could make the argument, however, that Canadian girls were actually freer from the domestic sphere than their European counterparts. The harsh realities of pioneer life, for instance, meant that even women from the upper middle class often played a direct physical role in the building of farms and homesteads, a fact demonstrated by the writing of sisters Susanna Moodie and Catharine Parr Traill. The early predominance of the middle class in Canada may also have contributed to a greater sense of freedom for young women. The harsh reality of existence in a new country, the absence of an ancient aristocracy, and the predominance of the middle class, necessarily freed Canadian women from some of the restraint imposed on their upper-class British counterparts. Women from across the social spectrum would have participated directly in many of the activities required for establishing a new civilisation. Evidence of this association of women with the daily work of building the nation is present in the realm of children's fiction. For a nation of women accustomed to participating to some degree in these pioneering activities, tales of "male" adventure in the wilderness may not have seemed part of a radically different sphere of existence.

Yet the fact remains that Canadian children's literature frequently, though not exclusively, followed the familiar European pattern of falling into the categories of either boys' or girls' literature. Furthermore, the role children could play in the nation's future varied accordingly. Young boys learned the lessons needed for them to grow into future workers and leaders, while girls were schooled in the lessons they would require to become the future mothers of this new nation.

Nineteenth-century Canada was, after all, still a place where it was unusual for women to pursue higher education and impossible for them to vote. With the changes in laws and attitudes towards women that took place in the early twentieth century, children's literature increasingly came to reflect the widening role of women in Canadian society through works such as L.M. Montgomery's *Anne* books, and Muriel Denison's *Susannah* series.

While much of early Canadian children's literature appears to fall into the traditional categories of boys' or girls' fiction, some subversion of literary conventions is also taking place. Just as colonial life saw a sharing of traditionally male tasks by Canada's early female settlers, there was a sharing of fiction between a male and female readership. While a majority of texts appear to exclusively address a male readership, many of them were actually written by women and likely read by an undeclared readership of young girls. Despite what first appearances may suggest, therefore, writers were not excluding girls from the new Canadian identity. Moreover, the most famous and enduring Canadian children's story from this era is L.M. Montgomery's *Anne of Green Gables*, whose strong female protagonist remains one of literature's most distinctly Canadian figures. Regardless of whether early works of Canadian children's literature are traditional female tales of domesticity or masculine tales of adventure, the important role they play in constructing an image of the Canadian reality remains the same. While the expectations of *how* young men could contribute to the building of the nation differed from the roles assigned to young girls, both groups were included in this process. What remains apparent throughout much of the literature from Confederation onwards is the sense that the Canadian child, male or female, holds the key to ensuring the nation's future, and that both boys and girls must learn the roles they can play in this undertaking.

Influences on Identity

With their belief in the formative and influential nature of children's literature, writers worked in a variety of ways to instil a sense of national spirit and patriotism in young readers. This identity was fashioned in part by the children's literature that writers from Europe and the United States were setting in Canada, which had an impact on the country's sense of its own identity. Similarly, early Canadian regionalism also had an influence on the wider national consciousness. The acceptance of certain depictions of Canada by both Canadians and non-Canadians, and a backlash against other portrayals, contributed to the complex and diverse nature of the Canadian identity.

Many British writers, fuelled by their own nationalist and imperial fervour, write of Canada as the great cornerstone of the Empire. In such works, Canada is a playground for the British and a symbol of England's imperial might. In writing of R.M. Ballantyne's work for children (some of which is set in Canada), Stuart Hannabuss states that it is through excitement and adventure that "boys are turned into men and young Britons turned into staunch colonists" (1989:

56). For those who believed that the colonies were a source of wealth for Britain and a means of relieving problems such as overcrowding at home, there was a vested interest in presenting the benefits (real or imagined) of colonial life, and inspiring younger generations to become enterprising colonists. Young Canadians also read such works, which could in turn influence their vision of themselves and their nation.

While British literary tradition was a powerful force in Canadian culture, today's concern with the influence of the United States on Canadian culture and society was already an important issue in the nineteenth century. Many Canadian writers were submitting their work to the larger literary market south of the border and were moving there to find work in the editorial offices of American magazines. American critics had a tendency to impose stereotyped expectations on Canadian writers, the most notable of which was that their literature would be "a celebration of nature" (Doyle 1990: 32–33). While there is evidence to suggest that the influence of American editors and critics probably led Canadian writers to conform to these expectations, there is also evidence of a Canadian resistance to the United States' influence on Canadian culture, and to its stereotyping of Canada. Writers from both the United States and Great Britain imposed their own expectations of what Canada represented, adding to the complicated nature of the nation's own sense of identity.

While some writers came to reject the colonial status designated to Canada by many European writers, others continued to embrace the theme of Empire. For some Canadian writers, the question of national identity centred on the country's interaction with other nations. Many in Canada were struggling to reconcile the ideology of empire with an increasing awareness of the need for independence. Canada was struggling with the apparently conflicting role of being both the coloniser and the colonial outsider. The nation's complex and sometimes difficult relationships with both America and Britain were deeply influential, and commonly appear as themes in early writing for children.

As Canadian writers attempted to define the country, a variety of definitions of what it meant to be "Canadian" emerged in children's literature. In many instances Anglophone writers display an ethnic bias, with many tales focusing on characters of British descent. Some writers exhibit the feeling that Canada needs to preserve its largely British population as the norm, defining the Canadian identity as being predominately Celtic or Anglo-Saxon at heart. Yet there are other stories from the late-nineteenth century that demonstrate a growing awareness and acceptance of Canada's diversity.

Both the French Canadian and the "Indian" are common figures in the work of Anglophone writers such as Egerton Ryerson Young and J.M. Oxley, and many of the portrayals of these characters reveal a nineteenth-century racial and ethnic prejudice. But if one looks beyond the frequent caricatures and stereotypes, the complex and integral relationship that both groups have to the concept of the Canadian identity becomes apparent. The process by which these diverse segments of Canada's population are included in the concept of national identity reveals the growing predominance of what can be termed "civic nationalism" in nineteenth-century Canada. This includes "all those who accept the nation's political beliefs, whatever their colour, gender, language, or ethnicity" (Tausky 2002: 795). The tension between this civic nationalism, and one based on language and race, is one of the forces at work in the construction of a Canadian national identity.

Even as racist attitudes appear to persist—and in some cases intensify—in the children's literature from the early years of the twentieth century, a greater awareness of the richness of native myth and legend appears in the work written in Canada. As the nation developed, writers displayed increasing interest in Canadian history. Some authors mythologised the nation's history and Canadians began increasingly to study figures from their own past, rather than simply those from European history. The period of French and English conflict in North America was a rich source of historical fiction, as were tales of war with, and victory over, the United States. Children's novels, short stories, and songs all became ideal means by which to explore the nation's past, and to develop pride in Canadian achievement.

Also of vital importance to the developing sense of national identity was the influence of the natural environment. The celebration of nature in Canadian children's literature was a popular trend that led to a lasting identification of Canada with the natural environment. While the country's landscape was incredibly diverse, the basic fact of nature's presence was universal. The few urban centres were islands in a sea of wilderness and Canada's rural populations could not ignore the power and beauty of their natural surroundings. In an age before mass communication, literature was a means by which Canada's geographically dispersed population could coalesce into a national community. The overwhelming presence of Canada's natural environment was something the people all shared and as such, it played an important role in the nation's literature, acting as a central point of identification for the Canadian nation.

The years between Confederation and the end of the first decade of the twentieth century were a period of great change within Canada. Consisting of only four provinces and fewer than three and a half million people in 1867, by 1873 the new Canadian nation stretched from the Atlantic to the Pacific and encompassed the vast arctic reaches. By 1885 the original main line of the Canadian Pacific Railway was complete, paving the way for the settlement of Canada's western territory. Under the leadership of Prime Minister John A. Macdonald the foundations of Canadian society were laid. That is not to say that the country was without its share of problems in those early days. Twenty years after Confederation the nation's population had not grown significantly, various provinces threatened to rebel, and tensions between the nation's French and English populations remained a worrisome issue. It was against this backdrop in 1896 that the Liberal Party took power and Sir Wilfrid Laurier became the Prime Minister of Canada, a position he would hold until 1911.

During the leadership years of Macdonald and Laurier, Canada faced a series of challenges and changes that helped to shape the evolving national consciousness. The opening of the West shed new light on the promise Canada held for development, bringing in new waves of immigration but also sparking the Northwest rebellion and the eventual assassination of Louis Riel. The controversy over the Boer War in 1899 managed both to inspire a new pride in Canadian military achievements while at the same time dividing the country over the questions of conscription and the undue influence of the British Empire. The settlement of the Alaska Boundary Question in 1903, which many Canadians saw as evidence of the British undercutting Canada's interests to protect their own relationship with the United States, galvanised the realisation within Canada that the nation's interests were not always served by loyalty to the Empire. Roosevelt called the American victory in the Alaska debate "the greatest diplomatic victory of our time," while Laurier in turn declared "So long as Canada remains a dependency of the British Crown, the present powers which we have are not sufficient for the maintenance of our rights" (LaPierre 1996: 295). The first years of the twentieth century witnessed these changing attitudes towards Britain and the United States and saw Canada's urge to shed its lingering colonial status and embrace its role as a truly independent nation.

From the midst of this turbulence emerged the growing voice of Anglophone Canadian writers who were articulating the nation's changing attitudes and new self-awareness. Children's literature certainly reflected these changes, and may very well have helped to influence them. As each successive generation of Canadian readers consumed the literature of their young nation, a sense of what it meant to be Canadian grew and strengthened. It was this early literature that sowed and helped mature many of the seeds of Canadian identity.

Chapter One
The View from Afar: British and American Perspectives

Children's literature has a lengthy history in Anglophone Canada, with the production of literature for young Canadians dating back as early as the eighteenth century.[1] By the end of the nineteenth century there was a large variety of juvenile literature being created by both Canadian authors and foreign writers who were exploring Canada's literary potential. While this study focuses primarily on Anglophone literature written by those born or resident in Canada, it also explores the impact that American and British writers had on the development of a Canadian identity. Non-Canadians were creating images of the country through their writing for both Canadian and non-Canadian children, and some of the attitudes that these outsiders brought to bear on portrayals of Canada and its people were shared by the country's own writers (MacLulich 1988: 24).

The literature written by foreign pens in the late nineteenth and early twentieth centuries clearly demonstrates that an image of Canada and its citizens was being shaped not only from within, but also from outside the nation's borders. In 1907, for example, Frenchman André Siegfried wrote a work for adults entitled *The Race Question in Canada*, an English-language version of which was published in London. While concerned with the question of Canadian politics, Siegfried's analysis of the relationship between the French and English in Canada betrays a distinctly French perspective on France's historic defeat in North America. It is a view marked by a lingering sense of regret when Siegfried observes: "To England is given the loyalty that has its origin in self-interest, for it is she who guaranteed the French of Canada their untrammelled liberty. But to France goes forth their hearts, for their memory of the land of their forefathers is ineradicable" (113–114). The author's examination of Canadian affairs is not an unbiased consideration of feeling and sentiment in Quebec, rather, it is coloured by France's own interests and by a European perspective.

Writers from Britain, America, and the European continent echoed such foreign commentary on Canada in their children's literature. Popular authors such as Jules Verne (1828–1905) and Rudyard Kipling (1865–1936) set children's tales in Canadian locales. Verne's Canadian works include such titles as *The Fur Country* and *A Winter Amid the Ice* while Kipling visited Canadian themes in such poems as "Our Lady of the Snows," and the short story "Quiquern," set in the Canadian Arctic. Other writers echoed the interest in Canada shown by these two successful authors. For example, French author Benedict Revoil's account of his hunting and trapping expedition to Canada in 1844 was translated from the French and published by T. Nelson and Sons of London as a book for children in 1887. Revoil lived in New York for nearly ten years during the 1840s and wrote several such texts on the topics of hunting and fishing. Titled *In the Bush and On the Trail. Adventures in the Forests of North America: A Book for Boys*, Revoil's work provides observations about Canadian climate and wildlife and demonstrates the interest that both the British and the French had in Canadian topics.

In the Footsteps of Wolfe: British Literary Conquests

Long after the political separation of Britain and Canada, the literary worlds of the two nations remained intertwined. British authors devoted much literary attention to Canada, developing its image as a land of wilderness and adventure in the process. R.G. Moyles and Doug Owram illustrate the incredible extent to which the British were writing and reading about Canada at the turn of the twentieth century in their study *Imperial Dreams and Colonial Realities: British Views of Canada, 1880–1914*. This offers an excellent account of the degree to which the ideals of British imperialism find expression in the Canadian themed stories written and read in Britain during the height of the Empire. The study focuses on nine stereotypical views of Canada and the manner in which British dreams of Empire frequently clashed with the reality of the lives and sentiment of the Canadian people themselves. Moyles and Owram demonstrate that a story relating to Canada could be found in almost every issue of *The Boy's Own Paper* between 1879 and 1967 and that the weekly periodical *Chums* published Canadian tales in roughly one hundred of its issues between 1892 and 1907 (Moyles and Owram 1988: 38). Included among the images of Canada popularised by these tales are the depiction of the nation as a loyal imperial subject, a sportsman's paradise, and a golden land of opportunity. In the process of revealing British views of Canada, this literature also reveals much about the way the British viewed themselves at this time:

> Just what the British thought of Canada, or what they thought Canada was, is graphically revealed in that literature, though it is a varied and often strange conglomeration, saturated by the ideals and vanities of a people engrossed in their own glory. . . . In other words, the literature embodied

the serious and the frivolous, offering acute observations and superficial commentary. It was, in fact, as varied as British society itself. (Moyles and Owram 1988: 6–7)

Many British children's writers gravitated towards Canadian themes and locales, and their work influenced the images of both countries.

Sheila Egoff and Judith Saltman attribute this interest in Canada on the part of British writers to the fact that its setting offered some freedom from the class restraints of England:

It is no accident that all the English boys' adventure stories of the nineteenth century were set in the colonies or on exotic desert islands. Class-conscious England was no place for younger sons or for those intent on improving their lot in life. But in Canada's forests, fields, and rivers only skill, courage, and ingenuity counted—not birth and breeding. (Egoff and Saltman 1990: 9)

While Egoff and Saltman exaggerate the degree to which writers of this fiction disregarded birth and breeding, it is true that Canada offered new possibilities for stories of adventure by British writers. Following in the footsteps of their political and military forefathers, British children's writers found a new world of literary inspiration and opportunity in the young country and set out to capture Canada on the page and in the imagination of their young audience.

While Canada was frequently portrayed as an exotic and very different place from England, its glories were also regarded as further proof of the might of Britain's empire. Regardless of whatever movements towards independence and nationalism may have been taking place within Canada itself, the writers of British children's literature frequently wrote of Canada as an extension of their own nation. Adventure narratives presented Canada as an exotic landscape and as an available playground for any Englishman brave enough to explore its shores. Many children's stories of the nineteenth century tell of English explorers and adventurers seeking fortune and excitement in a new land. John Cunningham Geikie's *Life in the Woods: A Boy's Narrative of the Adventures of a Settler's Family in Canada*, tells one version of this story. Geikie, more commonly known as the author of several theological texts, was born in Edinburgh in 1824 and served as a minister in both Canada and Great Britain. His children's novel features characters who leave Britain to go out as settlers to Canada but who eventually return to Britain with increased fortunes. Other works tell tales of British individuals and families who leave their homes permanently to start a new life as settlers in Canada.

"Bruin'"s *The Forest Home; or, Life in the Canadian Wilds* (*circa* 1875) is one children's novel that includes examples of both types of British characters; those who settle permanently in Canada, and those who return home at the end of their adventures. "Bruin" tells the story of the Macdonald family from England and their new life in Canada. Despite the Canadian setting of the novel, however, the social codes and practices revealed in the story are clearly British. For example, the class distinctions and racial stereotyping of the Welsh and Irish, which were a part of English life in the nineteenth century, are transported along with this family to Canada. This is largely evident through the character of the Macdonalds' servant Betsy, who has accompanied the family to Canada and who furnishes much of the story's humour. Betsy's Cockney accent and position as a servant reveal her status as a member of the working class. While Betsy's physicality equips her with the strength required for the chores of settler life, she appears less able than her employers to cope either emotionally or intellectually with the challenges of a new environment. She has an irrational and exaggerated fear of wolves and other wildlife and the Macdonalds find great amusement in teasing her about such matters:

> "If winter sets in now, after this Indian summer," said Harry, "the bears will go to sleep, I suppose, and we need not be so afraid of them as of the wolves."
>
> "Go to sleep!" cried Betsy. "What, all day and night! I never heard tell of such a thing."
>
> "Didn't you now?" said the doctor. "Why, Betsy . . . Don't you know that they make a warm feather bed for themselves, and scoop out a jolly little bedroom in the hollow trunk of a tree . . . and snore away in jolly style as long as winter lasts, dreaming of fat sows and little piggies? . . ."
>
> "I shall never feel safe here again," said Betsy—"never, never . . ."
>
> "You're a born Cockney," said Harry. "I thought you'd have got some sense out here in the backwoods of Canada, Betsy. We've been out here ever since last spring, and I believe you're just as big a coward as you were when we came." ("Bruin" c 1875: 17)

Harry's hope that Betsy would "have got some sense . . . in the backwoods" betrays a belief in the improving nature of Canada. Through their exposure to the new country the settlers ultimately evolve into wiser and braver beings. In these evolutionary terms, however, the genteel Macdonalds prove themselves to be better fit for survival in Canada than their servant girl. The fact that Harry makes much of Betsy's status as a "Cockney," demonstrates that he and his family are still keenly aware of, and keen to maintain, the social divisions and practices familiar in England at the time.

While the narrator and characters say many complimentary things about life in Canada in this novel, the perspective is clearly British. At one point, the narrator expresses annoyance at the thought that some people consider Canada to be superior to England. This annoyance emerges in a discussion of the attitudes of another young British emigrant, the character Jack Williamson:

Jack Williamson was a young man about Harry's age. . . . He was a thorough backwoodsman . . . and such a lover of the free life he led, that he used to declare he wouldn't exchange it with the richest nobleman in the kingdom; and as to going back to live and be cramped in "pokey little England"—catch him doing such a thing!

Only fancy calling our beautiful England a "pokey little place!" I must say I think it is taking a great liberty, don't you? And do you know that a Canadian gentleman once said pretty much the same sort of thing to me. He declared that he always felt half stifled when he came over to England, as if he couldn't get enough fresh air to breathe! ("Bruin" c 1875: 43)

In the defence of what is termed "our beautiful England" the narrator reveals that the novel's intended audience is one of English children. But by relating the feelings of both the unnamed "Canadian gentleman" who finds himself "stifled" on his visit to England, as well as those of British expatriate Jack Williamson, the narrator also provides a glimpse of some of the expressions of anti-imperialism already taking place in Canada at this time. The narrator does not endorse these sentiments, which run counter to the dominant refrain of imperial fervour in the nineteenth century. While the telling of the Macdonalds' story reveals unwittingly that there is some degree of "anti-England" sentiment among Canadians at this time, the narrator's expression of incredulity and indignation at the thought that some may find Canada a preferable place to live is very much in keeping with the English perspective that pervades this novel.

While the novel's setting may be Canadian, the views expressed in the text would not be unfamiliar to an English child. The attitudes towards class distinctions displayed in the novel, and the narrator's frequent comparisons between Canada and "our England," make it evident that this work is intended for a young English audience. It is through the character of young Ned Macdonald in particular that the author displays the ideal of English boyhood. In one of the novel's opening scenes, for instance, Ned displays strength of character as he risks injury by killing a bear that attacks the family sow: "Ned sprang into the stye, though it was a dreadfully dangerous thing to do, but he was as brave as any English boy can be, and besides he knew that the sow would be killed if he didn't kill the bear" ("Bruin" c 1875: 9). The view that Ned's bravery is a distinctly English quality is again emphasised after he sustains an injury in his encounter with the bear:

Ned had quite come to himself, but he didn't seem inclined to speak. He held Harry's hand as they went on, and bit his lips hard not to let a cry come when there was any jolting. He was a true English boy, and couldn't bear to make a fuss about the pain he felt. ("Bruin" c 1875: 12.)

The repeated emphasis on the fact of Ned's being an "English boy" underscores both the British perspective of the novel's narrator, as well as the fact that the intended readership is English.

Nevertheless, notwithstanding its bias, the novel contains many positive portrayals of life in Canada. For instance, regardless of the narrator's apparent shock that some would consider England a "pokey" place in comparison to Canada, this novel does contribute to the image of Canada as a healthy, clean, and invigorating environment. Perhaps the author even downplays the country's drawbacks, portraying it as a place in which the English have a vested interest, with the narrator acknowledging that some of the story's readers may one day grow up and "go to live in a new part of dear old Canada" and experience adventures of their own (3).

Such direct references to the continual waves of emigration from Britain to Canada are not uncommon in the British children's literature from this era. Canada continued to be promoted as a land of open spaces and great opportunity throughout the late nineteenth and early twentieth centuries. For example, in the *Boy's Own Annual* from 1906, there are many references to life in various parts of the British Empire, including Canada. The May 5, 1906 issue contains a letter to the editor from a John H. Crockewit of Battleford, Saskatchewan encouraging fellow British boys to start a new life in Canada as he has done:

> Dear Mr. Editor,—I am an old reader of, and subscriber to, 'The Boy's Own Paper,' and have not long left Bedford Grammar School. I am very well pleased with this country, and if any boy would like information respecting settling in the Canadian North-West, or has any questions on the subject he would like answered, I shall be delighted to write to him fully if he will address me here and enclose one shilling in stamps for a prepaid reply by return mail. I will explain in detail how I have fared out here, and what the prospects are, this being my second year in the West. I may add that the Canadian Northern Railway has just completed a line direct from Winnipeg to this town, and it is now possible to locate on a homestead comprising 160 acres of very desirable prairie land (which is steadily rising in value), within a few miles of the station. (Crockewit 1906: 496)

Crockewit's letter fuels the image of Canada as a land of great promise for England's young citizens. While British writers find Canada's differences from Britain a continual source of inspiration, they simultaneously describe Canada as a place where their young readers can feel at home.

This duality is made apparent in "Bruin'"s novel about the Macdonald family in which Canada, as different and exotic as it may at times appear, is described as a part of the British Empire and as a place with which English children are somewhat familiar:

> I daresay most of you know something about Canada, a country on the other side of the Atlantic, where it is dreadfully hot in summer and ever so cold in winter. . . . It belongs to us, you know, and most of the people

who live there are our own people. But it is very different to England in many ways, and for some things I like it much better. I think girls and boys have more fun over there than we can have here; for all through the long winter they have such capital skating. ("Bruin" *c* 1875: 3)

This narrative epitomises the ambiguous colonial position Canada held in the nineteenth century. While its differences are emphasised, and even exaggerated at times, it is simultaneously claimed as part of Britain. "It belongs to us" declares the narrator in this novel, emphasising the sense of ownership that many British writers maintained well into the twentieth century. Ironically, "Bruin'"s concept of British ownership of Canada is in direct contrast to John Bourinot's claim of Canadian ownership "from the Atlantic to the Pacific" in his article in *The Anglo-American Magazine* from February, 1900 (99). British children's novels such as "Bruin'"s, with its descriptions of Canada as both "dreadfully hot" and "ever so cold" and as both a distant land and a land of Britain's "own people," exhibit some of the contrasting portrayals of the nation that persisted following Confederation. Seen as a distinct, "new" and exotic land, yet simultaneously viewed as part of Britain, the literary construction of Canada by lesser-known British children's authors such as "Bruin", and the much more popular writers such as G.A. Henty (1832–1902) and W.H.G. Kingston (1814–1880), contributed to the nation's complex and multi-faceted image.[2]

While *The Forest Home; or, Life in the Canadian Wilds* is essentially a domestic tale of settler life, it also contains many familiar elements of the children's adventure tales set in Canada. There are incidents of hunting, canoeing, and fishing, and dangerous encounters with bears and local tribes. There is an emphasis on the real or perceived threats of Canada's wilderness, including its wildlife. The image of Canada as a place teeming with strange and exotic creatures was prevalent in children's literature throughout the nineteenth and early twentieth centuries. *The Empire Annual for Boys* from 1909, for instance, features an article by Llewellyn A. Morrison on Canadian wildlife entitled "A Chat with a Moose." Morrison describes his encounter with the majestic animal, describing its strength and beauty. The article opens with an epigraph that highlights some of Canada's attributes: "Canada—glorious land for the free, the bold, and the hardy!—boasts of great rivers, great lakes, great prairies, and great mountain ranges. It is but fitting that one of the greatest of four-footed beasts—the moose—should also be Canadian" (Morrison 1909: 211). The moose embodies the characteristics of freedom, boldness, and hardiness that Morrison sees as defining Canada and clearly establishes the symbolic link between Canada and the natural environment.

Morrison's article is just one of many examples of writing published for children in Britain that emphasise Canada as a land of wilderness and abundant natural assets. In his comprehensive index to Canadian content in children's literature in British and American periodicals, R.G. Moyles cites many examples of similar tales in British journals like *The Boy's Own Paper*, with titles such as

"An Adventure with Wolves: A Canadian Story," "Incidents of Forest Life in British Columbia," and "A Trip to Beaverland" (Moyles 1955: 21–22). Other texts from England, such as *Half Hours in the Wide West Over Mountains, Rivers, and Prairies*, contribute further to the image of Canada as a great wilderness. The first chapter of this non-fiction account of travels through Canada recounts a journey from Toronto, Ontario to Fort Garry, Manitoba by steamer and canoe. From the start the narrator manages to evoke a sense of the country's vast wilderness: "The first step in our journey was to get to Fort Garry, in the province of Manitoba. That step is for giants, being at least a thousand miles long" (*Half Hours*: 3). The author, however, refrains from exaggerating the scene and describes with relative accuracy the reality of the Canadian wilderness. He remarks on the immense size of the Great Lakes, but describes them as he actually encountered them, avoiding a tendency towards mythologising such places:

> Of all the great Lakes, Superior corresponds least to the ordinary conception of a lake. Day after day you can sail in the same direction over its deep crystal waters without seeing land. It breeds rains, storms, and fogs like the sea. . . . We heard from sailors stories of its strength and fury; but with the exception of a thundersquall with which it greeted us as we entered between its portals, Capes Gros and Iroquois, our sail along its shores was as delightful as warm suns, bracing air, and cool nights could make it. (*Half Hours* 1883: 4)

Without recourse to exaggerated tales of the perils encountered in Canada, the author of this work still manages to create a very clear picture of Canada as a land of immense size and natural diversity. At the same time, he promotes Britain's own claim on this land, implying that Canadians and British alike see Canada as part of the Empire:

> The persistent loyalty of Canadians comes to the surface in the names they give to almost every new settlement. The number of Victorias, Prince Alberts, and other royal-family names already in the north-west promises a good crop of confusions and annoyances in postal matters in the future. (*Half Hours* 1883: 6)

Such evidence of Canada's "persistent loyalty" to Britain emphasises the British perspective of this work.

Yet while Canadians are presented as loyal, they are simultaneously presented as somewhat different from the English. They are, it appears, products of their natural environment, which is pictured as having a strong influence on the habits of Canada's inhabitants. In writing of winter in Canada, the author of *Half Hours* remarks that "natives and old residents usually wear fur caps and gloves, but the Englishman, when he first goes out, feels no necessity for any change in his apparel. In a few years, however, he is glad to adopt the customs of the country" (*Half Hours* 1883: 62). The environment appears to determine the behaviour of the country's inhabitants and is portrayed as a highly influential force in Canadian life.

Works with some factual basis like *Half Hours in the Wide West Over Mountains, Rivers, and Prairies,* in which the glories and dangers of Canada's natural environment are emphasised, found their fictional counterparts in the adventure narratives of writers such as W.H.G. Kingston and R.M. Ballantyne. Amid the many non-fiction accounts of life in the Canadian wilderness published for children, there was a vast body of novels and short stories by British writers that pictured Canada as an exotic land full of promise and adventure in hunting and exploring for any young Englishman ready for the challenge. Again, while contributing to the image of Canada as a strange and wild land, writers such as W.H.G. Kingston emphasise Britain's connection to this land: "The climate is healthy and perfectly suited to British constitutions. The winter lasts five months; spring one, autumn one, and summer five" (Kingston 1890: 334). Kingston is concerned with the Canadian climate strictly as it relates to those British adventurers or settlers who may encounter it. It is through such observations that the continuing interest and involvement which Britain had in Canada following Confederation is made evident. While Canadians themselves were becoming increasingly independent from Britain and evermore loyal to their native country, there is evidence of a prevailing attitude in Britain that Canada represented one of the great jewels in its imperial crown.

This attitude emerges in an article originally published in *The Times* in August of 1886, which outlines the prominent place that Canada had in the Colonial and Indian Exhibition of that same year:

> Had the Dominion kept aloof what a blank there would have been any one can realise who looks at a plan of the Exhibition, and sees how Canada is spread almost all over the building, from the gateways of British Guiana and the West Indies on the one side to the frontiers of Natal and the Cape on the other, reaching south to the confines of New Zealand and stretching away into the North-West Territories of the arcades and the conservatory. (*The Times* 1886: 1)

Canada, it appears, is still the focus of much attention when it comes to determining Britain's power and influence in global affairs. The writer portrays Britain as having title over this vast, far-reaching region, and the rest of the article examines the history of Canada's development, and draws attention to its growing agricultural wealth. It also echoes some of the ideas concerning the Canadian character that were finding expression in the children's literature of both countries, highlighting a common belief in the industrious nature of Canadians: "In Canada, as elsewhere, the man who wants to succeed must be prepared for the hardest work and the endurance of hardships which, though disagreeable, will not hurt him if he has a decent constitution to begin with and gives it fair play" (*The Times* 1886: 5). British writers, it appears, were not simply aware of the different environment Canada offered; they also acknowledged specific needs and characteristics of the people who lived in such surroundings.

Some writers who set their works for children in Canada spoke with more authority on the subject than others. Although it is conceivable that many writers of the adventure tales set in Canada's arctic regions or expansive forests never set foot in such places, some did have an intimate knowledge of Canada. Among this group stands Robert Michael Ballantyne (1825–1894). Born in Edinburgh, Scotland, Ballantyne worked for the Hudson's Bay Company in Canada for six years, starting when he was just sixteen. Between 1841 and 1847 he lived in York Factory, Norway House, and Fort Garry, among other northern posts. Ballantyne's experience in Canada influenced 1856's *Snowflakes and Sunbeams; or, the Young Fur Traders: A Tale of the Far North*, a novel inspired by his own experiences as a young man working for the Hudson's Bay Company. While he lived most of his life in Europe, Ballantyne's experience in Canada lends a voice of authority to this novel and its Canadian setting. Ballantyne's writing displays both an intimate understanding of the Canadian experience as well as the perspective of a British onlooker.

In the case of other children's writers of the era, there is indeed some difficulty in defining their status as Canadian or British authors. Catherine Parr Traill (1802–1899), for example, is one author who is widely recognised for the influence she had on Canadian literature, yet who originally emigrated from England in 1832. Among her diverse works on botany and the experiences of settlers in Canada, Traill also published children's stories including the 1852 novel *Canadian Crusoes: A Tale of the Rice Lake Plains*. Unlike R.M. Ballantyne, Catharine Parr Traill settled permanently in Canada. Yet each of these authors illustrates the difficulty that exists in defining such nineteenth-century writers as either Canadian or British. In effect, writers such as Traill exemplify the dual perspective that characterises much of Canadian writing. In articulating the immigrant experience, these writers encompass the perspective of both the Canadian insider and the European onlooker.

Just as the perception of Canadian society varies in these nineteenth-century texts, so too does the treatment which British characters receive. Whereas some works clearly maintain a sense of the class and racial divides of nineteenth-century England, others take less notice of such distinctions. While characters continue to be distinguished as English, Welsh, Canadian, and so forth, the importance of such distinctions varies according to each particular author. In the work of British writer E. Everett-Green for example, there is an emphasis on the distinctions between French and English; "Ay, a white man—Frenchman. . . . He called us dogs of English, who were robbers of the soil where none had right to penetrate save the subjects of his royal master" (Everett-Green 1899: 23). In other works, it is the distinctions between the Irish, Welsh, Scottish, and English themselves that are emphasised. R.M. Ballantyne does this with a degree of wit and self-deprecation in *The Young Fur Traders*, as he ascribes different characteristics to the fighting styles of the English, the Scottish, and what he terms Canada's "half-breeds":

> Every nation has its own peculiar method of fighting, and its own ideas of what is honourable and dishonourable in combat. The English, as everyone knows, have particularly stringent rules . . . and count it foul disgrace to strike a man when he is down; although by some strange perversity of reasoning, they deem it right and fair to *fall* upon him while in this helpless condition, and burst him if possible. The Scotchman has less of the science, and we are half inclined to believe that he would go the length of kicking a fallen opponent; but on this point we are not quite positive. In regard to the style adopted by the half-breeds, however, we have no doubt. They fight *any* way and *every* way, without reference to rules at all; and, really, although we may bring ourselves into contempt by admitting the fact, we think they are quite right. (Ballantyne 1856: 306)

Ballantyne's commentary on the differing characteristics of the Scotchman and Englishman is echoed in many nineteenth-century children's narratives, in which there is an emphasis on the differences between the various "races" which make up the British people.

Nevertheless, there is also a tendency among some writers to promote what Katie Trumpener calls a "collective amnesia" (1997: 253), where the ethnic divisions within the British themselves are downplayed in imperial fiction: "This colonial tilt . . . whereby Scottish (and Irish) settlers misplace in transit their age-old anti-English, anti-British, and anti-imperial hatreds, appears to be both the cornerstone and the central mystery of empire" (Trumpener 1997: 253). According to Trumpener, the "dream of empire is that a long history of British ethnic strife . . . can be sublated into a new utopian community" (256). In the British children's literature that was set in Canada at the end of the nineteenth century, the varying emphasis on this British "ethnic strife" reveals that Canada was imagined as both an extension of Britain and its social realities, and as a distant land still in a primitive state, and free from the complications of English civilisation. Some truly saw Canada a new world with utopian potential.

"54–40 or Bust!" America's Literary Invasion of Canada

While influences from Britain and Europe shaped Canadian society and culture, Canada also developed as part of a wider North American scene. Just as children's writers in Canada were offering both positive and negative commentary on their neighbours to the south and featuring American characters and locales in their work, so too were their American counterparts engaging with Canada. On the part of writers of non-juvenile literature, this often took the form of political commentary. In February, 1886 for example, an American by the name of

Prosper Bender wrote an article entitled "The Disintegration of Canada" for a Boston publication, in which he outlines his views on the "serious family jars" afflicting Canada in the form of difficulties between the French and English populations (Bender 1886: 144). Bender questions the entire foundation of Canadian society in what he calls a "startling illustration of the serious difficulty of founding, by the great lakes and the shores of the St. Lawrence, out of the various, rival, jealous, and discordant races, a homogeneous, contented, and prosperous nation" (151). Bender's views also include a belief that Americans can regard themselves as an enlightening influence on the Canadian people:

> Nor can it be doubted that a powerful factor in the expansion of the Canadian mind, and in the liberalizing of Canadian feelings of late years, is an extensive intercourse with the United States, to which thousands of French as well as British Canadians annually repair. Among the results of this communication . . . must be set down a better feeling toward the United States, and a substantial respect for the hospitality, wealth, and energy of its people." (148)

The article also claims that many an aggrieved Canadian province has demonstrated a habit "of earnestly casting its eyes toward the American Union, for that relief and future protection from injustice deemed difficult of attainment at home" (152). Prosper Bender's confident prediction is that Canada is in a state of disintegration, and that annexation by the United States is an inevitable and logical outcome.

Attitudes such as this do not belong to the world of adult literature alone, and provide an example of some of the interaction between Canada and the United States taking place within the literary milieu of the late-nineteenth century. American publishers were producing books written by Canadians and many juvenile periodicals published in the United States featured stories and articles by Canadian writers. At the same time, American children's authors themselves were setting works of fiction and non-fiction in Canadian locales and featuring Canadian characters. An examination of this material reveals some of the ways in which American writers envisioned Canada, and how their views mirrored or contrasted the developing sense of national identity expressed in the work of their Canadian counterparts.

The role of the United States in the production of Canadian children's literature has long been fraught with negative and positive implications. In the June 1, 2001 issue of Canada's *The Globe and Mail*, Marina Strauss writes of the negative impact that the American literary market has on Canadian children's literature, claiming that "Canada is in danger of losing a vibrant piece of its national culture: the distinctly Canadian flavour of its kids' literature" (Strauss 2001: M1). To offset losses in the domestic markets, children's book publishers such as Groundwood Books are relying more on exports to the United States, and the Americanisation of titles, spelling, and locales is affecting Canadian books. Groundwood Books' representative Patsy Aldana is quoted as saying that "Americans have no interest in Canadian content" (Strauss 2001: M1). The truth is that Aldana's concerns over a lack of American interest in Canadian content, and her fear of writing being "de-Canadianized," have been part of the world of Canadian children's books since as far back as the mid 1800s, and there is evidence to suggest that American children's writers of the nineteenth century did in fact have an interest in Canadian content.

This engagement with Canada is clearly documented in several American texts from this time and is explored by James Doyle in his study of the images of Canada in American literature from 1775–1900. While Doyle notes that Canada never figured as prominently in American literature as Britain or Europe did, and that interest in Canada on the part of American writers declined after the nineteenth century, he does demonstrate that there was still a fairly substantial body of work pertaining to Canada up until that time. Nevertheless, Doyle dismisses the literary merit of much of this material:

> [T]here are no American literary masterpieces dealing with Canada. . . . When major writers . . . turn their attention briefly to Canada, the results are frequently disappointing in comparison to their best-known works. The American literary interest in Canada is most evident in the travel narratives and the adventure novel, genres that have frequently attracted the second-rate writer or the minor efforts of the first-rate one. (Doyle 1983: 2)

While one may take exception to Doyle's evaluation of the literary merit of these works and his summary dismissal of the travel and adventure genres, he is correct in identifying the popularity of such works among authors from the United States. What Doyle fails to note is that many of these works belong to the category of children's literature. This makes juvenile literature a particularly wealthy source of information regarding American perspectives on Canada. Certainly among the American children's writers active during the latter half of the nineteenth century stories of hunting, camping, and exploration in Canada's wilderness account for a large portion of their literature. Some other genres explored by American children's writers include animal stories and works of history and historical fiction.

One such text is *Queenston, A Tale of the Niagara Frontier* by Judge Jesse Walker, published in Buffalo by Steele's Press in 1845. This is an American book, with an American narrator, which aims to tell American children about the war of 1812. The old "Captain" narrates it, answering the young boy Harry's question about why the United States fought Canada. In keeping with the book's publication date (more than twenty years prior to Confederation), the Captain's answer equates Canada with Great Britain and places the blame squarely on the shoulders of the English, even while admitting that the Americans were the first to declare war:

"With the establishment of the independence of the United States, Great Britain was not exactly satisfied. Her acknowledgment of it was extorted rather from her fears than from her sense of Justice. She had not entirely laid aside the thought of conquering us. . . ."

"But," said Harry, "the war was declared by the Americans. How should they be the first to make war because England desired to conquer us?"

"There were other causes," said the Captain. "The government of England was always ready to excite jealousies among our people." (Walker 1845: 84–85)

Despite the clearly American viewpoint from which this history is told (noticeable in the failure to address America's sense of Manifest Destiny and its own attempts to conquer Canada), the Captain appears reluctant to criticise the British too strongly, recognising the current peaceful relations between the two countries. He tells Harry that war "is not between men, but between Governments. British and American officers will be personally good friends the day after a hard fight, and will be ready to fight again the next day, if their Country requires it of them" (Walker 1845: 74). This work, with its emphasis on the need for patriotism and national pride, is an early example of American children's literature that addresses the issue of Canadian–American relations, as it attempts to justify the American invasion of Canada during the War of 1812. In its efforts to justify these actions and portray them as necessary to the security and future of the United States, this text displays some of the inward-looking tendencies that Doyle identifies as characteristic of much American literature:

This egocentricity of American culture can, however, be related to a more comprehensive context than mere self-absorption. The intelligent and imaginative American who writes about Canada—or about any foreign country—is most likely to be preoccupied by a theme that pervades his national literature: the meaning of the New World. (Doyle 1983: 3)

Walker's *Queenston, A Tale of the Niagara Frontier* is one work that attempts to help American children understand their country's history and its position in the New World, in the context of its somewhat ambiguous relationship with Canada. In the process, it helps to shape a picture of Canada as a country of Englishmen on North American soil, whose perceived aggression towards the United States has been brought under control.

Canadian writers also helped introduce Canada to young American readers. One juvenile periodical published in the United States that demonstrates a strong interest in Canadian subject matter is *The Boys' World*, printed weekly by David C. Cook Publishing in Illinois in the early twentieth century. The May 18, 1907 and June 22, 1907 issues each contain stories by the prolific Canadian writer Marjorie L.C. Pickthall (1883–1922) that demonstrate Canadian content. Raised and educated in Toronto after emigrating from England at the age of six,

Pickthall was the author of several novels and hundreds of short stories. One such story, "The Day of Victory," from the May 18, 1907 issue of *The Boys' World*, tells the tale of a young boy named Ted who overcomes his fear of diving in order to save a younger boy from drowning. The events described take place on the 24th of May, which is Victoria Day, a uniquely Canadian holiday that celebrates Queen Victoria's birthday and her role in establishing Canada. Pickthall does not "de-Canadianise" her story and Victoria Day is a central element of the tale. For instance, as Ted leaves his house to join his friends in setting off firecrackers in celebration, his father muses on more appropriate ways to honour the English Queen:

> His father nodded indulgently across his littered desk. "Go on," he said, "and don't blow yourself to pieces. But I wish people would honor the day more nobly. One might do better things in memory of the great Queen-Empress than setting off rockets. A fault overcome, a spiritual victory gained, would be of higher value as a memorial than a hundred exploded squibs." (Pickthall 1907b: 1)

The symbolic Victoria Day holiday is central to this story's message of "spiritual victory," giving it a uniquely Canadian air and demonstrating that there was an interest in Canadian content among publishers of juvenile literature in the United States at the beginning of the twentieth century. It also suggests that young Americans were not merely interested in travel narratives and adventure novels, but were also consuming other types of stories about Canadian life and society.

Pickthall's story "All Together," which appears in the June 22, 1907 issue of *The Boys' World* is a further example of the ways in which American publishers and readers were exploring Canadian themes through children's fiction. Once again, Pickthall uses an important Canadian holiday as a backdrop, and "All Together" tells the story of four Canadian boys preparing to row in a regatta against an American crew on Dominion Day (July 1), the holiday that marks the anniversary of Canadian Confederation. Old Elliot, the boys' coach, is frustrated with their apparent inability to pull together as a team, and the crew's internal divisions serve as a metaphor for problems with Canadian unity:

> "See here," he said, more gently, "you *must* pull together. It's the same with a crew as it is with a country. If they don't pull together, it's all up with 'em. Macpherson, you're from Lanark, in Ontario; and Warwick, you're from Winnipeg; and Swenson, you're from New Brunswick; and Lalonde's from Quebec. You're all proud as can be of your home towns, and you'd like to come in with flyin' colors for the sake o' Perth and Winnipeg and Fredericton and L'Assomption. But you must drop all thinkin' o' that. If you want to win, you must just remember you're Canadians, and think o' Canada. Pull for the whole Dominion!" (Pickthall 1907a: 1)

Old Elliot's metaphor and the subsequent rousing plea "Don't let the Old Dominion take a back seat on Dominion Day!" (1), make this a story full of Canadian significance. The fact that the team is facing an American rival also takes on special meaning when one considers that at the time of the story's publication, the United States was viewed as a potential threat to Canadian sovereignty.[3] The threats of Canadian fragmentation and annexation are therefore implicit in Pickthall's tale. Yet its ending betrays a concession to the fact that it appears in an American periodical. The Canadian boys learn to pull together to honour their country on the holiday that marks the anniversary of the union of the various provinces, but their triumph lies in achieving team unity, rather than in defeating the American crew:

> A roar from every soul on the banks startled him. He saw one of the Washington House boys leaning forward excitedly, as if to grip hands with him across ten feet of water. And then, as the red ensign with the maple leaf, and the stars and stripes, fluttered up together to announce the dead heat, he toppled backwards into Macpherson's arms. His right hand dropped useless from the scull.
>
> "Guess that was my last race," he said faintly; "but it was a good one."
> The cheers told him he was right. (Pickthall 1907a: 8)

The joint victory of the American and Canadian teams allows Pickthall to stress the importance of Canadian unity without disappointing or offending the pride of her young American readership. The narrative's final episode also reinforces the notion of harmonious relations between Canada and the United States.

The appearance of Marjorie Pickthall's Canadian tales in *The Boys' World* in the spring of 1907 is an example of one of the ways in which Americans were involved in Canadian children's literature in the early twentieth century. She was one of many Canadian authors who regularly submitted work to American magazines during the 1890s and the first decade of the twentieth century (Doyle 1990: 30). This was occurring in the realm of both adult and juvenile literature, with American periodicals publishing several Canadian stories, poems, and articles per year. In addition to Marjorie Pickthall's stories of 1907, for example, *The Boys' World* also published Canadian writer Pauline Johnson's "Little Wolf-Willow" in December of the same year. While these tales retain much of their distinctly Canadian nature, one can question the degree of influence American editors and critics had on such material (Doyle 1990: 33). Ultimately, while offering uniquely Canadian references and details, Pickthall's tales espouse values, namely those of manly virtue and patriotism, which readers and publishers on both sides of the 49th parallel can embrace. Pickthall's stories reveal a conscious effort not to offend the sensibilities of their American readers, and her publication in American periodicals demonstrates both an American interest in Canada, and the fact that some Canadian writers needed, or wanted, their works published in the United States.

The publication of Canadian authors in the United States, and the existence of Canadian subject matter in works by American writers, illustrates the manner in which the United States could influence (for good or bad) the Canadian literary landscape. In his survey of Canadian juvenile fiction, Gordon Moyles observes that the publication of Canadian authors outside their home country is a positive sign of the influential nature of such writing:

> The fact that they, of necessity, published in magazines produced and chiefly circulated in Great Britain and the United States is not to be taken as a detriment, but rather as a compliment: having no outlet in their own country, they were accepted by such discerning writer-editors as Mary Mapes Dodge, and they gained an international reputation rarely accorded later writers of children's literature. (Moyles 1995: 8)

Moyles' index demonstrates that Canadian children's literature appeared frequently in such high-profile American publications as *Harper's Young People*, to which J.M. Oxley was a frequent contributor, and was often concerned with distinctly Canadian topics. Yet to some extent, Patsy Aldana's observation that Americans are not greatly interested in Canadian content, or rather that they are not particularly familiar with it, does apply to the late-nineteenth and early-twentieth century children's literature market. In the review section of the Canadian monthly family magazine *Our Home*'s September 1896 issue, for example, there is an excerpt from an American review of the Canadian book *Twok*. This review from the Philadelphia *American*, demonstrates that Canadian themes were not always familiar ones to readers in the United States: "The scene is Canadian, and this not very usual locale for a work of fiction gives the scheme novelty, which is enhanced by numerous clever realistic touches . . ." (*Our Home* 1896c: 45). The reviewer's observation that Canada is not a usual *locale* for works of fiction lends an almost exotic air to the Canadian scene. But it also betrays an ignorance of the number of American works of fiction in existence at this time that had Canadian settings. This particular reviewer appears either to be unaware of, or to be discounting, the number of children's works that his fellow Americans were setting in Canadian landscapes.

The comments of this reviewer underscore the somewhat ambiguous literary relationship between the United States and Canada at the end of the nineteenth century. When it came to children's literature, writers pictured Canada both as an exotic landscape, and as a mere extension of the United States. William J. Long's *Ways of Wood Folk* from 1899 is an example of a non-fiction work in which the author sees the Canadian setting merely as part of the larger North American landscape. This account of animal life in parts of the United States and Canada includes an account of an encounter with a moose in New Brunswick but places no special emphasis on the Canadian locale. Canada is merely an extension of the American playground for hunters and fishermen in this text. Numerous children's works echo this attitude, including James A. Rose's *A Boy's*

Vacation on the Great Lakes, which sees a group of American boys travelling by ship through the Great Lakes. Although the children do visit Canada during this vacation, the difference between the two countries is barely remarked upon. In effect, it is by this very absence of a distinction between the United States and Canada that American writers extend their ownership over Canadian soil.

Yet while some writers fail to note any serious differences between their homeland and Canada, others see a new and exotic frontier in this northerly land. One such American writer is Jack London. Born and raised in California, London spent part of 1897 and 1898 in the Yukon and saw unique characteristics in Canada and its landscape. The first chapter of *The Call of the Wild* details the arrival of the story's canine hero Buck into the Canadian north. The Canadian locale is central to this story and spells trouble for Buck: "Buck did not read the newspapers, or he would have known that trouble was brewing. . . . Because men, groping in the Arctic darkness, had found a yellow metal, and . . . thousands of men were rushing into the Northland" (15–16). His encounter with the Canadian wilderness teaches Buck many harsh lessons, but also proves to be a dangerous place for men lured by the promise of gold, but betrayed by their greed at a time "when the Klondike strike dragged men from all the world into the frozen North" (London 1903: 19).

Critic James Doyle dismisses this novel's Canadian setting as "little more than incidental local colour" which does not detract from the American significance of the Klondike gold rush or the American themes and experiences of the frontier and man's conflict with nature (Doyle *North* 148). "Ultimately," writes Doyle, "London's North is a super-national entity, an anonymous setting for the conflict between man and nature and for the "survival of the fittest" doctrine" (Doyle 1983: 148). Although similar stories were also being set in American locales such as Alaska, Doyle is somewhat mislead in his assessment here, for London's setting is *not* anonymous, it is clearly Canadian. As such, London's portrayal of Canada helps to shape a memorable image of the country as a land of primeval forces, led by the rule of natural law. With the detailed account of Buck's journey from the southern warmth of California to Canada's frigid lands, the comparisons between Canada and America are inescapable. London's depiction of "the Arctic darkness" and "the frozen North," are part of the author's vision of Canada as a strange and threatening place. He also presents a picture of Canadians themselves as a distinct group of people. Buck encounters many brutal dogs and men joining the rush for gold in the north, but it his Canadian owners who finally earn his respect, if not his love:

> Perrault was a French-Canadian, and swarthy; but Francois was a French-Canadian half-breed, and twice as swarthy. They were a new kind of men to Buck . . . and while he developed no affection for them, he none the less grew honestly to respect them. He speedily learned that Perrault and Francois were fair men, calm and impartial in administering justice, and too wise in the way of dogs to be fooled by dogs. (London 1903: 37)

These "swarthy" Canadians demonstrate fairness and justice in their handling of the dogs, and as a result, Buck gains some respect for them: "That was fair of Francoise, he decided, and the half-breed began to rise in Buck's estimation" (38). Of all the men portrayed in this novel, it is the Canadians who most clearly embody the virtues of fairness, justice, and respect for the power of their natural surroundings.

Jack London's popular novel, now considered a classic of children's literature, demonstrates many of the attitudes towards Canada current in late-nineteenth century America. Canada is both an extension of the United States, with its mineral potential fought over by men from around the world, as well as an unmistakably foreign and strange land. Its northern landscape has a nature and influence very different from that of the United States, being able both to corrupt and purify. Furthermore, London's depiction of the Canadian figures of Perrault and Francoise echoes some of the "Canadian characteristics" promoted in Canadian children's literature, including honesty, perseverance, and an intimate and valuable knowledge of the land. James Doyle describes this ambiguity in the portrayal and function of Canada in American literature as follows:

> The Canada that appears in nineteenth-century American literature is not always the country its own inhabitants know. But neither is it always the Canada of popular cliché, the country of frozen wastes and cheerful French woodsmen. . . . In the most artistically significant versions, the image of the northern country is a vague, enigmatic variation on the geographical and historical experiences of the United States, not quite impressive enough to constitute a serious challenge to the assumptions and values of the republic but prominent enough to be seriously contemplated and at times vigorously refuted. (Doyle 1983: 4–5)

Doyle argues that after the Revolution, American writers began to consider the implications of Canada's rejection of independence, and that Canada continued to "provoke reconsideration, in the minds of a few Americans at least, of questions relating to the vital centre of American political experience" (Doyle 1983: 4–5).

While Doyle is referring to adult literature, the image of Canada as a mere extension of the United States, but also a challenge to it, is also present in children's literature. Sometimes portrayed as a different and sometimes threatening place, writers simultaneously picture Canada as nothing more than an extension of America's playground. Popular children's writers such as St. George Rathborne (1854–1938), whose many pseudonyms include Oliver Lee Clifton and Warren Miller, wrote several stories of American boys seeking adventure in Canada among their "Canuck" neighbours. Rathborne's American-published novels with Canadian settings include *Rival Canoe Boys: or, With Pack and Paddle on the Nipigon* (*circa* 1902) and *Canoe Mates in Canada or Three Boys Afloat on the Saskatchewan* (1912), which tells the story of

American boys Cuthbert and Eli who are joined on their canoe trip down the Saskatchewan river by a Canadian boy, whom they call a "Canuck." Many similar children's works published in the United States during the nineteenth and early twentieth centuries, exhibit a variety of attitudes towards Canada and Canadians. For Canadian children reading these American publications, the image of their country was one of complexity and contradiction.

Following Confederation, young Anglophone Canadian readers had access to literature from Britain, the United States, Europe, and Canada. Many of these works dealt directly with Canadian themes and presented a multitude of images of the country and its people. This complex group of images all played a role in influencing Canada's own developing sense of national identity. From British works which claimed Canada as a loyal subject nation, to American literature that predicted the inevitability of Canadian annexation by the United States, writers described the nation in terms that were colourful, complex, and often contradictory. While some children's writers could offer personal experience to enrich their stories of Canadian life, others, including Canadians themselves, often betrayed an ignorance of the true nature and diversity of the country. One of the most prominent and recurring images was the depiction of Canada as a northern wilderness:

> The fictional Canada to which young English readers were transported was, on the whole, a monotonously restricted area: it was, to use one of the most popular definitions, the 'great North-West.' More than 85 percent of the so-called 'Canadian' stories in English juvenile magazines and novels were set in this ill defined and variously defined region, and the assumption must have been that the whole of Canada—if, indeed, there was any more—was exactly similar in both terrain and inhabitants. There was an occasional story set in the 'bush' of Ontario and less occasionally one . . . set in Nova Scotia, Newfoundland, or Labrador. . . . One could, for example, have read *The Boy's Own Paper* for almost fifty years and never have known that there were large cities like Montreal or Toronto, although every now and then a spoil-sport would point out that even Winnipeg had grocery stores and modern conveniences. (Moyles and Owram 1988: 40)

From the midst of this plethora and confusion of images, Canadian readers were finding the roots of what would come to be the major strains of national identity and Canadian nationalism in Anglophone Canada in the twentieth century.

Chapter Two
Forest, Prairie, Sea, and Mountain: Canadian Regionalism

In addition to the impact foreign literature had on Canada's self-image, Canadian regionalism also had serious implications for the Canadian national identity. The strong centralist perspective in Canada and the concentration of publishing houses in Ontario and Quebec influenced the nation's literature. As the western areas of the country came to be settled and developed, the sense of what constituted Canadian nationhood changed in accordance with the growing-pains experienced in the provinces of Manitoba, British Columbia, Alberta, and Saskatchewan. Children's writers from across Canada's diverse territories each contributed their own regional cultures and experiences to the developing sense of a national community.

The writings of the various regions of Canada also reflect the manner in which writers, educators, and politicians employed children's literature to construct a national identity and to promote a sense of unity. The publishing industry was concentrated in central Canada as the distribution figures of the nation's daily papers at the turn of the twentieth century demonstrate. In 1901, Ontario had fifty-five dailies, the Maritimes had twenty-two, Quebec had fifteen, British Columbia had a dozen, Manitoba and the Yukon each had fewer than eight, and the Northwest Territories had just one (Page 1972: 15). These figures reflect the reality of children's literature publishing as well. Yet while central and Eastern Canada (particularly Ontario) had a strong influence on the national culture, regional literatures for children also played an important role in educating young readers about Canada and inspiring them with a vision of a vast and grand nation.

Regionalism and National Character

While children's writers and publishers from across Europe, Britain, and America helped to shape the image of Canada in the late-nineteenth century, the juvenile fiction produced in Canada itself reveals a host of attitudes towards the country and its inhabitants. Following Confederation, Canada quickly became, and remains to this day, an incredibly diverse nation. The regional diversity of the country has had a lasting impact on all aspects of Canadian culture, including music, art, and literature. Northrop Frye explains this diversity, and its difference from American regionalism, as follows:

> In the United States, the frontier has been, imaginatively, an open-ended horizon in the west; in Canada, wherever one is, the frontier is a circumference. Every part of Canada is shut off by its geography, British Columbia from the prairies by the Rockies, the prairies from the Canadas by the immense hinterland of northern Ontario, Quebec from the Maritimes by the upthrust of Maine, the Maritimes from Newfoundland by the sea . . . everywhere in Canada we find solitudes touching other solitudes: every part of Canada has strong separatist feelings, because every part of it is in fact a separation. And behind all these separations lies the silent north, full of vast rivers, lakes, and islands that, even yet, very few Canadians have ever seen. The Mississippi, running north to south through the middle of the country, is a symbol of the American frontier and its steady advance into the sunset. The largest river in Canada, the Mackenzie, pouring slightly into the Arctic Ocean at what seems the end of the earth, is a symbol of the *terra incognita* in Canadian consciousness. (Frye 1982: 58–59)

Frye's account of Canadian regionalism speaks of both physical and imaginative divides. Geographic reality has an influence not only on questions of politics and economics, but also on the national culture. In his study of the concept of region in Canadian literature, historian William Westfall writes that Canada is a nation "balanced on a tension between a political feeling of unity and a host of regional identities," while at the same time acknowledging the difficulty in defining these distinct regions (1993: 336). The term region can imply political, economic, cultural, linguistic, as well as environmental distinctions. Familiar terms such as Atlantic Canada, Prairie, and Northern reflect the traditionally environmental approach to identifying regions within Canada, and "underline the strength and popularity of associating a region with a dominant physical feature" (Westfall 1993: 336). These terms underscore the important role that Canada's environment has played in shaping the country's identity. Westfall writes that landscape and climate "have created and nurtured strong regions and acted as a barrier against national unity. Consequently, we have strong regional identities within a relatively weak nation-state" (336). Few nations, however, are without some sense of distinct regional identities. While Westfall may be correct in saying that strong regions pose a potential threat to national unity, there is also evidence that this diversity can actually strengthen and enrich national culture.

In early post-Confederation Canada, writers of children's literature were exploring the country's different regions in a deliberate attempt to overcome these potential barriers against national unity. Writers were both portraying their own regions in the context of their place in the larger national scene, and actively developing the identities and images of other regions of Canada in an attempt to envelop these less populated and less familiar locales into the national fold. Frye observes that "culture has something vegetable about it, something that increasingly needs to grow from roots, something that demands a small region and a restricted locale" (Frye 1982: 62). In the children's literature of post-Confederation Canada, one can see this kind of cultural growth beginning to take place. This type of regionalism, while highlighting the diversity within Canada and enhancing local culture, also contributes to a sense of a larger national identity. Following Confederation, there continued to be discord among the various provinces and regions within Canada. Those writers who were concerned with strengthening national unity began to pay more attention to the various elements that made up the nation, in order to develop a greater understanding of these regions and the part each could play in the Canadian whole. At times the sense of national unity portrayed in this literature is an illusion, but in the very process of creating these fictions, writers were helping to ensure the future reality of a sense of nationhood and Canadian national identity.

Much of the English-language children's literature produced in Canada during the nineteenth and early twentieth centuries emanated from central Canada. For example, the majority of the works examined in this study were published originally in either Quebec or Ontario. The Ontario perspective pervades much of this literature, and influences the attitudes towards national identity and unity expressed in Canada's early children's narratives. The predominance of the centralist (and specifically Ontario) viewpoint results from several factors. To begin with, Ontario has a much longer history of settlement than provinces such as British Columbia, and Ontario had a far greater concentration of population in the nineteenth century. Second, it was one of the key provincial powers pushing for Confederation, which in 1867 consisted solely of Ontario, Quebec, New Brunswick, and Nova Scotia. The remaining provinces joined the Canadian union at different times with Manitoba becoming a province in 1870, British Columbia joining in 1871, and Prince Edward Island following suit in 1873. The year 1905 saw the creation of the provinces of Alberta and Saskatchewan, with Newfoundland being the last to join Confederation in 1949. It was the older, established centres in Quebec and Ontario, therefore, which were the prime centres of cultural production in the late-nineteenth century. As a result, the images of Canadian identity and nationalism put forth in much of the children's literature from this period reflect a strong centralist perspective, similar to that which Canadian historian and historiographer S.F. Wise observes in the work of today's Ontario historians:

[M]ost Ontarians, do not perceive the province to be merely a region, but rather a kind of provincial equivalent of Canada as a whole. . . . Ontarians have always regarded Confederation as primarily their creation, and the province as pivotal to its maintenance. . . . The idea of centrality, linked to the idea that the country as a whole is a field for the expression of Ontario's interests ("Empire Ontario," a phrase current at the turn of this century), continues to be a part of the province's political ethos. (Wise 1993: 413)

The idea that the nation as a whole is a field for the expression of Central Canada's interests is further evident in the concentration of many so-called national juvenile magazines and periodicals in the hands of a few publishers in Montreal, Toronto, and some smaller centres in southern Ontario.

This conflation of the ideas of "national" and "Ontario" emerged in politics as much as in culture. Nevertheless, despite this centralist perspective, there was some awareness of the Canada that lay beyond Ontario and Quebec. Tales of east coast provinces such as Nova Scotia found expression in the retelling of the histories of Acadia and Louisbourg. Children's writers from the East like James de Mille (1833–1880) of New Brunswick, and Nova Scotia's J.M. Oxley (1855–1907), lent a voice to this part of the country: De Mille with such novels as *The Lily and the Cross: A Tale of Acadia* (1874) and Oxley with works that included *Fife and Drum at Louisbourg* (1899) and *In Paths of Peril: A Boy's Adventures in Nova Scotia* (*circa* 1903). While both authors were highly prolific writers, it was children's writer L.M. Montgomery (1874–1942) who represented life in Atlantic Canada most famously. Montgomery's tales of life in Prince Edward Island were hugely popular, and *Anne of Green Gables* and the sequels that followed, with their detailed observation of life in the small, rural community of Avonlea, drew a vivid picture of life in Eastern Canada at the turn of the twentieth century. These tales of life in the very specific Canadian locale of Prince Edward Island were warmly received by young readers throughout Canada and abroad.

Despite its unique setting, Montgomery's *Anne of Green Gables* situates the story of life on P.E.I. in the context of the nation as a whole. With its examination of questions of difference and conformity, rejection and acceptance, duty and independence, and family and community bonds, all of which are pertinent to Anne's life in the small island society, the novel mirrors many of the issues that were of relevance to the wider national community. In their study of Montgomery's role in shaping Canadian culture, Irene Gammel and Elizabeth Epperly see Montgomery's close focus on region as an important part of her vision of the nation as a whole:

Montgomery constructs the nation not only through the window of regional difference, but through the window of a common set of values. The region is associated with . . . the pleasure of romantic identification with the landscape. . . . The nation, in contrast, is associated with labour, industry, duty, courage, and noble service. (Gammel and Epperly 1999: 7)

Through her depiction of domestic life in the small, rural (and fictional) community of Avonlea in Maritime Canada, Montgomery both constructs and reflects the larger concerns of Canada as a whole. The journey of the novel's eponymous and orphaned heroine, as she gradually finds a place of belonging in her new community and develops a strong sense of self, mirrors Canada's own journey towards claiming an identity for itself.

While Eastern Canada had children's writers like De Mille, Oxley, and Montgomery to give it a voice and to establish its place in the national consciousness, there were also writers who portrayed Western Canada in the juvenile literature of the late nineteenth century. While east coast writers like Montgomery were writing tales of domestic life in rural Prince Edward Island, or examining the social codes and practices of its larger urban centres, the rivers and plains of the Northwest Territories were the site of tales of adventure in the worlds of fur-trading, mining, and exploration. British Columbia figured in tales of the mining boom of the late 1800s, and the prairies of the West received much literary attention long before the actual political birth of Alberta and Saskatchewan in 1905. Unlike Eastern and central Canada, which had local writers to speak for them, the later period of settlement of the West meant that much of the literature devoted to it was also written by authors from the central and eastern regions of the nation. As the twentieth century progressed, the West gradually came to have its own writers such as Nellie McClung (1873–1951) to give it a literary voice. Born in Owen Sound, Ontario in 1873, McClung moved to Manitoba as a child. She celebrated life in the Canadian Prairies in a series of popular novels. McClung was also a keen political activist, devoted to the issues of women's rights and suffrage. In 1929 she was one of Canada's "famous five" who successfully fought to have women declared "persons" under the law. Works such as McClung's *Sowing Seeds in Danny*, first published in 1908 and read by children and adults alike, lent authority to the tales of western provinces like Manitoba. In telling the story of young Pearl Watson and her younger brothers and sister, McClung draws a picture of daily life in one of Canada's prairie communities and depicts the unique beauty of the western landscape. In the nineteenth century, however, the writing of the West by authors from other parts of the country largely "treated the west as a distant stage for an eastern drama" (Westfall 1993: 342). Yet the attention devoted to this "distant stage" in children's literature is in itself an indication of the symbolic impact that this vast and important region had on the national psyche in the years following Confederation.

As Canada grew as a nation, it quickly became clear that its western territories needed to be developed. With the purchase of vast tracts of land from the Hudson's Bay Company in 1869, the expansion of the country from the Atlantic to the Pacific was well underway. The Manitoba Act of 1870 saw the creation of that province and its inclusion in Confederation. The development of the West was not, however, without its share of trouble and controversy. The displacement of the land's original inhabitants, including the Métis, and the destruction of their way of life on the plains in order to clear the land for agriculture sparked the North-West "rebellions" of 1870 and 1885, and led to the eventual execution of Métis leader Louis Riel.[1] This settlement of the prairies forever changed the face of western Canada. While settlers came from other parts of the country in the hopes of capitalising on the great promise offered by this new frontier, the development of this region also sparked new waves of immigration to Canada. Between 1896 and 1914 more than two million immigrants came to Canada and the majority of these settled in the West. The efforts of these new inhabitants helped transform the Canadian plains into rich and productive, though challenging, farmland. The agricultural wealth of the prairies saw Canada producing hundreds of millions of bushels of grain by the first decade of the twentieth century, and helped to ensure the nation's economic security.

As the West gained real economic and political significance it also gained a new literary significance, and gave rise to a host of unique imagery. In reference to this imagery and history of the West R. Douglas Francis writes:

> There is an aspect of its history which transcends the decisions of politicians, the intricate workings of the economy, and the daily activities of its people; it exists in the mind. The history of the West has often been governed as much by what people imagined the region to be as the "reality" itself. (Francis 1993: 441)

This imagining of the region took shape in children's novels and periodicals from the late nineteenth century onwards. As the West gained importance in strengthening Canadian unity and avoiding political annexation of British Columbia by the United States, writers communicated its significance to young readers through this mixture of imagination and reality. In the July 1897 issue of Toronto's *Home and Youth* for example, the poem "The Glories of Canada" contains some romanticised imagery of the West:

> The prairies vast of Canada!
> Where sun sinks to the earth,
> In setting, whispering warm good-night
> To myriad flowers, whose blushes bright
> Will hail the morrow's birth.
>
> The prairie wealth of Canada!
> Whose dark, abundant soil,
> Unfurrowed yet, awaits the plow:
> Who sows shall have true promise now
> Of rich reward for toil.

What tho' the winter wind blows keen
When daylight darkly wanes!
A strong, true heart is hard to chill;
When seen afar, the home light still,
Shines bright across the plains.

The robust life of Canada
In cheery homes I see!
Tho' gold nor jewels fill the hand,
'Tis Nature's self has blessed the land,
Abundant, fair and free. (*Home and Youth* 1897b: 17)

Writing about the West and securing its place on the page and in the nation's imagination, was part of an attempt to secure its place in the nation's political union and economic future.

In fact, it was the West that gave rise to one of the most enduring symbols of Canadian national identity—the Mountie. First known as the Northwest Mounted Police in 1873, this organisation really entered the national consciousness after its initial march from Manitoba to Fort Whoop-Up in southwestern Alberta in 1874. The story of this cross-country march, the glories of which were celebrated in the literature of the day, is in itself a story of the East conquering the West. The fact that the journey was not in reality the undisputed success that many writers made it out to be did not diminish its status in the nation's imagination.

While the force came to be associated with Western Canada, it began its journey toward mythological status in central Canada. The Mounted Police heralded the lawful development of Canada's western territories, in direct opposition to the image of America's unruly "Wild West." Many writers of the time saw the Mounted Police force as something that had begun as a vision of Canada's Father of Confederation, John A. Macdonald. That he was not necessarily the integral force behind them is something Keith Walden points out in his study of the mythology surrounding this police force. But Walden illustrates the reason behind the symbolic connection between Macdonald and the Mounted Police:

It is obvious why so many writers wanted to see such a close association between Macdonald and the mounted police. By linking the two, it was natural to think that the vision which brought the force into being was part and parcel of the vision which had inspired Canada itself. Macdonald's interest seemed to imply that the formation of this dedicated corps was part of the act of national creation. The force, therefore, was an instrument of national growth and not a repressive, negating element in Canadian life. It was central to the Canadian experience and an essential element in the ongoing success of the nation. (Walden 1992: 109)

The Northwest Mounted Police, with their initial Great March from East to West, symbolised a unifying force within Canada. They were seen to draw the western territories into the Canadian whole in a lawful, disciplined, and just manner. The Mounted Police received treatment in numerous children's tales from the force's inception onwards. Once again, Moyles' index provides excellent evidence of the frequent appearance of such stories in children's periodicals, including such titles as J.M. Oxley's "Policemen of the Canadian Plains" (1889), W. Everard-Edmonds' "The Northwest Mounted Police" (1905), and A.L. Haydon's "The Lost Patrol: How the RNWMP Carried a King's Mail" (1912). These stories are part of the increasing attention that both politicians and writers paid to western Canada in the years following Confederation.

The Canadian children's periodicals of the day frequently incorporated stories about western Canada as a great source of entertainment, but these were also a means of educating the children of central Canada about British Columbia and Canada's other western territories. The presence of these informative stories betrays the fact that the main readership of these "national" magazines actually resided largely in Ontario and the eastern part of Canada. Nevertheless, this increasing awareness of the need to educate Canadian children about the western areas of the country illustrates the growing conception of Canada as a nation that spanned from coast to coast. And there is evidence that children from across the country read the national magazines published in Ontario and elsewhere in central Canada. In the March 1897 issue of Montreal's *Our Home* for instance, there is a collection of letters from satisfied subscribers from Manitoba, Ontario, Nova Scotia, New Brunswick, British Columbia, and even from the United States (*Our Home* 1897: 7). In the May 1901 issue of *The Canadian Boy*, there is a similar claim that the magazine "is a favorite . . . in many parts of Canada" and that "each month's issue circulates from Vancouver to Charlottetown and all through Canada" (*Canadian Boy* 1901: 38). There is also a letter to the editor in this issue from Professor E. Odlum of British Columbia calling *The Canadian Boy* "one of the most valuable papers in Canada" for "helping Canadian boys to be better men" (Odlum: 37). Odlum then goes on to promise that he will contribute to the magazine in the future, in order to inform its readers about his province, British Columbia:

> I shall write them a few short letters telling them of the wonderful riches of British Columbia, of its lovely and healthful climate, and of the many openings for spirited, wise and good boys. I shall tell them how the grand Canadian Pacific Railway Company has built its many splendid lines through the valleys and over the mountains, and also about the fisheries, the large lumber forests, vast mining interests, the farming and ranching opportunities, and other items of interest, and what I shall tell your boy readers will be of knowledge and not guess work. (Odlum 1901: 37)

Odlum's assurance that his accounts of British Columbia will "be of knowledge" indicates that he is aware of the tendency for his province's story to be written and told by the "guess work" of outsiders.

Canadian writers looked beyond their own communities to explore the diverse regions of Canada and to communicate a sense of national unity to their young readers. The emphasis on stories about western Canada mirrors the critical agitation for settlement of the West taking place in Ottawa. With the construction of railways, the development of a vast agricultural industry, and the accompanying waves of new immigration, the development of Canada's western territories became an issue of immense national and political importance.

With Ottawa being the seat of government in Canada, Ontario's influence in the shaping of the nation, both real and imagined, is undeniable. In the wake of nineteenth-century fears that the new confederation was still under threat both from American influence and from its own internal struggles, writers with an interest in strengthening the federal union were eagerly promoting the cause of national unity, while inescapably expressing a multitude of regional loyalties and identities at the same time. If, as Canadian historian Christopher Armstrong claims, "National loyalty flourishes not by overpowering other loyalties but by subsuming them and keeping them in a mutually supportive relationship" (Armstrong 1993: 59–60), then the literary attention paid to the country's various provinces and regions by Canadian writers can be viewed as part of this attempt to establish a sense of national loyalty and understanding in the nation's children. Nevertheless, if the predominance of this writing by Ontarians reflects "the desire of Ontarians to fasten their version of Canadian nationalism upon the rest of the country, making little copies of what they see as the 'real' Canada" (Armstrong 1993: 60), then the ideas of nationalism and national identity put forth in the children's literature of the late nineteenth and early twentieth centuries in fact reflect an image of the country that is strongly influenced by this centralist perspective.

Yet even Ontario's vision of itself was a mixture of imagination and reality. Writers accepted and perpetuated the image of Canada as a land of the north, with all the associated notions of Canadians being a hardy, industrious race, even though Ontario's primary centres of culture and power were concentrated along the province's southernmost reaches. But as time progressed, Canadian writers as a whole began to reflect a more accurate picture of their surroundings. As writers began to examine the unique diversity within their vast country, they began to lend a more authoritative voice to Canada's national literature. In his examination of the tradition of fiction in Canada, T.D. MacLulich acknowledges that by the end of the nineteenth century, most Canadian writers had moved away from strictly European models of fiction, and had begun to identify themselves as part of the rising Canadian bourgeoisie (MacLulich 1988: 36). Writers of children's fiction in the decades following Confederation were dealing directly "with the ordinary people and scenes of their native country"

(MacLulich 1988: 36). In spite of the concentration of people in central and eastern Canada, writers and publishers placed an increasing emphasis on representing the various regions of the country.

In 1893, a collection of stories written by Canadian school children containing tales from regions across Canada was published in Montreal. Selected and edited by Rev. Charles J. Cameron of Ontario, the introduction to this collection states that "Mr. Cameron does not claim to have selected the best stories, but rather stories representative of the different provinces" (Cameron: viii). The tales represent the writing of children from across Canada, including British Columbia and the Prairie provinces, and help to demonstrate that by the late nineteenth century, there was an emphasis on exploring the various scenes of the country.

As the century progressed and Confederation incorporated new provinces and territories, there was a sense that while the country was growing, it was also becoming a closer-knit community. Increasingly, the various regions of the country were drawn into a definitive national unit. As an 1896 article in *Our Home* indicates, the technological developments of the century had much to do with this:

> Yes, we are moving on, and the progress of the future will be greater than the progress of the past. We will move on by the lightning express instead of by the stage coach. The Dominion is fast becoming a network of railways, and railways induce immigration, bring distant towns into hand-shaking distance and build up trade. What Canadians as a people require more than anything else is confidence in the future. (*Our Home* 1896b: 1–2)

Children's writers of the late nineteenth century were witness to the changes that were bringing the various locales of Canada into "hand-shaking distance." The Canadian scenes depicted in their literature gradually incorporated the far regions of the country as these writers increasingly envisioned the country as a unified whole, stretching from coast to coast to the far reaches of the frozen north.

Chapter Three
A Question of Loyalties:
Britain and Canada

In his discussion of Canada's search for an identity following the upheavals of the Second World War, political scientist Blair Fraser made the following remarks in 1967:

> Up to and during World War II, Canada was preoccupied with her emergence from the status of colony. This process, which went on for two centuries, at no time got unanimous encouragement from Canadians. Many preferred to be colonists, and apparently some still do. . . . The fight for Canadian independence was never, on any significant scale, directed against the British. It was always a running fight among Canadians. . . . No sooner had the sense of identity been attained than it began to be questioned on other grounds, and from new aspects. (Fraser 1967: 1–2)

Fraser's study underlines the inherent complexity of Canada's "search" for identity. It also demonstrates that present-day perceptions and expressions of Canadian identity are part of a lengthy process of discovery and understanding. The study of nineteenth-century literature reveals that elements of what many consider to be the "Canadian identity" have been in existence for quite some time. Nevertheless, although there is evidence of Canadian nationalism in the late nineteenth century, this was of a complex, contradictory nature and shaped by complex and often opposing forces. One of the major influences on Canada's developing sense of identity was the nation's connection to Great Britain.

A major struggle within the Canadian psyche was between a lingering loyalty to Britain, and a growing awareness of Canada's need and desire for independence. This tension manifests itself in several ways in the children's literature of the time. On the one hand, there is literature that clearly promotes the country's imperial ties, while on the other there is literature that reflects a growing impatience with Britain and frustration with its continued meddling in Canadian affairs. In the first body of literature, British characters and traditions are seen to be worthy of emulation. In the second, they are often mocked and derided. In some instances, the young "Englishman" emerges as a figure of fun; a representation of outmoded, undemocratic practices, and the moral, political, and physical inferior of the children of the New World.

These contrasting views appear in the novels and juvenile periodicals published in Canada and designed specifically for Canadian children, providing evidence of an ongoing struggle between those who wanted Canada to forge its own path and resist continued British influence, and those who firmly believed in the duty of supporting the empire and the motherland. The complexities of Canada's association with Britain manifested themselves in the children's literature of the day and played a significant role in the construction of Canada's national identity and self-image.

God Save the Queen?

From the Queen's head on the currency, to the names of cities and towns across the country, evidence of Canada's relation to Britain abounds in the twenty-first century. It is, therefore, hardly surprising that Canadians still felt a British influence in the late nineteenth century. In economic terms, Britain's partnership with Canada remained of supreme importance well into the twentieth century. While trade with the United States gradually increased, Canada's most important trade relationship in the nineteenth century remained with Britain.[1] In addition to being such a strong economic presence, the United Kingdom also had a powerful cultural existence in late-nineteenth and early twentieth-century Canada. Children sang the British national anthem, waved the British flag, and read British books. Many juvenile periodicals of the day, while given "Canadian" titles, were in fact simply reprints of magazines or material previously published in England. Such literature included titles like *Young Canada: An Illustrated Magazine for the Young*, which was published in Toronto but had minimal Canadian content (Egoff 1992c), and *The Canadian Girl's Annual* published in London and containing primarily English content (Egoff 1992a). From 1880 to the early years of the twentieth century there were Canadian editions of Britain's *Boy's Own Paper* and *Girl's Own Paper* published in Toronto, which again did not provide much in the way of Canadian content (Vann and VanArsdel 1996: 103). The strong presence of British literature continued well into the late nineteenth century and J. Don Vann claims that during this period "Canadian children and adolescents were supplied with imported titles, or made do without periodicals" (103).

While Vann is correct in saying that Canadian children read foreign periodicals, and although it is true that they may not have had as much choice in the way of home-grown periodicals as their English counterparts, there were, nevertheless, several nineteenth-century children's magazines and newspapers designed specifically for the Canadian market. Yet while many of these claim to promote national pride and spirit, they are often simultaneously promoting pride in, and loyalty to, Britain. In these magazines, stories of the Royal Family, British history, and British politics abound, but often appear alongside stories of Canadian events and daily life.

One such magazine, published in southern Ontario, is *The Canadian Boy; A Journal of Incident, Story and Self-Help*. This was one of several juvenile periodicals published in cities and towns in Canada following Confederation. Usually produced by small local publishers, these periodicals included weekly and monthly publications with annual subscription prices ranging anywhere from twenty-five cents to two dollars. From the editorials and subscription information in the back pages of these magazines, it appears that many had national circulation, though the life span of most does not on the whole appear to have been lengthy. *The Canadian Boy* was an illustrated monthly, with a subscription price of one dollar per year, or ten cents a copy. According to an article in the issue from May 1901, the magazine had a large national readership:

> *The Canadian Boy* is growing. . . . This magazine is a favorite already in many parts of Canada. Counting boys and their friends at least ten thousand persons will read this number of *The Canadian Boy*. By the end of the year we expect to have thirty thousand readers. We commend this journal to all friends of boys in Canada. . . . Each month's issue circulates from Vancouver to Charlottetown and all through Canada. Agents are at work everywhere. (*Canadian Boy* 1901)

The title page describes this periodical as a "Bright, Patriotic, Helpful, Entertaining" magazine for "Young Canada." The "Patriotic" nature of this magazine, however, is not always clear, and as such it is representative of the ambiguity surrounding the concept of Canadian identity. While there is a great deal of Canadian content, many issues also contain excerpts from British writers and political figures such as Rudyard Kipling and Joseph Chamberlain. Several articles and illustrations relate specifically to England. A photograph of the British Houses of Parliament in London, for instance, serves as the frontispiece of the August 1902 issue, even though there is no article or story relating to these buildings. Nevertheless, this type of juxtaposition of British imagery with Canadian subject matter is a common occurrence in such journals, which contain many stories and articles concerning Canada's relationship with Britain.

The first story in this issue of *The Canadian Boy* illustrates the complex nature of the relation between Canadian and British interests. "The Hero of Camp Roberts" by Margaret Strang is, in essence, a story of one boy's bravery while on a local camping trip with his cadet group, yet it opens with a reference to the war in South Africa. This war functions as a model of Canadian heroism for the story's young protagonist, but this perspective on the hostilities in South Africa ignores the controversy surrounding Canada's involvement in this conflict. The

Boer War, which began in the autumn of 1899, marked a bitter divide in Canadian thought at the turn of the twentieth century. As a former colony, many Canadians and many in Britain expected the country to contribute soldiers to support the British side in Africa. While Colonial Secretary Joseph Chamberlain pressured Sir Wilfrid Laurier and other members of Canada's Parliament to commit troops to the effort, sentiment in Quebec was strongly opposed to Canadian participation and Quebec politician Henri Bourassa even threatened to resign his seat in Parliament over the issue (LaPierre 1996: 266). While Britain had requested 10,000 Canadian troops, the Laurier government eventually agreed to send a volunteer battalion of approximately 1,000 men, equipped and trained in Canada, to fight under British command in Africa (LaPierre 1996: 269). While this initial number of volunteers was significantly smaller than the figure proposed by Great Britain, the debate over whether to send any troops at all highlighted a major division within Canada (one largely between French Quebec and English Ontario), between those who thought Canada was not doing enough to support the Empire and those who thought that the country was being sold-out for, and sacrificed in the name of, British interests.

Prime Minister Laurier's decision to dispatch soldiers in the face of public pressure can be viewed as "testimony to the growing strength of the imperial cause" (Berger 1969: 171). Yet even the overt imperialism of the day was connected to a sense of Canadian nationalism, with the widely held belief in English Canada that the country's support of the Empire would be rewarded with more direct influence over imperial foreign policy (Berger 1969: 172). A poem entitled "Destiny," for instance, which appeared in a collection of verse for children in 1891, expresses this desire on the part of England's former colonies to share in the power of the Empire:

Awake! awake! old England,
　　Rise from thine island lair;
The sun of empire dawning,
　　Gleams on thy dew-wet hair.

Outstretch thy limbs majestic!
　　Peal out the thund'rous roar!
Thy lion brood will greet thee
　　From every sea and shore

Temptations now beset them,
　　Foes from behind, before;
Her children look to England,
　　They wait the lion's roar—

The royal invitation
　　To the lion brood afar,
To share the royal burden,
　　Be it in peace or war.

To share the royal honour,
    Bright guerdon of the day!
When England and her offspring
    Shall join in equal sway.

Awake! awake! old England
    Rise from thine island lair.
Thy lion brood are longing
    Thy destiny to share. (Moberly 1891: 22)

The poem's mention of "Temptations" refers to Canada's relationship with the United States. It alludes to the fact that Canada faces the prospect of aligning itself with the United States, insinuated by the suggestion of "Foes from behind, before." In a sense, there is an implicit threat that if Canada does not "join in equal sway" with England, then she may look elsewhere for new alliances. The desire, therefore, is not merely to "share the royal burden," but to share in England's power and "royal honour" as well.

Those pushing for continued loyalty to the Empire believed that participation in "peace or war" should result in greater power for Canada. Even among proud supporters of England and the South African war there was a feeling that aiding Britain would ultimately allow Canada to gain a more powerful position within the Empire. As Carl Berger explains:

> What divided those who called themselves nationalists from those who preferred to be known as imperialists was not the question of whether Canada should manage her own affairs and have the power to formulate a foreign policy expressive of her interests; what divided them was disagreement over how these powers were to be acquired and for what purposes they were to be employed. The imperialists saw the British Empire as the vehicle in which Canada would attain national status; the anti-imperialists were so convinced of the incompatibility of imperial and Canadian interests that they saw all schemes for co-operation as reactionary and anti-national. (Berger 1969: 173–4)

The divide over Canadian participation in the Boer War, therefore, was not merely one between Anglophone and Francophone parties but was one that affected relations among English Canadians themselves. Even so, this split was most pronounced between English and French Canadians, with the latter being strongly opposed to the thought of Canadians engaging in what they considered to be a solely British war against a non-British minority with which they themselves identified (Berger 1969: 172). This debate manifested itself in many ways during the course of the war in South Africa. The English-language newspaper the Montreal *Star* was a vocal supporter of Canadian participation in the South African War, and is even credited with forcing the Laurier government into participating in this conflict (Rutherford 1982: 231). There were riots between French and English parties in Montreal during the period of the Boer War (LaPierre 1996: 270), and the country felt the implications of this racial division long after the hostilities in Africa came to an end. Ultimately, by the time the war concluded in May 1902, Canada had spent nearly three million dollars, had sent over seven thousand men to participate, and had witnessed its own "battle" on home soil.

Margaret Strang's story in *The Canadian Boy*, however, makes no mention of the controversy surrounding Canadian involvement in South Africa. Rather, it is a tale aimed at Canadian boys, which holds forth as an example of heroism the story of Canadian men faithfully serving the Empire. At the story's opening Strang writes:

> The military spirit had always been strong in our town, but it had been strengthened and fostered by the outbreak of the South African war, when two of our boys left home to join that first contingent of brave Canadians, who left for South Africa to fight for the Motherland, and to show the world, that though lacking in experience, there were none of the whole British Empire who could fight more bravely. (Strang 1902: 3)

Strang clearly promotes fighting for the "Motherland" as an honorable and noble pursuit for Canadian boys. Yet the story's message of imperial duty and loyalty is not as straightforward as it may first appear. While the author expresses loyalty to the Empire and writes of the town's excitement at being "honored by the presence" of the Duke and Duchess of Cornwall and York, she tempers these imperialist sentiments with a pride in Canadian achievement. Of the town's response during the Boer War she says that "the war columns of the newspapers were always eagerly scanned by men and women, boys and girls, eager to see what 'our boys' had been doing. The Canadian Contingent was, of course, considered by us the main part of the British army" (3). Balanced with the sense of duty to the Empire, is home-town pride in Canadian achievement. There is evidence in Strang's story that those who support the Empire match this with a belief in Canadian accomplishments. The Canadian "we" is clearly distinguished in the minds of these townspeople from the British Imperial "we." While loyalty to Britain and her army is declared, there is also evidence of a desire to be something more than a "British" soldier.

This complexity of the Canadian position, which lies somewhere between identification with Britain and identification with Canada, is again seen in an advertisement for a picture entitled "In Memoriam" in the back pages of this same issue of *The Canadian Boy* from August 1902. The ad describes the picture, dedicated to the memory of those who fought in the wars in South Africa, as "a souvenir of our brave boys who have given themselves for the honor of Canada and to prove their loyalty to the mother country" (*Canadian Boy* 1902a: 47). Here too is an example of pride in Canada co-mingled with pride in the empire—a dual sense of identity that is not always a comfortable one to wear.

There are other articles in this 1902 issue of *The Canadian Boy*, however, whose messages are much less ambiguous. These give clear evidence of an existing attitude that English morality, history, and achievements mark the goals which Canadian children should strive to attain. One such article, "Play the Game," is straight from the pages of the British juvenile periodical, *Boys of the Empire*:

> Why is it that our King rules over millions of our bronzed and swarthy brothers in India who have sworn allegiance to their foreign Emperor? Because almost every Briton has played the game, whether in peace or war, ever since the day we first landed on that great continent.
>
> Why are the names of Livingstone, Stanley, and Moffat passwords with nations of South Africa? Because the natives knew a promise given by a Briton was a deed performed; that we respected the natives' point of view and played the game fair and square. (*Canadian Boy* 1902b)

Such sentiments, in an article also claiming "there is nothing finer than a healthy British boy!" are a clear indication of the emphasis that many Canadians still placed on British values and traditions at the turn of the century. The fact that *The Canadian Boy* borrowed this material directly from a British publication is further evidence of the strong relationship that still existed between the two countries. *Boys of the Empire* was edited by Howard Spicer and published in London by Andrew Melrose. It called itself "A Magazine for British Boys All Over the World" but its published aim was "To promote and strengthen a worthy imperial spirit in British-born boys." It also ran in conjunction with a highly popular "Empire League" which was designed to encourage this spirit of Empire in young boys (Walker 2003). The sharing of material between such an overtly imperialistic periodical and Canada's own *The Canadian Boy* is evidence that some children's writers in Canada were still promoting so-called "British" values and imperial ties in the early twentieth century.

Ironically, however, this particular article actually serves to underscore a key element of the often uncertain relation between the two nations. It is evident from the tone of this piece that the young male "Briton[s]" to whom it is addressed are seen to share the perspective of the imperial master. It is they, and their King, to whom the natives of India and South Africa have "sworn allegiance." Yet the Canadian child was neither a conquering Briton, nor a "swarthy" native brother. He was in fact, in the terms of this article, both the coloniser and the colonised. For when Canadian boys were set the example of their brave elders going to fight in South Africa, they were also told that this was part of their duty as a *colony*. The repeated description of Britain as a "motherland" unmistakably implies that it is something quite separate from, and (in keeping with familial hierarchy) something superior to, Canada. The motherland is authoritative and expects its Canadian offspring, like their "bronzed and swarthy brothers in India," to swear allegiance. Toward the end

of the nineteenth century, the Canadian child reader faced a confused rhetoric
that identified the Canadian as equal and identical to the Briton, while
simultaneously (and paradoxically) putting forth the notion of the need for
allegiance and loyalty to this supposed equal.

The contents of a book of Canadian poetry intended for children and
published in Toronto in 1891 offer further evidence of the existence of this
competing sense of loyalty. Some of the poems included in this collection are
infused with a great sense of patriotism and pride in Canada, while others
unmistakably advocate the need to maintain loyalty to England. One poem
which stresses the importance of such loyalty is "Brothers Awake!" written by
Aimee Huntingdon of Pictou, Nova Scotia. The poet scorns those who wish to
cut ties with England, fearing this will lead to annexation by the United States:

> Brothers awake! There are traitors around us,
>   Seeking their country and ours to betray;
> Striving to sever the links that have bound us
>   To dear Mother England for many a day.
>
> List to their pitiful, cowardly croaking,
>   Bidding us barter our heritage grand;
> Bend, like dumb cattle, our necks to the yoking,
>   Yield unto strangers our glorious land.
>
> Surely too long we have borne with their scheming;
>   Now let them learn that forbearance is o'er!
> Teach them that Canada's sons are not dreaming;
>   Brothers awaken! and slumber no more.
>
> Say, shall not we, whom our country has nourished,
>   Fight for her weal 'gainst the treacherous crew?
> Shall it be said that foul treason has flourished
>   'Neath the proud folds of the Red, White and Blue.
>
> Never! With courage undimmed and undaunted,
>   Crush, ere it blossoms, the seed they have sown;
> Back in their teeth fling the boasts they have flaunted,
>   Pause not, nor rest, till the day be our own.
>
> Croakers and cravens and patriot-haters,
>   Soon shall their schemes in the dust be laid low;
> Then shall this land of ours, freed from the traitors,
>   To her bright destiny joyfully go. (Huntingdon 1891: 21)

Huntingdon calls attention to the historic connection between Canada and
England in her attempt to convince a new generation to maintain this loyalty.

Such efforts to emphasise the ties between the two nations relate in part
to the issue of race. While the question of competing French and English

interests had always been an issue in Canada, increasing immigration from new ethnic and linguistic groups led to an increased emphasis on the subject of race. The September 1897 edition of the children's magazine *Home and Youth* provides evidence of the importance placed on immigration. What is also clear is that there is a desire on the part of some to control who enters the country:

> This news of our mineral wealth and of the magnificent harvests that are being reaped from the fertile lands of our Northwest is finding its way throughout Europe and the United States, with the result that the tide of population is already beginning to set in this direction. While population and capital are the most important requisites to our advancement, we desire only population of the right sort—such as will compare favorably with that which we already have—in order that we may continue to be characterised as a nation by intelligence, industry, and integrity. (*Home and Youth* 1897a: 1–2)

So while one can see from this that there was an ongoing desire to increase Canada's population, children also had exposure to a rhetoric that exhibits a fear that the "wrong type" of incoming population could corrupt the nation. At the same time that England feared its population would be overrun by people from across its own empire, so too was English Canada (itself one of these holdings) clinging to a sense of racial unity (Galway 2004: 44). British immigrants on the whole tended to hold a relatively privileged position, as it was generally held that their language skills and their technical skills, born of England's industrial society, would allow them to be more easily assimilated into a Canadian way of life (McCormack 1993: 334). This is not to say, however, that native born Canadians never felt any resentment toward British immigrants.[2] Friction could exist even between those of very similar heritage and experience. Yet comparatively speaking, groups from the United Kingdom were more readily welcomed than those from distinctly different linguistic, racial, and cultural backgrounds.

From Confederation onward, the number of new immigrants arriving in Canada rose steadily each year with few exceptions. In 1867, there were just over 10,000 new immigrants who arrived in Canada; by 1911 this number had risen to more than 300,000 (Avery 1995: 11). In 1891, 76 percent of Canada's foreign-born residents had been born in Britain; by 1921 46 percent of the foreign-born population was of non-British origin (Avery 1995: 22). Most of these new immigrants were from southern and eastern European countries, but people from China, Japan, and East India were also in Canada by the 1880s. In the face of these changes, just as French Canadians desired policies such as separate schools and language protection to protect their culture and identity, there was a feeling among some British-Canadians that their heritage needed protection from the growing population of immigrants from non-Anglophone backgrounds

(Galway 2004: 44). This fear is one reason why the frequent promotion of continued ties to England appears in much of the children's literature of the day.

Yet even in the publications that were most loyal to Britain, there is a simultaneous emphasis on promoting a sense of "Canadian" achievement. Perhaps the complexity of Canada's early sense of nationality is best demonstrated by the contents of the July 1, 1893 edition of the Toronto weekly magazine *Pleasant Hours*. This issue marked the 26th anniversary of Confederation and contains many stories honouring Canadian achievements. At the same time, however, there appears a song by James L. Hughes (1846–1935) that reveals the ongoing presence of imperial fealty in Canada. Hughes, as part of his job as Inspector of Schools for Toronto, was responsible for introducing kindergarten to Toronto's Public Schools and believed in the creed that "it is better to kindle a child with ideals than to cram him with ideas" (Pierce 1924: 68). In addition to his interest in education, Hughes was also Grand Master of the Grand Orange Lodge of Ontario West. Writing in 1924, his biographer describes Hughes as coming from "one of the most aggressively patriotic families in the Dominion" (Pierce 1924: 124), but also outlines Hughes' ardent imperialism:

> [H]e is an imperialist in that he believes that our highest destiny lies within the Britannic household. For this he has worked unceasingly most of his lifetime. Few men in Canada have been such persistent and capable ambassadors between this country and the mother land. . . . Dr. Hughes made the first address at the founding of the League of Empire in London, England, in 1907, and has attended every meeting of the League since it was founded. He is Vice-President of the Canadian branch. (Pierce 1924: 125)

Hughes' belief in this imperial union is clear in his song "Canada to England":

> Oh! Mistress of the mighty sea!
> Oh! Motherland, so great and free!
> Canadian hearts shall ever be
> United in their love for thee.
>
> *Chorus*:
> Yes, Motherland! Dear Motherland!
> Beneath the Union Jack we'll stand,
> A part of the Imperial whole;
> From sea to sea, from pole to pole;
> On woodland height and fertile plain
> True British subjects we'll remain.
>
> Thy power shall faith and hope impart,
> Thy liberty inspire each heart,

Thy justice ever guide me right,
Thy honour be our beacon light!

[*Chorus*]

We share the glories of thy past;
Thy sailors brave beneath the mast,
And soldiers true on many a field,
Have taught Canadians not to yield.

[*Chorus*]

We'll build a nation great and free,
And greatest in its love for thee,
No other fate could be so grand
As union with our Motherland! (Hughes 1893: 104)

Hughes' lyrics celebrate the British Empire, and put forth the argument that Canada should maintain imperial union.

Hughes, who believed in the power of education, felt that it was important to promote the ideals of nationalism and imperialism to children. He founded the Public School Cadet movement and saw such activities as part of the process of instilling imperial loyalty in Canadian children:

> "I intended to speak on the Cadet movement as the only logical and economical and truly developing plan for preparing the men of the Empire to be ready for service to their country, if such service was ever required. I was the first to start the Public School Cadet movement and I, therefore, knew more about its national and ethical values than any other man in the Empire." (Pierce 1924: 131–132)

Hughes's words were prophetic. When "Canada to England" appeared in *Pleasant Hours* in 1893 it was read by the same generation of children that later faced the prospect of the First World War. This event would reveal the true cost of active loyalty to the "motherland" and many would come to see this as the moment when Canada truly came into its own as a nation (Galway 2004: 41).

Oh Canada!

While there is much material in the children's novels and periodicals of the late nineteenth century to suggest that loyalty to the British Empire was still being promoted as a duty to which all Canadian children should aspire, there is also material that illustrates a growing sense of frustration with Britain's ongoing interference in Canadian affairs. This literature demonstrates a developing awareness of Canada's distinct needs, aspirations, and achievements. Alongside the children's literature promoting imperial ties, the Canadian child reader was served stories of Canadian life from coast to coast in which the glories of the country were promoted. This increasing perception of Canada's individuality had, in actual fact, been emerging for quite some time. Canada had really begun to come into its own as a nation after the passing of the British North America Act in 1867. One can surely argue, in fact, that if there was not already a concept of Canada as something distinct and unique from its "mother country," the move towards Confederation never would have taken place.

Many children's texts from the nineteenth century contain evidence of an existing body of citizens that wanted Canada to forge its own path and resist continued British influence. *The Young Canadian*, published weekly in Montreal in the 1890s, is one such magazine. On the editorial page of the September 23, 1891 issue, it states that the magazine's aim is "to foster a national pride in Canadian progress, history, manufactures, science, literature, art, and politics; to draw the young people of the Provinces closer together; and to inspire them with a sense of the sacred and responsible duties they owe to their native country" (*Young Canadian* 1891c). It then goes on to describe itself as "a means of providing for the people of the Dominion a thoroughly high-class Magazine of Canadian aim, Canadian interest, and Canadian sentiment" (*Young Canadian* 1891d). It is clear from such statements that this was no accidental promotion of national pride. Patriotism was seen as a genuine need, and a growing reality.

As the century progressed, there was an increasing belief that Canada needed to move away from British influence. Some, particularly French Canadians such as Quebec politician Henri Bourassa, believed that Canada needed to become independent and could only achieve this by breaking imperial ties. Bourassa promoted the view that Canadian independence would lead to the harmony between Anglophone and French Canadians that the nation needed to prosper (Levitt 1870: 180). While others may have shared the belief that independence and participation in the Empire were mutually exclusive, not every Canadian thought it was necessary to sever all ties with Britain. Nevertheless, the nineteenth century witnessed a growing clash between Canadian nationalism and British imperialism. While Britain was certainly preoccupied with issues of imperialism in this era, many of its most prominent colonies were experiencing a new wave of nationalism that was increasingly at odds with Britain's imperialist aims (Careless 1953: 315). In Canada, this nationalism developed in response to several issues raised by apparent impediments to Canada's ability to self-govern. While the British North America Act of 1867 established Canada's independence, it still did not allow Canada to act independently in foreign affairs. Yet it was becoming clear that with Britain negotiating on its behalf, the country's interests were not always represented adequately. One catalyst of the movement towards greater self-governance was the debate over the Alaskan Panhandle.

Shortly after Confederation, the U.S. purchased Alaska from Russia and then, interpreting the boundary, claimed that American territory lay between the

Yukon and the Pacific coast. The Klondike gold-rush of 1898 made clear the importance of this territory. Canada argued that portions of the Panhandle lay entirely within its borders, but in 1903, in an arbitration commission chaired by the British Chief Justice, the land was awarded to the Americans, largely in an effort to preserve favourable relations between Britain and the United States (Careless 1953: 320–321). The judgement led to a lingering resentment towards Britain for undercutting Canada's interests. A volume on Canadian history from 1908, while written on the whole from a pro-British stance, records the reaction in Canada as follows:

> It would be difficult to exaggerate the resentment and anger felt in Canada over this result. It fulfilled and justified all the gloomy apprehension with which the Canadians had regarded the outcome of the tribunal. The newspapers burst into a frenzy of denunciation. . . . The anti-English sentiment in Vancouver was so pronounced that a theatre crowd howled down the strains of the national anthem. It was generally felt by the Canadians that this was another surrender by Great Britain of Canadian rights to American greed. . . . And so much resentment still remains . . . that it will be impossible ever again for Canada to agree to allowing an Englishman to cast the deciding vote in any tribunal regarding important Canadian rights. (Tracy: 1043–1045)

Indeed, this incident did galvanise the movement toward greater self-determination on the part of Canada in matters of international policy.

Acts such as the howling down of the national anthem (which at this time was still the British national anthem "God Save the King") are evidence of a strong and highly emotional strain of anti-English sentiment. The debate over the Alaskan Panhandle was not the first source of this feeling, though it was ultimately one of the most visible causes. In actual fact, the outcome of the tribunal was reminiscent of the Treaty of Washington of 1871, in which a joint high commission (whose only Canadian representative was Prime Minister Sir John A. Macdonald) met to discuss the questions that had arisen out of the U.S. Civil War. As the Alaskan incident would show thirty years later, when it came to preserving good relations between Britain and the United States, Canadian interests were often set aside (Careless 1953: 198–199). The newspapers and journals of the late nineteenth century contained expressions of a growing dissatisfaction with Britain, and Canadian literature began to call for greater independence.

Strong evidence of this desire to move away from British influence appears in *Canada First. An Appeal to All Canadians.* The name of the author of this lengthy piece of verse is simply "A Toronto Boy," and his poem is an excellent expression of contemporary Anglo-Canadian thought on Canada's relation to Britain. It addresses such issues as the younger country's inability to take control over its own foreign affairs:

Let Eighteen-eighty, close Colonial life,
　　And Canada, a Nation now become!
We court no bitter feelings, war, or strife,
　　But we must have an Independent Home.

A colony, a Nation ne'er can be,
　　And proud ambition rises with our years.
Our aim is noble, 'tis this land to see
　　A Greater Britain, founded without tears.
　. . .

Thus, Canada a manly course would steer;
　　To treat *direct* with nations now would choose;
On equal footing meet them as their peer,
　　Nor henceforth, rights and claims by proxy lose.
(Toronto Boy 1880: 3–4)

The poem underscores the bitterness felt over Britain's decisions in matters such as the Treaty of Washington which, among other things, granted the Americans open access to Canada's Atlantic fisheries. It also foreshadows the bitter debates that emerged over conflicts such as the Boer War:

In British legislation, we've no voice;
　　Our fisheries are sold, nay, giv'n away;
The Yankee 'cute can o'er the gift rejoice,
　　Whilst we, for Fenian raids, receive no pay.

We have no voice in wars that Britain makes;
　　Why should we be in danger when these rage?
We would an *ally* be, if Britain shakes:
　　But freemen we must be in this free age. (Toronto Boy 1880: 17–18)

The idea of freedom is an important one in this poem. It is not simply a matter of Canada having the freedom to make important decisions, but is also a question of individual freedom and equality. In rejecting the authority and influence of Britain, this poet is also rejecting the class restraints and inequalities of the Old World:

Not to our lands have emigrants, in shoals,
　　Flocked from the British Isles to swell our ranks;
　. . .

"For us," say they, "the land, where freedom bright,
　　Lifts up our manhood, long time crushed by pride
Of king, queen, prince, duke, lord and squire and knight;
　　Henceforth, where all are equal, we'll abide.

"We'll choose no British *colony* for home;
   We will be *citizens*, free men among.
Now forced from Britain far away to roam,
   We join the great Republic from her sprung!

"You have self-government, we do not doubt;
   But cling to monarchy, in form and name.
. . .

"You now have knights, Canadian born and bred,
   Soon native lords may rise, in pride and power;
Next, for yourselves you'll choose a crowned head;—
   Adieu to Independence from that hour!" (Toronto Boy 1880: 5)

The desire to move away from British influence is evident in the poem, and the poet draws a distinction between the potential corruption of the monarchical system, and the perceived superiority of Canadian democracy.

Of greatest significance to this study is the attention the poet draws to the role of Canada's children in building the nation. He stresses the need for a national literature for these young citizens; "The Poets of this Nation must appear! / We want our ballads—none are written yet! / Canadian lilts and songs, the youthful ear / Ne'er hears when nurse or mother soothes her pet" (Toronto Boy 1880: 15). This poet reiterates the belief that there is a connection between literature, children, and the strengthening of the nation. While he fears that this literature for the young has not yet been developed, in actual fact, many such ballads, lilts, and songs did already exist. Many of the sentiments expressed in this poem also found their way into the Canadian children's literature of the period.

In some instances, the young Englishman becomes a figure of fun, such as in Valentine Williams' novel of 1889 *The Captain of the Club; or, The Canadian Boy*.[3] This novel tells the story of Jack Brady and his group of young friends growing up in the town of Scugog in southern Ontario. During the course of the story, they meet an English boy by the name of Percy Fitzwobble, who has come out to Canada to learn the art of farming. From his introduction, Percy is painted in comical colours:

He pointed to something smoking a cigar, something between a boy and a man, dressed in a ridiculously wide pair of pants of a very large-checked pattern, shoes that turned up their toes higher than his instep, a high crowned hat with a narrow curled brim, and a short overcoat of light gray, with a large cape that covered most of his arms. He wore drab kid gloves and a very heavy cane. There was the least possible suspicion of a fawn-colored mustache on his lip, but it might have been only the smoke of the cigar, and the right side of his thin face was twisted and wrinkled out of shape in a difficult endeavour to hold a very large eyeglass. This specimen was anywhere from sixteen to nineteen years of age, and he spoke in a shrill voice. A few foppish boys were in his party. (Williams 1889: 98–99)

Percy Fitzwobble, whose name and style of dress alone are comical, also speaks in a "shrill voice" and has a lisp (99). It is apparent that the Canadian boys consider this young Englishman to be an extremely strange creature. In many respects, Percy is greatly inferior to his new friends. His dress suggests that he has had a pampered upbringing and is not used to hard work, while the mention of his "foppish" companions suggests a degree of effeminacy. When it comes to athletic ability, Percy takes a clear second place to his Canadian friends. On a snow-shoe tramp through the woods, for example, Percy has difficulty because of his inappropriate dress and his inexperience, appearing comical in his failed effort to keep up with the Canadians.

In addition to offering the narrator an opportunity to compare physical strength and ability, Percy's character also allows for a comparison between Canadian and British politics. For example, one of the discussions that Jack and his friends have with Percy concerns the different attitudes towards war in the two countries. Percy sees a lack of military strength in Canada, and questions how the nation could go to war:

> "You do lack a great many things, though," remarked Percy in a superior manner. . . . "Faw instance, thaah's the navy. How could you go to waw with Fwance, now?"
>
> "We have no fear of war," answered Jack; "we interfere with nobody, and will have enough work for a century filling our country with settlers and making them happy."
>
> "But can't you suppose the case? Suppose the Gweat Powahs declared waw. How stwong would youah land fawses be?"
>
> "If some quarrelsome nation attacked us," said Jack warmly, "the brave men that Heaven has given us will do their duty. You have perhaps read, Percy, in English history, that a nation of quiet citizens have more than once been a match for her strong armies, and so it may prove with us." (Williams 1889: 127)

While Percy cannot understand the idea of a nation without strong military structures and impulses, Jack Brady's response expresses an implicit contempt for the "quarrelsome" and militaristic nature of other nations. He presents a view of Canada as a nation of peace and "quiet citizens"—a notion that remains a central part of the Canadian identity.

But Percy's discussion with the boys from Scugog goes beyond questions of military organisations to the basic structure of society itself. Williams' novel expresses a strong distaste for the rigid and oppressive class system still thriving in Britain. The democratic and egalitarian nature of Canadian society comes as a bit of a shock to Percy Fitzwobble, a young English aristocrat. He demonstrates this through his reaction to the winter scene in Scugog where the Canadian boys show him the town's giant toboggan run:

> "Do the ladies and gentlemen all tuhn out faw their wecweation?"
>
> "Yes, everybody, old and young," returned Jack. "If a stranger came to Scugog in winter, and wanted to see its best samples of men, women, and boys, he'd find them here. . . ."
>
> "Well, that's not bad. And it ansahs vewy well in this countwy: but it would nevah do in England."
>
> "How is that," asked Billy.
>
> "Why, you see, the gentwy wouldn't stand it to have the common people sharing this slide, faw instance. They'd wathah considah it an invasion of thaah pwivileges." (135–136)

Percy's answer does not satisfy the Canadian boys, and Billy O'Neill expresses his contempt for what he sees as the pretensions of aristocratic British society.

Billy's response to the English boy's justification of English social practices underlines a strong dislike of Old World aristocratic privileges:

> "Privileges?" said Billy. "Then why don't they send them out of England? Why do they let working people live in the same country?"
>
> "It's the easiest mattah in the wohld. Who'd pay the went, foh instance? Who'd look aftah the gahdens? and who'd be the sehvants? Ansah that, now."
>
> "It's all bosh," replied Billy hotly. "They help to feed the gentry, and the gentry shouldn't stick their noses up. And, besides, who fights battles for England, and wins them, too. Is it the gentry, or the common people, as you call them? What do you say to that?"
>
> "Percy, I'm afraid you're a snob," remarked Smithy. "But we'll give you a year back north to reform; and when you go home to England, if you're not put into jail for trying to drive the lords and all the gentry into the sea, with the rest of the codfish aristocracy, why, then I'll change my name and call myself Jones, or Brown, or Robinson." (Williams 1889: 136)

Ultimately, Canada does prove to have a beneficial effect on the young Englishman, who returns home with a new respect for democratic values. Valentine Williams uses the interaction between his Canadian and English characters to express a sense of Canadian superiority in matters such as physical strength, work ethic and social equality. In so doing, he also draws a portrait of a country no longer dependent on a European "motherland."

Increasingly, writers promoted the view that Canada had the potential to be a great nation in its own right. Literature and education were two keys means used to help communicate this to the nation's children. In the September 23,

1891 issue of *The Young Canadian,* there is an advertisement for a $500.00 prize to be awarded for a suitable manuscript for a book on Canadian history. This illustrates the existing feeling that more needed to be done to educate Canadian children about their country and the events of its past (*Young Canadian* 1891b). This interest in educating children does not merely lie in the betterment of children themselves, but stems in part from the feeling that such education is a means by which to achieve national aims and ambitions.

Further evidence of such efforts to emphasise Canada's distinct identity is Valentine Williams' discussion of the nation's past. In *The Captain of the Club,* Williams presents a view of Canadian history through the voice of Jack Brady that can make Canadian children proud:

> "But what a history she has, though still in her youth. Think of the early discoverers and settlers of Canada, the kind of men they were, the difficulties of soil and climate they had to conquer, and the dangers they met from savage men and savage animals. We had the solitary Jesuit making his way through a forest then trackless, and his only hope and reward to spread the gospel and civilize the Indians. Then came the old nobles from France and the young gentlemen of honorable family and finished education working side by side with the humble but strong man of toil. What a beginning for a great nation! A populous country grew up in a solitude, with churches, schools, and devoted citizens. Then came a war; in fact, it was always war; but a war came, and with it a change of rule. Then see the people twice defend their homes and country against a powerful nation, and even rise against their own rulers for a greater amount of freedom. And now, with growing fortunes and increase of citizens, how Dear Old Canada, our mother and our pride, stands strong and hopeful of the future, knowing that her sons will increase her dignity and uphold her honor among the nations of the earth." (125–126)

Jack's speech about Canadian history is certainly patriotic and it is clearly propaganda. Despite the obvious errors and omissions in his account (or perhaps because of them), it is striking evidence of a strong sense of national identity and history that was already present in Canada. Two years prior to *The Young Canadian*'s call for a book on Canadian history, Valentine Williams was already providing his own proud version for the child readers of Canada.

In addition to addressing the subject of Canadian history, Williams also addresses the issue of class structure, a subject that other writers also deal with. In the September 23, 1891 issue of *The Young Canadian* there are two articles that reveal some of the existing attitudes towards labour, class, industry, and immigration, and the role they can each play in achieving national aims. The first is an endorsement of the value of the labouring middle class, highlighting the importance of the worker to the future of the nation:

Let no young Canadian despise the lot in which he is actually placed. Let him think twice before he forsakes the farm for the town, the workshop for a profession. The great procession of our successful men comes from the ranks of patient, persevering work. The large majority of our men at the tops of our trees have not come there by chance, much less by birth. The metal out of which our young nation shall be built lies more in raising our occupation to our own earnest level than in a false notion about imaginary levels of labour. Though we hear more of the captain than of the private, it is the private's work and not the captain's that tells. The unwritten life, the unsung history, is, after all, the backbone of national strength. Every young Canadian who does his best where he is—just where he is—and makes himself an indispensable factor in his own peculiar circumstances, does more for the realization of a grand future of Canada than if he broke free and rushed madly after deeds of prominent service.

. . . Great men are not secured from great men. They are created from great workers. Luxury enfeebles. Difficulties sharpen the intellect. A steadfast purpose, an unconquerable perseverance, carry everything before them. (*Young Canadian* 1891e: 553)

Here are some of the cornerstones of what is often declared to be Canadian sentiment: a literal expression of the iconic beaver's symbolic example of labour and perseverance. Like the sentiment expressed by the Canadian boys in Williams' novel, this pictures Canadian society as one created and supported not by a ruling aristocracy, but by the people.

Although the nature of Canada's relation to Britain still complicated the notion of patriotism at this time, many works of children's literature demonstrate an increasing awareness of the elements that make Canada a unique country. Some of these also clearly promote a sense of loyalty to Canada itself. One such piece, included in 1891 in a collection of verse for children, is E.G. Nelson's "My Own Canadian Home." Edwin Nelson was a bookseller from St. John, New Brunswick, who first published this verse in 1887. There were a variety of musical accompaniments to the song, one of which reportedly sold one and a half million copies by 1896 (Canadian Encyclopedia 2003). The piece was so popular in the nineteenth century that it became known as "Canada's National Song" and was adopted as the official song of St. John in 1967 (Canadian Encyclopedia 2003). Nelson's work, published as a poem in this collection, is a strong display of Canadian sentiment:

Though other skies may be as bright,
    And other lands as fair;
Though charms of other climes invite
    My wandering footsteps there,
Yet there is one, the peer of all
    Beneath the bright heaven's dome;

Of thee I sing, O happy land,
　My own Canadian home!

Thy lakes and rivers, as "the voice
　Of many waters," raise
To Him who planned their vast extent,
　A symphony of praise.
Thy mountain peaks o'erlook the clouds—
　They pierce the azure skies;
They bid thy sons be strong and true—
　To great achievements rise.

A noble heritage is thine,
　So grand, and fair, and free;
A fertile land, where he who toils
　Shall well rewarded be.
And he who joys in nature's charms,
　Exulting, here may view—
Scenes of enchantment—strangely fair,
　Sublime in form and hue.

Shall not the race that tread thy plains
　Spurn all that would enslave?
Or they who battle with the tides,
　Shall not that race be brave?
Shall not Niagara's mighty voice
　Inspire to actions high?
'Twere easy such a land to love,
　Or for her glory die.

And doubt not should a foeman's hand
　Be armed to strike at thee,
Thy trumpet call throughout the land
　Need scarce repeated be!
As bravely as on Queenston's Heights,
　Or as in Lundy's Lane.
Thy sons will battle for thy rights,
　And freedom's cause maintain.

Did kindly heaven afford to me
　The choice where I could dwell,
Fair Canada! that choice should be,
　The land I love so well.
I love thy hills and valleys wide,
　Thy waters' flash and foam;
May God in love o'er these preside,
　My own Canadian home! (Nelson 1891: 23–24)

With its picture of Canada's natural beauty, evoked in images of "mountain peaks" and "azure skies," and its appeal to the memory of historic Canadian events such as the battle of Lundy's Lane, Nelson's verse struck a chord with Canadians of the day. On July 7, 1890, one year prior to the publication of this piece in this collection for children, the *Press Newspaper* of Woodstock, New Brunswick demonstrated that many considered Nelson's song a good representation of the nation:

> The national song, "My Own Canadian Home" has been set to music by Morely Mclaughlan, of St. John, and chosen by the military to be sung at the great meeting of riflemen on Surrey Common, England, the accompaniment to be played by the band of the London Scottish Regiment. This piece will be played shortly by all hands throughout Canada, and so become familiar to the ears of all. (*Carleton County Home Page* 2003)

The evident popularity of this song is an indication of the warm reception that overtly patriotic Canadian pieces were receiving by the end of the nineteenth century. The sentiments expressed in Nelson's song echo those in other children's literature of the period. Like the September issue of *The Young Canadian* from the same year, "My Own Canadian Home" emphasises the importance of labour and hard work, and pictures Canada as a place "where he who toils / Shall well rewarded be." It also contributes to a picture of Canada as a land of beauty and freedom, for which her citizens will bravely die. Above all, Nelson's poem underscores a preference for Canada above all other nations, presenting it as a place that one can happily call home. While Canadian children continued to read British literature and to be schooled in the traditions of British society well into the twentieth century, this poem is an example of the increasing body of Canadian literature that was promoting a sense of pride in Canada itself, above all other nations.

As the nation struggled to define its relation to Britain, writers made the effort to instil pride and loyalty in Canada itself in its young citizens. In order to achieve this end, they promoted certain perceived strengths of Canadian life in their literature. As a result, Canadians gradually came to define themselves in much more precise terms than simply "Britons abroad." Comparisons to Britain helped to develop such notions of Canada as a place that rewarded hard work and based promotion on effort and achievement rather than on birth. There is also evidence to suggest that this literature was teaching young Canadians that the class divisions of the old world were to be overthrown in this newly emerging nation.

Chapter Four
Due South:
America and Canada

Some have argued that the Canadian identity is a negation, consisting simply of "not being American." It is even said that the quest for an identity is in itself the country's most defining feature. A September 2000 article in the *Washington Post* puts forth the argument that "nothing so characterizes [Canada's] identity as the absence of a distinctive national identity" (Pearlstein 2000). According to the American author Steven Pearlstein, it is simply a matter of time before Canada is absorbed by the United States. He argues that one of the reasons for this "absence" of identity is a lack of history:

> Over the years, Canadians might have coalesced around a shared sense of history but for the fact that they have so little of it they consider worth remembering. The country never fought a revolution or a civil war, pioneered no great social or political movement, produced no great world leader and committed no memorable atrocities—as one writer put it, Canada has no Lincolns, no Gettysburgs and no Gettysburg addresses. (Pearlstein 2000: A01)

Such claims as these clearly show the contemporary relevance of the question of Canadian national identity, as well as the continuing tendency for Canada to be measured in terms of the United States.

Canada's relationship with the United States played a significant role in the development of Canadian national identity following Confederation. The common interests and history of these two young, North American societies meant that the two nations had many common characteristics, and each saw something to admire and enjoy in the other. Yet Canadians had not forgotten the threat posed by the United States: originally a military adversary, the American republic became a new type of threat in the nineteenth century as many Canadians left for the United States in order to pursue the opportunities offered by its more substantial economy. Political tensions also arose over new developments in Britain's relationship with each country. Just as some writers were expressing negative feelings towards Britain, so too were others painting negative pictures of the United States in an attempt to secure national loyalty in Canadian children.

Canadian–American Relations

By the 1867, these two North American societies already shared a long and involved history. Regardless, the differences between the two countries were marked early on. British North America, notwithstanding its fears of annexation and the relatively slow consolidation of all ten provinces into Confederation, never intended to be the final jewel in the American crown. Early economic policies made this evident, and Confederation itself was in large part an attempt by the individual colonies of British North America to avoid absorption by the southern republic. As Canadian economic historian W.T. Easterbrook has argued, the resolution to build a new North American nation was planned and carefully executed preceding 1867:

> [I]t is apparent that there was no realistic alternative to acceptance of the challenge of nationhood. The construction of canals and early railways underlined the decision to avoid continental integration with the United States. The general strategy is clear in expansionist policies designed to integrate British North American possessions and to strengthen the British connection. (Easterbrook and Aitken 1956: 381)

While these deliberate efforts to construct a nation that would be both different and independent from the United States are indisputable, America maintained a powerful and unavoidable impact on Canada.

In addition to the significance of American–Canadian relations themselves, the United States was an important factor in the changing relationship between Britain and Canada during the nineteenth century. For example, one of the main arguments for maintaining strong ties with Britain was that this would help prevent Canada's annexation by the United States. On many levels, Canada's rebellious neighbour played as large a role in developing the nation's sense of unity and identity as its imperial motherland did. For if Canadian children were gradually learning that they were not British children, they were actively being taught that they were not Americans either. And yet the relationship between the two nations was a complicated one. For one thing, Canada clearly had many things in common with the United States that it did not share with England. Geographically, the two countries had more in common with each other than either did with Britain. They also shared economic ties which meant that America had a certain amount of influence over Canadian concerns. While

Britain remained Canada's prime trading partner and source of foreign investment until the mid-twentieth century, the American influence was nevertheless felt early on. The first U.S. branch plant in Canada is believed to have appeared around 1860 (Pomfret 1981: 140); by 1890 the number of branch plants had increased to fifty and in 1912 there were 209 such U.S. operations in Canada (Pomfret 1981: 89).

In addition to the increasing degree of this type of U.S. ownership of industry in Canada, the United States also dominated the North American publishing scene throughout the nineteenth century. This meant that much of the children's literature read in Canada was in fact published south of the border. A 2000 article in *The National Post* argues that the American influence on domestic literature is still a problem today. In writing of the debate over the need for Canadian writers to secure U.S. publishers, journalist Kenneth Harvey claims that the American market does affect what is produced and read domestically, and outlines the reasons why Canadian writers must appeal to publishers and readers in the United States:

> They must do so to make a decent living at their trade, because not only do the Americans control the success of a Canadian writer by making it necessary to find fame in the United States, but they dominate the shelf space in Canadian bookstores. . . . Canadian books do not sell well in Canada because they are given second-class status by most bookstores. (Harvey 2000)

Harvey's further claim that Canadian publishers "make money peddling overrated, over-publicized American books to complacent Canadians" comes very close to the nineteenth-century reality of the book trade in Canada. The issue of copyright law and protection for Canadian literature was a contentious one throughout the nineteenth century.[1] Although Canada had its own cheap reprint industry in both French and English, it was comparatively small and much of the demand for affordable editions was supplied by both the United States, which sent cheap American books and pirated reprints of British copyrights, and the United Kingdom, which began in the 1880s to export inexpensive "colonial editions" throughout the Empire (Parker 1985: 225). Harvey's assessment of the need for Canadian writers to be published in the United States is also true of the situation in the nineteenth century:

> Professional authors had to find publishers abroad, not only for renown and recompense, but often out of a lack of appreciation and the means to survive at home. It was a bitter pill to swallow, and the point was made constantly by authors . . . Sarah Jeannette Duncan . . . explained . . . that 'the market for Canadian literary wares of all sorts is self-evidently New York, where the intellectual life of the continent is rapidly centralizing.' She concluded that this situation would influence the way Canadians

wrote, with 'an eye upon immediate American appreciation,' and 'in the spirit and methods of American literary production.' (Parker 1985: 234)

The difficulty Canadian writers faced in being published in their home country was something shared by authors of children's literature. Even beyond the 1890s, "Canadians had trouble getting Canadian editions for their works, or sometimes the Canadian 'edition' was no more than a copyright formality" (Parker 1985: 235). The influence of the American publishing industry was felt equally by writers of adult and juvenile literature.

In *The Captain of the Club*, published in New York, the author is aware that he is in part addressing an American readership. After observing that "American boys will hardly know what is meant by 'Separate Schools'" the narrator proceeds to explain in some detail the structure of the educational system in Ontario (Williams 1889: 10). Separate schools in Quebec, and Catholic schools in Ontario, were protected under the British North America Act and were intended to protect the interests of Canada's French (and predominately Catholic) population. The explanation of the separate school system that appears in Williams' novel is clearly for the benefit of those "American boys" who have no knowledge of such things. Nevertheless, despite his acknowledgment of his American readership, the author proceeds to make comments that are not necessarily flattering to these readers. With respect to the school systems in the two countries he writes that the "system of public and separate schools is a benefit granted in Canada to the religious feelings of the people, and is a measure of justice which Catholics in the United States should but do not enjoy" (Williams 1889: 11). In this early passage in the novel, the author is already exhibiting a tendency to promote Canada's perceived superiority over other nations. This theme is clearly evident in the later passages in which the Canadian boys discuss their country's merits with the English boy Percy Fitzwobble. Whereas those later conversations reflect badly on Britain, some of the novel's earlier commentary promotes the idea of Canadian superiority over Americans. Williams' discussion of separate schools is not simply used as an example of this perceived national superiority, but is also in keeping with many pro-Catholic sentiments throughout the novel. According to the novel's title page, the publisher, J.P. Kenedy, is "Publisher to the Holy Apostolic See, Excelsior Catholic Publishing House" in New York, which accounts for the novel's somewhat lengthy vindication of Canada's protection of the educational rights of the Catholic minority.

In addition to arguing that Canadian children have a great benefit in the separate school system, Williams also presents them as physically superior to their American counterparts. They can even, the reader is told, paddle their canoes with enviable skill:

It was a pretty affair, with a blue stripe painted around it from bow to stern, and two paddles, as light as feathers, lying on the side. It looked so frail and delicate that very few American boys would have liked to step into it in a hurry, and it would have made them envious to see the ease and carelessness with which these two Canadians slipped into their places, put away their poles, and pushed out into the river. (Williams 1889: 4)

While this passage may simply appear to be some exaggerated Canadian pride on the part of the author, it actually highlights a common theme in the children's literature of the era. As in the novel's later scenes depicting the athletic superiority of the boys over their English friend, there is an emphasis here on the physical superiority of the Canadians. Ideas concerning physical strength and ability were tied closely to arguments surrounding nationhood in the nineteenth and early twentieth centuries. Reflecting in 1939 on the Boy Scout Movement which he had helped to instigate more than thirty years earlier, Lord Baden-Powell outlines this belief in the connection between physical prowess and strong nationhood:

[The Scouts'] development . . . is mainly got through camping and backwoods activities, which are enjoyed as much by the instructor as by the boy. . . . Therefore the aim of the Scout training is to replace Self with Service, to make the lads individually efficient, morally and physically, with the object of using that efficiency for the service of the community. . . . The effects of this training . . . have exceeded all expectation in making happy, healthy, helpful citizens. (Baden-Powell 1939: 9–10)

In Britain, many children's writers had already drawn a connection between the future of the British Empire, and the physical strength of its young citizens. In *Tom Brown's Schooldays*, published in 1857, Thomas Hughes emphasises the importance of sport in the education of Britain's young men. He places the role of physical activity above academics, writing, "The object of all schools is not to ram Latin and Greek into boys, but to make them good English boys, good future citizens; and by far the most important part of that work must be done, or not done, out of school hours" (Hughes 1857: 67). The relation between physical ability and citizenship is one that was expressed in much of the nineteenth century's literature for boys. Valentine Williams' treatment of a similar theme illustrates that Canadian authors were also making this connection and beginning to envisage Canadians as a race or ethnicity that was distinct from both the English and the Americans. It also marks the beginnings of a long tradition of competitive sports between Canada and America that is tied up with questions of national identity and patriotism.

It is particularly significant that canoeing is the sport in question in this opening passage from *The Captain of the Club*. Along with the beaver and the maple leaf, the canoe is one of Canada's major iconic symbols. Canoes, as Canadian educators James Raffan and Bert Horwood have noted "were born of the physical landscape and are ingrained in the Canadian cultural landscape.

On stamps, coins, and labels, in visual art, sculpture, stained-glass windows, and advertising, canoes are omnipresent" (Raffan and Horwood 1988: 1). The canoe is of great historical importance, having been the key method of transportation for the early fur traders, whose commercial exploits were what led to the eventual settlement of Canada by Europeans. It is also a symbol of the country's inescapable wilderness and wealth of fresh water lakes and rivers. In such a vast country where roads, railroads and canals are relative rarities, this "frail and delicate" boat was in fact one of early Canada's most important and reliable forms of transportation.

To this day the canoe remains one of the most reliable means of travelling through vast areas of Canada that are still otherwise inaccessible, and it played a different role in national development in Canada than it did in the United States:

> People of young nations tend to be restless and roving. . . . But rovers, adventurers and explorers had to have conveyance in a land without roads. In the United States it was the horse and the covered wagon that stamped their image on the psyche of the American people. In Canada, it was the canoe. Until the railway was punched through to the West, the canoe remained the fastest means of crossing Canada. (Roberts 1988: 107)

Valentine Williams was only one of many Canadians to celebrate the canoe in song and poetry. Poet E. Pauline Johnson, whose Mohawk name "Tekahion-wake" is fittingly translated as "two rivers flowing side by side" (Johnston 1997: 20), wrote one of the most memorable odes to the canoe in Canadian literature. Johnson first wrote "The Song My Paddle Sings" in 1892:

> West wind, blow from your prairie nest!
> Blow from the mountains, blow from the west.
> The sail is idle, the sailor too;
> O! wind of the west, we wait for you.
> Blow, blow!
> I have wooed you so,
> But never a favour you bestow.
> You rock your cradle the hills between,
> But scorn to notice my white lateen.

> I stow the sail, unship the mast:
> I wooed you long, but my wooing's past;
> My paddle will lull you into rest.
> O! drowsy wind of the drowsy west,
> Sleep, sleep,
> By your mountain steep,

Or down where the prairie grasses sweep!
Now fold in slumber your laggard wings,
For soft is the song my paddle sings.

August is laughing across the sky,
Laughing while paddle, canoe and I,
Drift, drift,
Where the hills uplift
On either side of the current swift.

The river rolls in its rocky bed;
My paddle is plying its way ahead;
Dip, dip,
While the waters flip
In foam as over their breast we slip.

And oh, the river runs swifter now;
The eddies circle about my bow.
Swirl, swirl!
How the ripples curl
In many a dangerous pool awhirl!

And forward far the rapids roar,
Fretting their margin for evermore.
Dash, dash,
With a mighty crash,
They seethe, and boil, and bound, and splash.

Be strong, O paddle! be brave, canoe!
The reckless waves you must plunge into.
Reel, reel,
On your trembling keel,
But never a fear my craft will feel.

We've raced the rapid, we're far ahead!
The river slips through its silent bed,
Sway, sway,
As the bubbles spray
And fall in tinkling tunes away.

And up on the hills against the sky,
A fir tree rocking its lullaby,
Swings, swing
Its emerald wings,
Swelling the song that my paddle sings. (Johnson 1904: 155–156)

Johnson's poem was a staple in many anthologies and school readers for Canadian children well into the twentieth century. Valentine Williams' use of the canoe as a symbol of Canadian strength and ability is part of a lengthy tradition in Canadian children's literature, and is a particularly appropriate image to use in order to contrast Canada and the United States.

Williams also uses this passage concerning the canoe in another significant manner. In addition to exhibiting an attitude of superiority over Americans, this scene also provides an opportunity for the narrator to reflect on the role of indigenous populations in Canadian history. After describing the boys' handling of the canoe, the narrator makes the following observation:

> It reminded one of those days, not so very long past, when the redskinned Indians, in the little boats they had invented, paddled along the same river, and went fishing in the same places where boys with white skin now held the land, and rowed about in canoes as skilfully as Indians could. (Williams 1889: 4)

This passage recalls the days when indigenous groups still held the land in Ontario, but it does not speak of a violent or unjust transition of power. Rather, the modern scene is transposed upon the older one, and the "boys with white skin" are pictured as having become "natives" in their own right. These boys are neither young Americans nor British boys "of the Empire"; they are firmly rooted in their Canadian soil.

Although the rivalry between America and Canada is often presented in the light-hearted tone of friendly competition, much of the children's literature of the late nineteenth century also demonstrates a more serious recognition of the fact that America poses a threat to Canada's welfare. In the country's earliest days this was the threat of invasion, but at the end of the nineteenth century the United States was feared for its ability to draw Canada's population south of the border. Canada had a history of losing both native born Canadians and immigrants to the United States. New and established Canadians alike were attracted by growing industries in the south and by the fertile lands of such states as Michigan and Ohio (Currie 1960: 65). The concern raised by this trend was heightened by the fact that in terms of sheer numbers, the United States was a giant compared to Canada. In 1860, seven years prior to Confederation, the United States already possessed a population of over 31 million and by 1900 this had risen to more than 75 million (Easterbrook and Aitken 1956: 396–397). These numbers meant that in addition to concern over its ability to drain Canada's population, the U.S. was also seen to pose the continued threat of annexation.

Concern over population numbers was something that was expressed in literature for young Canadians. For example, there is a discussion of this in an issue of *The Young Canadian* that was published shortly after the Canadian census of 1891. In its reference to these census results, it highlights some of the key concerns and insecurities of certain sectors of the population. Commentary on population figures underscores a latent and lingering fear of absorption by the United States; a fear based on the idea that bigger might just mean better after all:

> Everybody seems surprised and disappointed because our population is so small. Of course, all Canadians, and young Canadians especially, want to grow into a great nation; and it was generally taken for granted that we were growing much faster than the census shows. Many expected to find our numbers over six million, while it turns out that they are under five. It seems clear that we ought to have grown more rapidly than we have done; for evidently many have left the country whom we should have retained, and we have not succeeded in attracting as many people from other countries as we should have liked. What is the cause of this, it would take a wise head to tell with certainty; but there is one thing clear . . . that all Canadians, young and old, should unite in making their country as attractive as possible, both to its present inhabitants and to newcomers, so that . . . we may have reason to rejoice over our growing numbers and our growing prosperity. (*Young Canadian* 1891a: 553)

Here then, in September 1891, is evidence of an early fear of the "brain drain" from Canada to the United States that continues to spark concern today. It was a fear based on the very real movement of people across the border. By 1900, more than one million former Canadians had relocated to the United States (Avery 1995: 10), and many of these were people who had originally immigrated to Canada from abroad. This outward flow of established Canadians and newcomers was of concern to a country struggling to increase its population. As a result, we can see in this passage from *The Young Canadian* the promotion of what has long been a central and key focus of Canadian policy; namely, an emphasis on the need for immigration.

In addition to promoting immigration in order to increase Canada's population, something also needed to be done to address the problem of people leaving Canada for the U.S. Anti-American sentiments were one of the weapons used in an attempt to stem this tide. There was a hope that by promoting the idea of Canada's superiority its young citizens would remain loyal and avoid leaving to pursue opportunities in the United States. A brief essay in the August 1902 issue of *The Canadian Boy* entitled "Why Go to the United States?" is an example of the existing view that the United States is a threat to Canada: "It may be that some of our readers will some day have inducements offered to them to go over to the neighboring republic. Many Canadian Boys are there now, and doubtless more will follow, but we think that the number will gradually less [*sic*] till the 'exodus' disappears altogether" (*Canadian Boy* 1902c). The anonymous author optimistically puts forward the notion that Americans will in fact be the ones to leave their country for Canada:

> Why pass over the line? The tide is already turning the other way. The citizens of the United States are flocking by thousands into Canada,

attracted by our agricultural, industrial, and mineral wealth. The more of them who come the better, provided that they respect our laws and become loyal citizens of this country! (*Canadian Boy* 1902c)

In view of this supposed influx of Americans across the border, the author questions why any citizen of Canada would wish to head south:

And if they find this a good country to come to, why should we think of leaving it for the land they forsake? There is plenty of room for us at home, plenty of room for that industry, honesty and ability which made our young men sought after by employers in the United States. Our own country needs us, and very great should be the inducement which would take any of the patriotic sons of Canada off there [*sic*] native soil. (*Canadian Boy* 1902c)

In reality, however, the tide did not turn as the essayist had hoped, and population movement continued to be in a southward direction. America continued to be seen as a threat to Canada's welfare and the nation's child readership was increasingly warned of its drawbacks, and told of Canada's benefits.

Once again, it is *The Canadian Boy* of August 1902 that provides an example of the manner in which these sentiments were presented to Canadian children. "A Young Canadian's Manly Stand," by Margaret MacTavish, tells the tale of a Canadian studying at an American university who resolutely observes the Sabbath even though his fellow students choose to use the day for study. His declaration that he does not study on Sunday is met with disbelief by his U.S. companions:

"Not study on Sunday!" exclaimed Aubrey Hunter. "How on earth do you expect to keep up?"
"Where do you hail from, anyway?" asked Harty Watson.
"I come from Canada," responded Roberts. (MacTavish 1902: 9)

The perceived association between Roberts' strength of character and his nationality is made clear in this exchange of dialogue. While the boy faces temptation from those around him, he is steadfast in his resolve, and is true to his values. At the end of the tale, the "loyal young Canadian" successfully passes his examination, while his American counterpart sees his health give way as a result of his heretical study habit. The result of his failure to follow the Canadian's lead is lamentable and the reader is told that "instead of being a help to his family, he found himself for a long time a charge upon those whom he hoped to help" (MacTavish 1902: 10). By avoiding the bad habits of the American students, the Canadian boy ends up triumphant. Once again, the message presented to young Canadian readers is that in moral as well as physical character, the northerners are superior to their southern neighbours.[2]

The kind of anti-American sentiment found in MacTavish's story is not limited to works concerned exclusively with Canada's relationship to the United States. This relationship was also a factor in Canada's association with Britain. While not all Canadians who advocated greater self-government and less control by Britain were secretly plotting Canada's future union with the United States, some imperialists used this fear of American power to promote Canada's ties to Britain. This relation between imperialism and anti-American sentiment is apparent in a poem entitled "This Fair Canadian Land." This poem was included in a collection for children and contains some strong evidence of anti-American views:

How fair is this land which the might of our fathers
Bequeathed to their children to have and to hold;
From lonely Belleisle, where Atlantic foregathers,
To Mackenzie that down thro' the ages has roll'd!
Yes, fair is the land, with its great inland waters,
Vast links, forg'd of God, in the national chain,
That shall teach our brave sons and our virtuous daughters
To attune heart and voice to the patriots' strain;
    Then patriots say, Shall alien footsteps stand
    In triumph on this fair Canadian land?

O, Britain, dear Britain, ever glorious nation!
Whose strong arm in peace nigh engirdles the earth:
Canadians turn yet, aye, in proud exultation
To the mother of nations that gave to them birth.
Oh, where be the hearts that in trait'rous illusion
Would barter for pottage a birthright so fair;
On each be the brand of dark shame and confusion,
And the stews of sedition his crime-haunted lair.
    God make his hope but as the rope of sand,
    And one and indivisible this land.

Of the people who dwell in the land on our borders
We are kinsmen—not lovers—and can never be one;
Apart lies our future, and He will afford us
The help of His arm till our destiny's done.
We like them, but yet are their ways not as our ways;
There, the marriage-tie's but a tale that is told;
There, the Bench and the Forum are equally powerless
When Justice and Honour are ravish'd by gold.
    Peace, an' they will— nay more—a friendly hand,
    But not one foot of our Canadian land! (Cockin 1891: 9)

This poem makes a strong statement about the United States and the future relationship between the two North American nations. The poet adds greed and corruption to the list of negative traits attributed to the United States by some Canadian writers. As "This Fair Canadian Land" demonstrates, there was a tendency among the children's writers of the period to discourage Canadian youth from idolising or emulating their neighbours.

These attempts to distance Canada from the United States were being made in adult literature as well. Canada's daily press played a crucial role in developing the nation's sense of identity in which, once again, the spread of anti-American views played a part:

> Central to the nationalist credo in English Canada was the country's un-American heritage, more presumed than proved of course: the boundary, stated the Toronto *News* (13 January 1888), divided 'two peoples different in their form of government, in thought, in mode of life, in aims, in idiom[;] almost the only point of similarity is that the English tongue is generally spoken in both.' (Rutherford 1982: 160)

In order to secure loyalty to Canada, a negative picture was painted of the United States. Among the inferior qualities which were believed to characterise the republic were included greed, corruption, physical inferiority, aggression, and a lack of piety. By contrast, this picture helped to shape a positive image of Canada itself as embodying all those qualities that America, supposedly, did not.

By creating and promoting negative stereotypes of the United States, these authors were picturing Canada as its opposite, and emphasising certain political and social ideals that were considered to be essential to the Canadian way of life. Through this literature, Canadians began to be characterised in such terms as loyal, generous, honest, cooperative, peaceful, strong, brave and industrious. In response to the perceived threat America posed to Canada's growth and development, the periodicals and novels of the day also stress the continuing importance of immigration to the nation's future and prosperity. And while some elements of British society were supposedly being rejected, it is also clear that the English traditions of law and justice, rather than the traditions of the United States were a crucial part of Canada's basic foundation. These were just some of the political and social ideals that were helping to shape the country's growing sense of identity.

The influence Canada's relations with both Britain and America would have on the development of a national sense of identity is perhaps best demonstrated by the words of Prime Minister Sir Wilfrid Laurier. Following the decision over the Alaskan boundary dispute in October 1903, President Roosevelt declared it "the greatest diplomatic victory of our time" (LaPierre 1996: 295). By contrast, Laurier had some prophetic words about the future of Canada's relations with both the British and the Americans:

> I have often regretted that while the United States is a great and powerful nation, we are only a small colony, a growing colony, but still a colony. I

have often regretted also that we have not in our hands the treaty-making power which would enable us to dispose of our own affairs. . . . So long as Canada remains a dependency of the British Crown, the present powers which we have are not sufficient for the maintenance of our rights . . . if ever we have to deal with matters of a similar nature again, we shall deal with them in our way, in our own fashion, according to the best light we have. (LaPierre 1996: 295)

Just what "our way" and "our fashion" meant was shaped in large part by the literature of the late nineteenth and early twentieth centuries. In the face of the tug-of-war relations between Canada, Britain and America, this question of loyalties led to a new defining sense of Canadian identity, which found great expression in the children's literature of the age.

Chapter Five
Sleeping with the Enemy?:
The Figure of the French Canadian

If we love Canada and are desirous that she should prosper and attain the proud destiny that a bounteous nature has so well fitted her to attain to, we must develop throughout this broad Dominion a just national spirit founded upon mutual interest, mutual respect, mutual confidence and mutual affection.

(R. Prefontaine, Mayor of Montreal)

While English-speaking Canada was developing a new sense of national identity and a notion of what it meant to be "Canadian" towards the end of the nineteenth century, there was still an ambiguity about to whom exactly this identity applied. Canadian writers of the time acknowledged the impact of ongoing immigration to Canada and the incorporation of these new citizens into Canadian society, but the place of French Canadians in this vision of the nation remained complicated.

The identities of Anglophone and Francophone Canada are bound together, and the influence of French Canada on the national culture has always extended well beyond the provincial boundaries of Quebec. Nowhere is the complexity of this relationship more apparent than in the Anglophone children's literature in which the figure of the "French Canadian" frequently appears. "Le Canadien" can have many guises, including those of Explorer, Fur-Trader, Woodsman, Hunter, Settler, Habitant, Enemy, and Comrade. These representations of the French Canadian underscore the complicated relationship between Canada's two central ethnic and linguistic groups. Sometimes painted as an enemy, sometimes painted as a friend, the figure of the French Canadian demonstrates the ongoing struggles between these two groups, as well as the continuing importance of this relationship to a growing sense of a unified national identity.

The French Canadian: Friend or Foe?

The issue of French-Anglo relations in Canada has long been of central importance both politically and culturally. Yet the very attempt to classify people according to these categories (as if each in itself is not extremely diverse and complex) misrepresents the multifaceted nature of Canadian society. Regardless of their many differences, the French and the British in Canada share a lengthy history, which a repeated emphasis on such divisions undermines. It seems to have been the tendency of many nineteenth-century writers to focus on the differences and animosity between these groups rather than on their common bonds. The rich history of conflict over French and English holdings in North America was a common theme for many writers of children's literature. Major historical events including the fall of Louisbourg (1758) and the Battle of the Plains of Abraham (1759) feature in the works of children's writers such as G.A. Henty, J.M. Oxley, and E. Everett-Green. Writers of such historical fiction often draw a clear divide between the French and the English, with the relationship between the two groups portrayed as one of great animosity. While the English represent noble ambition and progress, writers often portray the French-Catholic society as corrupt and backward-looking. In these works, the French Canadian is often seen as a threat to the future development of Canadian society.

In British author E. Everett-Green's 1899 novel *French and English: A Story of the Struggle in America*, the French are frequently (though not exclusively) portrayed in a negative light. Evelyn Everett-Green (1856–1932) was a prolific writer of children's fiction who produced more than 200 juvenile novels in her career, many of them aimed at young girls. Many of her stories were works of historical fiction, perhaps inspired by her mother's own work as a historian (Skelding 2001: 123). While she is now out of print, Everett-Green was one of the most widely read children's writers of the late-nineteenth and early twentieth centuries, and a survey conducted by the *Girl's Realm* in 1898 places her within the top six favourite girls' authors in Britain (Skelding 2001: 123). Her historical novel about the battle between France and England for control of North America is one example of the way in which some children's writers portrayed the French in Canada in a negative light. Indeed, it is the treacherous act of a Frenchman that sets the events of this story in motion.

When a group of English settlers come under attack and are murdered viciously, the French receive the blame for the disruption of this community:

> "It was the French who came and spoiled our happy home. If they had let us alone, perchance we might have been there still, hunting, fishing . . . at peace with ourselves and with the world. But they came amongst us. They sowed disunion and strife. They were resolved to get rid of the English party, as they called it. . . . [T]hose in whom the sturdy British spirit flourished they regarded with jealousy and dislike. . . . If they

could have done it, I believe they would have taught the Indians to distrust us English; but that was beyond their power." (Everett-Green 1899: 44–45)

Such strong statements of anti-French sentiment are not uncommon in the literature of the day. In this particular novel, there is a sense that the French and English characters have strong allegiances to their respective ancestral homelands, and that neither side perceives itself as "Canadian." In the novel, the criticism of the French appears to centre on the impact of their actions on England, rather than the effect these may have had on the Canadian nation itself, which is in keeping with the fact that the author was British. The attitudes towards French society expressed in Everett-Green's novel in many ways reflect existing attitudes at the *fin de siècle*, when many saw France as a place of decadence and degeneration. The author transposes the view of the French as potentially corruptive onto the North American scene, but in this novel the figure of the treacherous Frenchman embodies a threat to English civilisation as a whole, rather than a detriment to Canadian society specifically. The fact that her negative portrayal of the French is inconsistent complicates Everett-Green's view of the French Canadian. In this particular novel, some French characters appear in a more sympathetic light than others. Yet despite these occasional positive portrayals, Everett-Green's work remains an example of a view that the French in Canada are a potential threat to society, and a potential foe to Anglo-Canadians.

Everett-Green was not the only British author to take a page from history and write of French–English relations in North America. G.A. Henty also exploited the past military conflict between these groups in such works as *With Wolfe in Canada* (1887). Henty tells the tale of an English boy named James Walsham who finds adventure in Canada after joining the English regiment responsible for the defeat of the French at Quebec under the leadership of James Wolfe. In his preface to the novel Henty outlines the significance of these events, not just to the future of Canada, but to the future of France and England:

On the issues of that struggle depended not only the destiny of Canada, but of the whole of North America, and, to a large extent, that of the two mother countries. When the contest began, the chances of France becoming the great colonizing empire were as good as those of England. . . . The loss of her North American provinces turned the scale. . . . Never was the shortsightedness of human beings shown more distinctly than when France wasted her strength and treasure in a sterile contest on the continent of Europe, and permitted, with scarce an effort, her North American colonies to be torn from her. (Henty 1887?: 5–6)

Henty is clearly writing as an English author, whose primary concern is how these events affected his own country. Nevertheless, his depiction of the French in Canada contributes to the image of the French Canadian as a rather backward figure; a representation prevalent in the work of other writers.

In explaining the history of the battle for North America, Henty outlines the state of affairs leading up to the conflict between France and England. He attributes the French loss in some degree to what he perceives as incompetence and backwardness. Henty writes:

> The Canadian population were frugal and hardy, but they were deficient in enterprise; and the priests, who ruled them with a rod of iron, for Canada was intensely Catholic, discouraged any movements which would take their flocks from under their charge. Upon the other hand, the colonists of New England, Pennsylvania, and Virginia were men of enterprise and energy, and their traders . . . carried on an extensive trade with the Indians . . . thereby greatly exciting the jealousy of the French. (Henty 1887?: 152)

Henty here portrays the French Canadians as quite inept, and attributes a portion of their failure to the prominent position of the Catholic Church in this society. Such portrayals of the French Canadian of Canada's past likely influenced the way in which this figure appeared and functioned in other children's literature of the nineteenth century.

Yet the portrayal of such characters was not exclusively negative. While writers such as E. Everett-Green and G.A. Henty looked to a time in Canada's past when active conflicts did indeed take place, other children's authors of the period were writing works that more accurately reflected the post-Confederation face of Canada, with the French and English no longer at war with one another. While the literary tradition of painting the French Canadian as "foe" continued, a more positive portrayal was simultaneously taking place. In these works, the Frenchman was more likely to appear in the guise of a woodsman, a fur-trader, or a farmer than that of an enemy on the battlefield.

Canadian author J.M. Oxley's novel of 1895 entitled *The Young Woodsman, or Life in the Forests of Canada* is one example of the manner in which the French Canadian was appearing as a friendly figure in the Canadian children's literature of the age. This novel tells the story of an Anglo-Canadian boy named Frank Kingston who, following the death of his father, finds work as a chore-boy in a lumber camp near the Ottawa River. Frank is an honest and pious boy, who has clearly borrowed his moral code from the English imperialist tradition. Much of his character and his background are revealed in the opening pages of the novel when the reader is given a clear insight into the tradition in which he has been raised:

> [T]here was a shelf in his room upon which stood an attractive array. Livingstone's "Travels," Ballantyne's "Hudson Bay," Kingsley's "Westward Ho!" side by side with "Robinson Crusoe," "Pilgrim's Progress," and

"Tom Brown at Rugby." Frank knew these books almost by heart, yet never wearied of turning to them again and again. He drew inspiration from them. They helped to mould his character, although of this he was hardly conscious, and they filled his soul with a longing for adventure and enterprise that no ordinary everyday career could satisfy. (Oxley 1895: 16)

In this obvious homage to some great works of children's literature, Oxley perhaps betrays a hope that his own literature may have an influence on moulding character in his young readers. He certainly establishes the very British nature of Frank's upbringing, value system, and cultural heritage.

Despite Oxley's emphasis on the British heritage so clearly embodied by major English authors like Kingsley and Thomas Hughes, Frank's arrival in the lumber camp introduces the boy to a much more varied society than that represented by his favourite literature. Oxley's description of the collection of men at the lumber camp betrays some racial and cultural stereotypes typical of the time, but it also underscores the existing diversity within Canadian society:

They were "all sorts and conditions of men"—habitants who could not speak a word of English, and Irishmen who could not speak a word of French; shrewd Scotchmen, chary of tongue and reserved of manner, and loquacious half-breeds, ready for song, or story, or fight, according to the humour of the moment. Here and there were dusky skins and prominent features that betrayed a close connection with the aboriginal owners of the continent. (Oxley 1895: 45)

Oxley's descriptions of various groups are in keeping with some of the thinking of the day. English anthropologist John Beddoe, for instance, was one of several anthropologists to examine the differences among the various European "races" in the late nineteenth century and outline what he considered to be distinct racial characteristics. In one of his studies on European anthropology Beddoe writes:

It is an invidious thing to draw national characters, and to point out their defects. But how seldom do the English produce a great orator, or the Welsh, though undeniably brave, a great soldier. The Spaniards have always been cruel, the French boastful, the Italians crafty and cunning, the English lovers of fair play, respecters of wealth, sufferers from "mauvaise haute." (Beddoe 1912: 188)

Oxley echoes Beddoe's thoughts on what he perceives as differing racial characteristics among Europeans. His description of the lumber camp not only explores the diversity within the British community, with distinctions drawn between Irishmen and Scotchmen, it also hints at the complex relations between the French and the Indians,[1] and the "half-breeds" who claim an ancestral connection to both these groups.

Indeed, it is only the English who are not distinguished in Oxley's initial description of the camp, suggesting that he considers this group to represent the established Canadian "norm." Perhaps this is also a reflection of the ideas expressed by Beddoe, who ranks the English as superior in matters of honesty, justice, and modesty. Oxley's depiction of the relations between the many groups that help form the lumber camp, however, indicates that in Canada, friendship between various ethnic groups is both possible and necessary. From among this diverse crowd the people who befriend Frank include Foreman Johnston, a fellow Anglo-Canadian, and the French Canadian Baptiste, the camp's friendly cook. Baptiste defends Frank against the jealousy of the "half-breed" Damase, and he and many of his fellow French Canadians are portrayed in a positive light. In spite of their linguistic, religious and cultural differences, a strong friendship forms between the young boy and the camp cook. The figure of the French Canadian here, as embodied by the character of Baptiste, is markedly different from the sworn enemy of the English of Everett-Green's novel.

Oxley's portrayal of the lumber camp demonstrates an ability for disparate groups of people to work in harmony. Nevertheless, there remains a sense of distance between the French Canadians and the other woodsmen: "Fully one-half of the gang were French Canadians, dark-complexioned, black-haired, bright-eyed men, full of life and talk, their tongues going unceasingly as they plodded along in sociable groups. Of the remainder, some were Scotch, others Irish, the rest English" (Oxley 1895: 50). Oxley's portrait of these men as "sociable" and "full of life" is positive, yet there is an implicit sense that the French woodsmen are somewhat exotic, with their dark complexions and black hair denoting their status as non-English "foreigners." Once again, while the British elements of the camp (particularly the English members) are given little characterisation, the perceived differences in the French, from their complexion to their conversation, are emphasised, establishing them as something distinct from the norm.

Through the emphasis on their dark skin and dark hair, and the comparative description of the sociable French and the "loquacious half-breeds," Oxley also establishes a link between the French Canadians and the Indians. Once again this is in keeping with the ideas of anthropologist John Beddoe who sees a connection between the French and Indians in North America, which he holds to be a threat to the Anglo-Americans:

> The birth-rate tends to decrease among the pure Anglo-Americans, while the French-Canadians, strongly crossed with native Indian blood, are multiplying with alarming rapidity; and the American military statistics seem . . . to indicate that the climate is less suitable to the blond than to the brunette. (Beddoe 1912: 183)

Here in Beddoe's observation is an implicit distinction between the "blond" and fair Anglo race, and the "dark" and swarthy French and Indian people. While the French and Indians in Canada were two distinct groups of people, in many ways they appear equally exotic in Oxley's tale when compared to the "norm" represented by the British contingent.

In this novel, the character of Damase most clearly embodies this idea of the "other" as an outcome of the association between the French and the Indians. Oxley suggests that because Damase is a product of a union between French and Indian, he is far more treacherous and threatening to the young protagonist than perhaps he would be if he were not, to use the author's words, a "half-breed." Historian H.L. Malchow discusses the late Victorian view that people of mixed ancestry were somehow unnatural and threatening:

> The racial and sexual cross-boundary confusions implicit in the idea of "the half-breed", the problem of secret identities betrayed by readable signs of difference, of fated, unstable natures torn between two worlds, of a violent contradictory combination of opposites—of villain and victim, masculine and feminine—makes the mixed race as constructed in nineteenth-century British popular culture as an *essentially* Gothic type. . . . There was . . . a pre-war representation of the dangers of "bad blood" and cultural-cum-racial pollution as a kind of threatened vampirism. (Malchow 1996: 103)

Certainly J.M. Oxley's portrayal of Damase supports Malchow's argument that it was not uncommon for such figures of mixed race to be viewed as threatening and potentially corruptive.

Frank's relationship with Damase is not the only one in this novel that is potentially unstable. While the overall harmony in the camp suggests that different races can work well together, the division in the camp over Frank's difficulty with Damase demonstrates that the friendly relations between the French Canadians and the other workers are of a tenuous nature. When Frank has a confrontation with Damase, who scorns the importance Frank places on reading the Bible, the young protagonist senses a division of loyalty among the members of the camp. It is one based largely along racial and linguistic lines:

> From this time forth he could see clearly that two very different opinions concerning himself prevailed in the shanty. By all the English members of the gang, and some of the French, headed by honest Baptiste, he was looked upon with hearty liking and admiration . . . by the remainder of the French contingent . . . he was regarded as a stuck-up youngster that wanted taking down badly. (Oxley 1895: 72)

Oxley's portrayal of French Canadians in *The Young Woodsman* is somewhat ambiguous, with both negative and positive stereotyping taking place. Nevertheless, Oxley does reflect an increasing tendency in Canadian literature to position the figure of the French Canadian as a friendly associate of the English, rather than as a decided foe.

There are two factors that might explain the difference between his portrayal of the French and those by Henty and Everett-Green. To begin with, while the two latter authors were setting their novels in the past, Oxley was writing about a time in which relations between the two groups had improved substantially. The portrayal of French Canadians such as Baptiste mirrors the changing nature of the relationship between English and French Canadians, which had improved significantly between the eighteenth century (the historical setting for both Henty and Everett-Green's novels) and the late nineteenth century, the period during which all three authors were actually writing. Second, Oxley himself was Canadian while Henty and Everett-Green were both English. While these two British authors did help to shape an image of Canada and Canadians, their work also reflects prejudices and attitudes that were of direct relevance to England and its own relationship with France. Their negative portrayals of francophone characters, therefore, while still influencing how literary representations of the French Canadian developed, are actually in large part a reflection of the relations between two European nations. J.M. Oxley, on the other hand, was more accurately reflecting the relationship between French Canadians and English Canadians. It was a relationship that had improved in many respects by the end of the nineteenth century.

While relations between the two groups were far from perfect—a fact that the debate surrounding the Boer War at the turn of the twentieth century would highlight—one can also argue that the last decade of the nineteenth century marked a turning point in these relations. In July of 1896 Sir Wilfrid Laurier became the seventh Prime Minister of Canada and the first French Canadian to hold the post; something which is unlikely to have occurred just a few years before.[2] With such developments taking place in the political arena, the stage was set for children's writers to put forth a new vision of the French Canadian. This figure began to embody several of the characteristics that many would come to consider quintessentially "Canadian." Certainly, the term "Canadian," or "Le Canadien," itself initially referred exclusively to French Canadians, but was adopted by the nation as a whole. Indeed, some of the most familiar cultural symbols of Canada, from the snowshoe to the toque, were commonly associated with the figure of the French Canadian fur-trader. While the French Canadian remained a distinctive literary character in Canadian children's literature in the early twentieth century, he ceased to be defined solely as an enemy of the English or as a threat to Canadian society.

Yet the growth of friendly feeling between Canada's varied ethnic groups was not instantaneous. Animosity between French and English Canadians persisted well into the twentieth century as the nation continued to reassess Confederation and provincial autonomy. There is certainly much evidence to support the view that some still saw the French element in Canada as a hindrance to the nation's development. In December of 1889, for instance, Conservative Member of

Parliament D'Alton McCarthy delivered a speech in Ottawa outlining his views on the use of the French language in Canadian schools:

> [A]s a citizen of Ontario—of the Dominion—I heartily endorse the sentiment . . . that we ought, and ought at once and for all time, to put an end to the teaching of our children, or any portion of our children, either French Canadian or English, in any other language than the language of the country in which we live. (Cheers.) I say further . . . that we will not support or tolerate in this Province, no matter which political party may advocate them, any half-hearted measures to carry that object or reform into effect. (Loud cheers). (McCarthy 1889: 4)

McCarthy was staunchly in favour of eliminating the use of the French language in Canada. He goes on to say in this speech that he does not see the French Canadians as simply possessing the desire to preserve their own heritage, but as ultimately planning to gain control of the nation:

> I think the French Canadian desires, not merely that he should have his language, as his Institutions and his laws, in the Province of Quebec; but his ambition is to carry it to the Province of Ontario, and thence to Manitoba and the North West, and ultimately, if he can, to subdue this country to Frenchmen, or to make of it a French nationality. And he will die game. There will be no backdown on the part of the French Canadian. (McCarthy 1889: 26)

McCarthy's speech reiterates the view of the French Canadian as a threat to the ultimate success and future of the Canadian nation. His call is not for harmony and cooperation, but for assimilation.

McCarthy was not alone in expressing such sentiments. In 1911 a paper appeared that echoed this notion of the French Canadian as a danger, claiming, "If we do not put forth well-directed efforts to make loyal and educated citizens of the people of . . . Quebec they will become a menace to the state, seriously retarding the growth of the nation . . ." (Anon 1911: 4). Like McCarthy, this author sees the French Canadian as a potential threat to the nation. Once again, the key to overcoming these threats is thought to lie not in an effort to achieve mutual understanding and respect, but in the instilling of "British" values in the French Canadian (Anon 1911: 4), and the stamping out of features of French culture, particularly the influence of the Roman Catholic Church. This author presents a condescending attitude toward the French people, and even his effort to be complimentary is painfully flawed:

> The habitant as we find him to-day . . . is the product of British rule. . . . And this habitant created under British rule is incomparably the finest type of the French people. In solid worth—honesty, industry, kindly

disposition, politeness—he commands respect, and if the causes were removed which have kept him unprogressive, he would astonish those who decry him, for the habitant and his children are naturally bright and have the capacity to take a foremost place among the peoples of this continent. Those who speak disparagingly of the habitant are ignorant of the qualities which lie latent within him, awaiting the touch of the spirit of truth. (Anon 1911: 18–19)

Literature such as this demonstrates some of the problems that lingered between the French and the English in Canada into the early years of the twentieth century.

As the writing of D'Alton McCarthy and others demonstrates, the literature in English-speaking Canada at the beginning of the twentieth century reflects both an element of anger directed towards the French Canadians and an idealised, yet patronising, attitude towards these "habitants." In the midst of these conflicting and equally unsatisfactory approaches, many authors of children's' literature were striking a middle ground. Among the many contrasting portrayals of French Canadians in literature, there was a body of work that emphasised the commonality between all Canadians, be they Anglophone or Francophone. The most familiar appearance of this interpretation of the French Canadian seems to be in works intended for use in schools, including history textbooks and readers. In some instances, portraying shared interests and history simply means anglicising or appropriating French-Canadian culture, the extent of which varies from work to work. While this literature still contains both negative stereotyping of the French Canadian, and kindlier, yet patronising portrayals, it nevertheless bespeaks an awareness of the fact that Canada's two main cultural groups share inextricable bonds.

This is clearly evident in the historical narratives produced in Canada following Confederation, when many Canadians were anxious to preserve and strengthen the new union of provinces. While some authors were interested in stories of conflict, many Anglophone writers were treating French historical figures as important and influential players in Canada's past, and seeing the history of French Canada as an essential part of their own society and character. In many ways, these works demonstrate both an accommodation and an appropriation of the figures and events significant in the culture of French Canada. In Henry H. Miles' *The Child's History of Canada* (published in Montreal in 1870 and intended for use in the Elementary Schools), figures such as Samuel Champlain and Jacques Cartier are noted for the key roles they played in Canada's development. Henry Hopper Miles (1818–1895) was an author and a teacher who immigrated to Quebec from England in 1845. While Miles' attitude towards French Canada is somewhat ambiguous at times, his understanding of the need for good relations between Quebec and the rest of Canada is clear. This is in keeping with the fact that Miles' textbook was intended for use in both English and French schools, including both Protestant and Catholic institutions (Egoff 1992b). In discussing the fall of Quebec into the hands of the English in 1759 under the leadership of English General James Wolfe, Miles downplays the lasting effects of Wolfe's conquest on the psyche of the French people, as well as the subsequent attitude of the French Canadians toward the British:

> Of course, it seemed strange, at first, to the French Canadians, to be under any other ruler than the King of France. It would seem the same to ourselves now, if, all at once, we found ourselves not the subjects of the good Queen Victoria. Perhaps the Canadians would have cared more about the change than they did, if Louis XV had been a good King. But he was far from being that. . . . So, in course of time, the French Canadians, came to be at least as loyal to George the Third as they had been to their former king. (Miles 1870: 107–108)

Miles portrays the French in Canada as being mildly disturbed at the sudden regime change but then quite content and satisfied to be under British rule. This version of events fails to take into account the difficult realities of the situation, when many French Canadians experienced distress over the defeat of Montcalm and France's loss of its North American territories. Miles' account of events also reveals his assumption that the French were undoubtedly blessed to fall within the benevolent compass of British imperial rule. Largely forgotten texts such as Miles' work on Canadian history are worthy of further examination by those concerned with the tradition of historiography in Canada, and with the changing portrayal of the developing relationship between the French and English elements in the country.

While Miles displays an imperialistic assumption that the French in Canada should be grateful for the perceived enlightenment brought by British rule, he also betrays a need to feel that French and English Canadians will live in harmony together. Miles inadvertently reveals some of the existing problems in 1870, however, when he relates an account of the Constitutional Act of 1791 that created Upper and Lower Canada:

> Other changes were made at this time, in 1791. They were made by the King and Parliament of England, who wished the Canadians to be contented and happy. When the Province of Quebec was thus made into two, settlers who could not agree about religion and other things, had it in their power to live as far apart as they pleased. (Miles 1870: 116)

This statement rather undermines the historian's earlier observation that as of 1792 the French and English in Canada were "no longer on bad terms with each other" (Miles 1870: 115). Nevertheless, Miles attempts to reconcile the histories of "French" and "English" Canada, and in effect presents these as the foundation for a unified Canada.

In 1893, Copp Clark published Agnes Machar's and T.G. Marquis' *Stories from Canadian History Based Upon "Stories of New France."* The title itself, which indicates a view of the stories of "New France" (the term given to France's early holdings in north-eastern North America) as being in essence stories from *Canadian* history, conceives of French and English Canada as a unified whole, rather than as two distinct halves. The bulk of the tales in Marquis' work concern events and figures from French Canada's past, and the chapters include such titles as the "Story of Champlain," "The First Great Siege of Quebec," and the "Story of Bréboeuf." Not only does Marquis' collection demonstrate that authors were trying to reconcile separate notions of "French Canadian" and "English Canadian" history, it also reveals an interest in French subject matter among English-speaking Canadians. The Anglophone Canadian children's periodicals of the late nineteenth century also demonstrate a growing awareness of the French contribution to Canadian society.

Children's authors were not the only ones to recognise the importance of building a better understanding of the French Canadians among Anglophone readers. In 1902 Byron Nicholson (1857–1916), author of several texts on Canada and Quebec, published a book about French Canadians from a "patriotic motive" in an attempt to correct what he sees as "misapprehensions" held by many English-speaking Canadians (Nicholson 1902: "Preface"). Nicholson claims in the book's Preface that his goal is to "supplant feelings of racial strife and bitterness by those of national brotherhood and a common citizenship," but to do so by avoiding some of the patronising attitudes displayed by other writers:

> In so doing he [the author] has tried to avoid giving his readers an unduly favourable opinion concerning those of whom he writes, or to represent them as being in every way the most admirable and lovable people that can be imagined; for indeed, human nature as seen in them is very much like human nature as seen in others. (Nicholson 1902: "Preface")

In his book, Nicholson argues that Canada's national unity depends upon a good relationship between French and English elements, and that the key to developing this is building a true understanding of the French Canadians. It is the same premise of the children's works of authors Miles and Marquis, as they attempt to teach children the role of the French in Canadian history.

One also finds evidence of an interest in French subject matter in the July 1, 1893 issue of *Pleasant Hours*. This Dominion Day issue features a ballad by Thomas D'Arcy McGee (1825–1868) about Jacques Cartier, who is described by the magazine's editor as both "intrepid and chivalrous" (McGee 1893: 102). Born and raised in Ireland, McGee moved to Canada in 1857 where he became a politician and an avid supporter of Confederation and the development of Canadian literature (Burns 1988). Before he was assassinated in 1868, McGee had written more than 300 poems, many of them centred on figures from

Canada's past such as Jacques Cartier. This particular poem was first published in 1858, in a collection called *Canadian Ballads, and Occasional Verses*. The Preface to this volume demonstrates that the poet himself believed in the importance of providing a national literature for the nation's youth. McGee writes:

> The Author of the Ballads contained in this little volume presents them to the younger generation of Canadians, as an attempt to show . . . that by those who are blessed with the divine gift of poesy, many worthy themes may be found, without quitting their own country.
>
> That we shall one day be a great northern nation, and develope [*sic*] within ourselves that best fruit of nationality, a new and lasting literature, is the firm belief, at least of those to whom this volume is mainly addressed. . . . Simply as an offering of first-fruits, I present this little volume to the young people of Canada. (McGee 1858: vii–viii)

McGee's feeling that there is an important relationship between literature, nationalism, and "the young people of Canada" is further demonstrated by the inclusion of his poem "Jacques Cartier" in the juvenile periodical *Pleasant Hours*. In view of McGee's hope for strong national unity in Canada, his choice of Jacques Cartier as a figure for his ballad is significant. It demonstrates both awareness and acceptance of the role French Canadians played in the development of the nation. The decision to include his poem in this periodical's Dominion Day issue further illustrates some of the positive treatment of French figures in late-nineteenth century children's literature.

While people from all periods of French Canada's past were increasingly being treated as important Canadian heroes, children's writers were also beginning to address the role of the French Canadian in contemporary society. In the August 1897 issue of *Home and Youth*, there appears a "Patriotic Song" by Canadian songwriter H.H. Godfrey (1858–1908) entitled "The Land of the Maple." The third verse and the chorus of this song read as follows:

> In Canada, dear Canada all dwell in unity.
> The Saxon, Gaul and Celt agree with Scots to keep us free.
> Though we be four, yet are we one if danger chance to be,
> Thus may it be for ever 'neath the spreading maple tree.
>
> *Chorus*:
> Oh the land of the maple is the land for me, the land of the stalwart the brave and the free the Rose and the Thistle, the Shamrock and "Lis"
> all bloom in one garden 'neath the maple tree. (Godfrey 1897: 8–9)

Godfrey first arrived in Canada in 1874 where he worked in a piano factory in Montreal, was a church organist, and proceeded to compose many patriotic songs with titles such as "When Johnny Canuck Comes Home," written during the Boer War (Canadian Musical). This version of his song "The Land of the Maple" contains a note explaining that "Lis" is pronounced "Lee" and is the French word for Lily, the necessity of which somewhat undermines the song's claim that Canada is a country of unity and mutual understanding. The need to explain the significance of the "Lis" to an English audience betrays a certain level of cultural ignorance about the "Gaul" in Canada. Furthermore, the reduction of Canada to only four groups—English, Irish, French, and Scottish—clearly marginalises the other ethnic and racial groups that were already helping to shape the Canadian nation in 1897. At the same time, however, Godfrey's very attempt to teach Anglophone audiences about French culture is evidence of an effort to build understanding. The vision of Canada put forth in Godfrey's "patriotic song" is one of a nation that is diverse, yet united.

There was a close link between Canadian politics and cultural production following Confederation. In the May 1901 issue of *The Canadian Boy*, published in Cobourg, Ontario, there is a contribution from R. Prefontaine, the French mayor of Montreal, which demonstrates that politicians themselves were directly aware of this relationship. Prefontaine wrote his article specifically for *The Canadian Boy*, illustrating his awareness of children's literature as an important venue for political debate and influence. The editor of the magazine states that in his "message," the "mayor of Canada's largest city shows how boys can help to promote unity and strength of citizenship" (Prefontaine 1901: 16). Prefontaine's use of the term "citizenship" is particularly interesting here, as it implies a strong dedication to Canada and to improving national unity, even though legal recognition of the term "Canadian citizenship" did not exist until 1946.[3] Titled "French and English Boys in Canada," the mayor's article acknowledges that Canada needs harmony between French and English elements. Instilling this belief in children is a key part of the process, and is something Prefontaine sees as his duty as a political figure:

> As you have given me this opportunity to speak directly and frankly to the English speaking boys of Canada, I would like to say to them what I often remarked to my fellow countrymen of French lineage and speech:— If we love Canada and are desirous that she should prosper and attain the proud destiny that a bounteous nature has so well fitted her to attain to, we must develop throughout this broad Dominion a just national spirit founded upon mutual interest, mutual respect, mutual confidence and mutual affection. (Prefontaine 1901: 16)

Prefontaine's article is aimed at a child audience and as such, it is an excellent example of the relation between politics, propaganda, and children's literature. It demonstrates a conscious decision on the part of political figures to utilise this literature as a means of disseminating political thought, and promoting national unity.

While many English writers were interested in French subjects Prefontaine's essay provides an insight into French thought on the topic of Canadian national identity and sentiment. Prefontaine demonstrates that the desire for national unity does not lie with English Canada alone:

> The undeveloped and unbounded natural resources of Canada offer a tempting field of operations to the Canadian boy, which cannot fail to excite his ambition. My earnest hope is that . . . he will not lose sight of the . . . importance of assisting in the cultivation of a spirit of national pride and national respect, which shall animate the whole Canadian population from the Atlantic to the Pacific, and weld them into one harmonious community. (Prefontaine 1901: 16)

Prefontaine's use of the word "cultivation" acknowledges the fact that writers for children were not just reflecting the realities of national unity and identity; they were constructing them as well.

In the midst of his optimistic view of the nation's future, Prefontaine acknowledges the existing tensions between French and English Canadians. Yet he sees both sides playing an active role in the growth of mutual understanding and acceptance:

> Since my advent into public life, I have witnessed great advance in the direction of a unification of the Canadian peoples. We French Canadians appreciate more than we used to the good qualities and many virtues of our fellow-countrymen of Anglo-Saxon origin and English tongue, and the English Canadians, I find, are growing to like us better every day and are discovering in us good qualities and virtues their fathers never dreamt of. (Prefontaine 1901: 16)

While the author here recognises the history of conflict between Canada's two main ethnic groups, he also believes that hope for the future lies in the next generation. He acknowledges that "more remains to be done before old animosities are entirely eradicated and old sores healed up," but says of the "healing process" that "it is for the Canadian boy to help it along" (Prefontaine 1901: 16). For Prefontaine, there is no doubt that the young Canadians to whom he addresses his work can have a great influence on the nation's future.

Prefontaine was writing at a time when divisions between French and English Canada were clearly visible, as the country had recently been divided over the issue of sending troops to the Boer War. Increasingly, however, Canadian writers were addressing the need to overcome these divisions. John Boyd writes in his essay on Canadian nationalism in 1911 that French and English Canadians can be proud of their respective heritage, but "the interests of our own country must always be of paramount importance and have the first consideration from all of us" (Boyd 1911: 15). Boyd is calling for Canadians to put Canada first, and

Prefontaine's article in *The Canadian Boy* is evidence that some Canadians were turning to the next generation to salvage the dream of national unity. According to Prefontaine, evidence of a brighter future could already be seen in the French and English boys of Montreal:

> I have been pleased to observe in this good City of Montreal, the spot where the races meet, that French and English boys mingle more freely together, and know each other better than they did when I was a boy. Some years ago, the French Canadian boys used to regard their English speaking neighbors as their natural enemies, and vice versa. . . . Such things are unheard of now, and French and English boys, associating together in play, are forming friendships which will doubtless . . . have a powerful influence in banishing from Canada the ugly demon of racial suspicion and hatred. (Prefontaine 1901: 16)

Prefontaine trusts "that the day in question may not be long delayed," yet acknowledges that the ideal state of affairs has not yet been reached (16). He looks forward to the day when "we shall have a united nationality in Canada, which will place our country at the very front among the nations of the world, and the brightest gem in the Imperial Crown will shine with brighter lustre than ever" (16). For Prefontaine, Canadian nationality must encompass both French and English, and the lack of such a unified identity will prevent Canada from taking her rightful place "among the nations of the world." For the French mayor, and the English editors of *The Canadian Boy*, a unified nationality is a goal for which young Canadians must strive, and one their literature can help to achieve.

Chapter Six
Flint and Feather: The Figure of the Indian

While the French Canadian played a changing role in children's literature and in constructions of Canadian identity, the figure of the "Indian" was also a staple of stories set in Canada. The position of the Indian in this literature was, like that of his French counterpart, often ambiguous. There are many similarities between the ways in which writers portray French Canadians and Indigenous peoples in their children's narratives. Just as French Canadian characters are both the friends and the foes of English-speaking Canada, Indians appear as both "noble savages" and fierce warriors.

While there are conflicting portrayals of the Indian in post-Confederation literature, children's fiction nevertheless demonstrates a growing awareness of, and in some cases an increasing appreciation for, the unique culture of First Nations people and their role in shaping Canadian identity. Writers such as Ernest Thompson Seton and Pauline Johnson did much to bring a new awareness of native culture to young Canadian readers, and to incorporate elements of these traditions into the collective Canadian identity. As Anglophone writers negotiated these relationships in their literature, Canadians were becoming increasingly aware of the diverse elements in their society.

The Indian in Children's Literature

The Indian is a recurring character in nineteenth-century children's literature set in Canada, variously referred to as a "redskin," "savage," "half-breed," or the ubiquitous "Indian." Sheila Egoff and Judith Saltman argue that, while Indian tales and legends themselves were not popularised for children until the mid-twentieth century, "Native peoples were certainly not neglected in early adventure stories; nineteenth-century writers treated them with respect as woodsmen and guides and frequently allowed them to mock the ineptitude of the white men"

(Egoff and Saltman 1990: 13). While the figure of the Indian as a valued guide in the wilderness is one manifestation of this character in children's literature, Egoff and Saltman's comments downplay many of the more negative representations of such figures, which include the role of both the buffoon and the treacherous enemy. It also ignores the fact that the Indian character in the role of guide was still in a position of servitude. Furthermore, the repeated portrayal of the Indians' superior skill in the outdoors figures them as closer to nature than their white counterparts, which underscores their perceived distance from civilisation, which the white man's ineptitude only emphasises.

In many historical novels written by Europeans and North Americans in the nineteenth century, much is made of the threat Indians pose to settlers in Canada and the United States. Stories of the historic battles between French and English reveal that both sides enlisted the help of various tribes to aid their cause. The use of such "allies" is looked upon in very different lights, however, according to the perspective from which history is being viewed. In E. Everett-Green's *French and English: A Story of the Struggle in America*, the French are portrayed as having instigated a series of attacks by the Indians on a group of innocent English settlers:

> For after years of peace and apparent good-will on the part of the Indians . . . a spirit of ill will and ferocity was arising again; and settlers who had for years lived in peace and quietness in their lonely homes had been swooped down upon, scalped, their houses burnt, their wives and children tomahawked—the raid being so swift and sudden that defence and resistance had alike been futile. What gave an added horror to this sudden change of policy on the part of the Indians was the growing conviction . . . that it was due to the agency of white men. (Everett-Green 1899: 11)

For Everett-Green, the horror of this murder and destruction does not lie merely in what she describes as the barbarity of the Indians themselves, but rather in the knowledge that white Europeans could enable such acts. While the French and English have their differences they are united by race, making any alliance with the Indians appear to be one of unthinkable betrayal: "There was peace between the nations. Nor had it entered into the calculations of the settlers that their white brethren would stir up the friendly Indians against them, and bring havoc and destruction to their scattered dwellings" (Everett-Green 1899: 24). In this condemnation of the French tactics of warfare, the narrator also suggests that the Indians themselves are fickle and easily swayed by the influence of others. The "friendly" Indian can, it appears, turn savage at any moment.

The band of Englishmen that resolves to fight the French and restore peace to British settlers in Everett-Green's novel sees this savagery as essentially non-English in nature. One character implies that the French have approached similar levels of savagery, but that the English settlers "must not, and will not, become like the savage Indians" (119). Inherent in this declaration is the fear that the white European in the New World is in danger of becoming the savage. Disgust with the allegiance between the French and the unfriendly Indians in the novel suggests that the intermingling of white and non-white races gives rise to feelings of shame and anger. As H.L. Malchow writes:

> [I]t is the half-breed who becomes the threatening creature of the boundary between white and non-white, a living sign, and emblem of shame. Either innocent and sympathetic or deformed and demonic, they were visible reminders of what came to be felt as a white fall from grace, a perpetual witness against the weak or dissolute natures that created man.
>
> (Malchow 1996: 103)

Everett-Green implies that there is a sense of unnaturalness and shame associated with the French side's plotting with the Indians against fellow white men. Indeed, the English find it an easier matter to understand the Indians' role in their suffering than they do to forgive the French for joining in this "savage" behaviour. By proclaiming their own distance from such savagery, the English find another way to assert their superiority over the French.

In addition to being violent aggressors, the Indians in Everett-Green's novel possess many other negative attributes. The young French girl Corinne describes them as a "plague," and as greedy and selfish, saying, "they eat up a week's rations in three days, and come clamouring for more" (137). She also describes them as "fiends" and "devils," and regards them as "insolent and disgusting and treacherous" (137). The young Ranger Fritz tries to assure Corinne that not all Indians fit this profile:

> "[T]here are Indians who are gentle and tamable, and are some of them even sincere believers in our Christian faith. I have seen and lived among such in the lands of the south. But here they have been corrupted by the vices of those who should teach them better. It is a disgrace to England and France alike that this should be so." (137)

While Fritz acknowledges that there are differences among various Indian communities, his description of the "gentle" southern Indians is clearly patronising, and his suggestion that they are "tamable" likens them to creatures of the wild that should be domesticated. As Edward Said and others have observed, this notion of the need to "tame" and control the native was central to the progress of imperialism. As Said writes:

> For the European of the late nineteenth century, an interesting range of options are offered, all premised upon the subordination and victimization of the native. One is a self-forgetting delight in the use of power—the power to observe, rule, hold, and profit from distant territories and people. . . . Another is an ideological rational for reducing, then

reconstituting the native as someone to be ruled and managed. . . . Third is the idea of Western salvation and redemption through its "civilizing mission." (Said 1994: 131)

Fritz's appraisal of the Indian population in Everett-Green's novel demonstrates what Said cites as late-nineteenth century attitudes towards the native. While on the surface he appears to defend the Indians, he in fact demonstrates what Said describes as a rationale for reducing the native to "someone to be ruled and managed." Fritz's claim that the Indians have been "corrupted by the vices of those who should teach them better," namely, white Europeans, positions the Indian as essentially inferior to both the English and the French.

While Everett-Green's novel condemns the French for utilising Indian forces in their war upon the English, it simultaneously attempts to absolve these "white brethren" of the worst atrocities by placing the blame on Indian forces that even such an important personage as the French leader Montcalm is unable to control (Everett-Green 1899: 189). Apportioning blame to Indian forces is something that emerges in other literature of the period. In a non-fiction account of the history of Upper Canada, titled *Pen Pictures of Early Life in Upper Canada* and published in Toronto in 1905, the author touches upon the same events that are the subject of Everett-Green's fiction. In this instance, however, it is not those Indians who sided with the French whom the author blames for committing atrocities; it is those who supported England's cause. The story of the Rangers of Everett-Green's novel is based upon a real-life group of United Empire Loyalists known as Butler's Rangers. While the novel portrays these people as victims of the French and Indians, *Pen Pictures of Early Pioneer Life in Upper Canada* acknowledges the fact that these men were engaged in "a guerilla warfare against the revolutionary party of the United States" ("Canuck" 1905: 21). According to this historian's account of events, the Rangers were accused of "laying waste to the country, destroying property, and burning buildings" (21), but they were unfairly blamed for many acts of violence:

> Many atrocities were laid to their charge, however, which were quite unsupported by the facts, and where offences were committed the actual facts were greatly exaggerated. . . . Most of the Indian tribes of New York State sided with Great Britain and made frequent raids on the American settlements. It is possible that the onus of their evil work may have been placed upon Butler's Rangers. . . . It is quite probable that many of the atrocities attributed to the Rangers were perpetrated by the Indians connected with them, and whose . . . ferocity . . . the Rangers themselves were unable to restrain. ("Canuck" 1905: 21)

Conveniently, it appears, the Indians are to blame for atrocities attributed to both the French and the English, thereby absolving the Europeans of any responsibility for the most barbarous acts of their war with one another. In post-

Confederation Canada, the old rivalry is downplayed by placing the greatest blame on another group altogether—the Indians.

The portrayal of indigenous groups in such works reveals an image of the Indian not simply as a fierce warrior, but as a threat to civilisation and the establishment of a Canadian society. While it is apparent that the French, English, and Americans all enlisted the help of Indian tribes in their various conflicts, the degree of violence reportedly perpetrated by these allies suggests a degree of "savagery" that goes beyond the bounds of proper military conduct. The repeated suggestion that European forces could not "control" the acts of their Indian allies shows that some saw these non-white and non-European people as a threat to civilisation and as a force that they needed to curb. This figuring of the non-white race as a perceived threat that needs to be controlled is another characteristic of empire that Said observes:

> But of course the natives could not really *all* be made to disappear, and in fact they encroached more and more on the imperial consciousness. And what follow are schemes for separating the natives—Africans, Malays, Arabs, Berbers, Indians, Nepalese, Javanese, Filipinos—from the white man on racial and religious grounds, then for reconstituting them as people requiring a European presence, whether a colonial implantation or a master discourse in which they could be fitted and put to work. . . . The indolent native again figures as someone whose natural depravity and loose character necessitate a European overlord. (Said 1994: 167)

Pen Pictures of Early Pioneer Life in Upper Canada reinforces this view of the native, in this case the Canadian Indian, as inherently separate from the white settler and as a potential threat to settler society.

Repeatedly in both British and North American children's literature of the nineteenth century, the Indian emerges as a threat to settlers (whom authors tend to portray as innocent victims). Ironically, stories of Indian "raids" suggest unlawful encroachment on the land of the settlers, as in the novel *The Forest Home; or, Life in the Canadian Wilds* discussed in Chapter 1. Among the many predictable incidents in this work, which include fighting wolves and bears, hunting for food, and making maple syrup, the family from England at the centre of this story must also contend with Indians who kidnap their young female relative, Tiny, who is visiting from England. Tiny's kidnapping is the result of a series of unfortunate encounters with the local Chippewa tribe. These begin with a rash assumption on the part of the Welsh character Sam that the first Indian he encounters has been trying to kill him:

> "What a queer looking animal!" cried Ned; "it must be an Indian. I say, Sam, I'd advise you to take care what you do; these fellows are more like demons than men, so have a care."

"If he was ten thousand demons, I'd let him see that he can't do whatever he likes with a Welshman," said Sam, boiling with rage. ("Bruin" *c* 1875: 89)

Sam's anger at what he immediately perceives as a threat is the first in a series of encounters between the white settlers and the members of a local tribe. In the second major incident, the Cockney house servant Betsy shoots at an Indian who appears in the family home and the family fears a reprisal. In the words of Jack, "A Redskin will run almost any risk for the sake of revenge" (162), and when Tiny goes missing her family immediately assumes that the hostile tribe has kidnapped her. The novel's plot reaches its resolution when Tiny's relatives rescue her from the hands of the enemy, whose violent deaths are depicted:

[T]he squaw in the first canoe flung up her arms . . . fell over the side . . . and completely overturning the boat, was drowned. Her two companions made frantic efforts to right the canoe . . . but the one that had been wounded finding himself sinking, seized hold of the other, and as neither of them knew anything of the art of swimming (it being rarely practised by that people, their horror of drowning being only exceeded by their dislike of clean water), both speedily sank, one in a fierce grip to save himself, the other in a savage attempt to free himself from the grasp of his dying brother warrior. ("Bruin" *c* 1875: 166)

After they save Tiny, her friends and cousin exult in their triumph crying "Hurrah! We've beaten the villains hollow! What glorious fun" (167). The reduction of the deaths of several Chippewa to a moment of "glorious fun" further de-humanises the figure of the Indian, and the novel closes with the return of the young people to their family home, which they have made a safer place by helping to remove the Indian threat.

This novel clearly demonstrates what Said has identified as the dominant imperial power's perceived need to control and subdue the potentially violent native. The threat of the "savage" to established Canadian order is depicted in stories of combat between Europeans and Indians and in tales of raids on settlers and farmers. But the implied threat to society which the uncivilised Indian poses also appears in more subtle forms in children's literature. In J.M. Oxley's *The Young Woodsman or Life in the Forests of Canada* for instance, Frank finds himself threatened by the woodsman Damase, who resents the boy and his influence with the foreman Johnston. Damase is the story's villain, whose Indian heritage is seen as something shameful:

Although he scorned the suggestion as hotly as would a southern planter the charge that negro blood darkened his veins, there was no doubt that some generations back the dusky wife of a *courier du bois* had mingled the Indian nature with the French. Unhappily for Damase, the result of his

ancestral error was manifest in him; for, while bearing but little outward
resemblance to his savage progenitor, he was at heart a veritable Indian.
(Oxley 1895: 62)

Terms such as "ancestral error" and "unhappily" indicate a prevailing attitude
that an Indian heritage is not something of which to be proud.

While Damase displays little physical resemblance to other Indians, the
narrator implies that he has inherited definitive racial characteristics. The Indian
"personality" is apparently a fixed reality determined by one's blood, and the
description of Damase's character betrays the existing stereotypes of Canadian
Indians:

> Greedy, selfish, jealous, treacherous, quick to take offence and slow
> to forgive or forget, his presence in the Johnston gang was explained by
> his wonderful knowledge of the forest, his sure judgment in selecting
> ... timber to be cut, and his intimate acquaintance with the course of
> the stream down which the logs would be floated in the spring. (Oxley
> 1895: 62)

Oxley's narrator not only suggests that Damase has inherited his negative
personality traits, but also implies that the Indian's understanding of nature is
akin to an instinct, rather than a difficult skill that is learned.

In Oxley's novel, their differing attitudes towards religion and, by extension,
towards established societal moral codes, instigate the conflict between Damase
and Frank. Damase rejects Frank's practice of reading the Bible and scorns
his religious values. This pattern of a "savage" refusing the Christian faith is
another incarnation of the motif of the uncivilised Indian rejecting
enlightenment and threatening the progress of civilisation. Religion played a role
in shaping commonly-held attitudes towards Canada's indigenous people. In an
1884 speech to the Y.M.C.A. of Winnipeg, Reverend Dr. Bryce, a professor at
Manitoba College, addresses the issue of Canada's Indian population in terms
that clearly reflect elements of missionary zeal and, to borrow Kipling's phrase,
the "white man's burden":

> During the summer it was my lot to be for a considerable time in the
> country ... known as the Lake of the Woods and Rainy River districts
> ... [T]he most familiar sights that meet the eye are bands and parties of
> the aborigines of our country, not now decked in the fantastic garb in
> which the red man was wont to disport himself, but still forming a
> picturesque feature of the region. The Indian agent found ... throughout
> that wide district, in charge of a certain number of bands, is a
> representative of the wise care taken under British control of the inferior
> races committed to our rule. ... It is well for us ... to remember that we
> have dispossessed the Indian. ... Since we have taken the red man's

country we should remember our obligations to him. But in addition to this the poverty, misery and ignorance of the Indian appeal to the sympathy of any one who has a spark of generosity or pity in him. If men are impelled to cross the ocean to better the condition of heathen and degraded nations, surely the cry of the race disappearing before the onset of the white man, like mist before the rising sun, cannot be unheeded by us. (Bryce 1884: 1)

From reducing the Indian to a "picturesque feature of the region," to invoking the call to "better" so-called inferior races, Bryce underscores some of the perceptions of the Indian that appear in the children's literature of the period. Bryce credits the influence of the European settler for producing an "advanced" class of Indian:

> For fifty or a hundred years the Indians of this district have been under the influence of Europeans. Much of their intercourse with the whites was hurtful, yet the Hudson's Bay Company, with a wise self-interest, if from no higher motive, treated the Indian well; . . . The Hudson's Bay Company Indian, indeed, almost formed a distinct type of red man. He was an easy-going, light-hearted mortal, shrewd in trade, agile on foot or in canoe, fond of his ease, and taking on very much the character of his immediate superiors, good or bad as they chanced to be. (Bryce 1884: 2)

Bryce here presents the Indian as easily malleable, formed for good or bad by the influence of his European master. This is the same suggestion of fickleness made in Everett-Green's novel, in which the native tribes are portrayed as capable of switching allegiances between French and English on a whim. Ultimately, Bryce represents the "good" Indian as being a product of the efforts of the white man.

The reality of the situation in early Canada is that many of the efforts of the European settlers would have failed if it were not for the help of the land's native populations, who were essential to the development of the Canadian fur trade. In Egerton Ryerson Young's 1896 novel *Three Boys in the Wild North Land: Summer*, the adventures of his three young protagonists from England, Scotland, and Ireland depend in large part upon the guidance of the local Indians. In this novel, the Indians appear in a very different light from the violent and aggressive figures portrayed in many other literary works. In her study of early Canadian children's books, Sheila Egoff champions this type of treatment of Indian characters:

> There is also much to be said for the picture of the Indians that is given in these older books. While most of the modern writers on this theme look back at the Indians through history, many writers of the nineteenth century could write about them from first-hand knowledge. Thus their Indian characters are not just primitive warriors; they are often shown in

their natural contemporary role as masters of woodcraft and as guides for white men in the forest. In Egerton Young's *Three Boys in the Wild North Land* . . . one Indian is shown to be far more sensitive and generous than most of the white adult characters. (Egoff 1967: 254–255)

Egoff's interpretation of these portrayals is somewhat problematic. One may ask, for instance, what is "natural" about the role of an Indian as a guide for white men. It does, however, draw attention to an image that contrasts the depiction of the Indian as a violent enemy of the settler.

Yet in Egerton Ryerson Young's work, much of this difference is accounted for by the introduction of Christianity to this "quiet, lonely region":

Here the only inhabitants were the fur traders, with their employees, and the dignified, stoical Indians. The only signs of habitation were the few civilised dwellings . . . where dwelt and traded the officers and their families . . . and not very far off was the Indian village of the natives, where the most conspicuous buildings were the church and parsonage of the missionary, who had been marvelously successful in planting the cross in these northern regions, and in winning from a degrading superstition, to the blessings of Christianity, some hundreds of these red men, whose consistent lives showed the genuineness of the work wrought among them. (Young 1896: 15)

Young's work is coloured by his missionary zeal, and the accuracy of what Egoff would term his "first-hand knowledge" is in question. His account is also underpinned by a set of binaries between the "civilised" whites and the "uncivilised" Indians.

While he attributes much of the success of these Indian communities to the white man's effort to Christianise them, Young does exhibit a somewhat more enlightened view than some of his contemporaries. For example, this work displays a more accepting attitude towards the notion of mixed race than is presented in Oxley's work. Here, the mingling of Indian blood with that of the *courier du bois* is not attributed to "ancestral error" but to a practical, and acceptable, reality:

In those remote, lonely regions there are not many white families from which the young gentlemen in the service can select wives. The result is, many of them marry native women, or the daughters of mixed marriages contracted by the older officials. These women make excellent wives and mothers, and, being ambitious to learn, they often become as clever and bright as their white sisters, to many of whom they are superior in personal appearance. (Young 1896: 96)

According to Young's narrator, such unions can result in perfectly successful, happy households and the mingling of European and Indian blood does not represent an imminent threat to civilisation in the New World. He observes that the tourist could go into "many a cozy home . . . and never would he dream that the stately, refined, cultured woman at the head of the home . . . if not of pure Indian blood, was at least the daughter or granddaughter of a pure Indian" (96–97).

In many ways, simply by considering the possibility of such marriages, Young is somewhat ahead of his time. Unlike J.M. Oxley's portrayal of the potentially disastrous results of mixed race unions, as exemplified by the figure of Damase, Young sees no threat in this type of marriage. If anything, this is a means of further enlightening the Indian race, a view that is in keeping with the early nineteenth-century representations of mixed-race culture discussed by H.L. Malchow:

> [T]here had prevailed a more sanguine opinion, common at the beginning of the century, that traces of blackness were likely to disappear over time into the larger pool of more vigorous European blood. The half-breed had been often viewed sympathetically not as a racial danger to whites, but as a superior—and useful—class of black, or, alternatively, as an object of sympathy . . . unfairly rejected, martyred by both worlds. (Malchow 1996: 103)

Young certainly acknowledges both "pure-blood" and "half-breed" Indian women as "useful" to their white husbands. He also regards a successful Indian as one who has been Christianised and who has adopted the habits and customs of Canada's settlers of European descent. It is, in essence, a call for assimilation. The "heathen" Indian, meanwhile, must remain on the periphery of Canadian society.

Young takes pains to emphasise the inherent superiority of the civilised man when he describes the physical competition between his three young British protagonists and the local Indian children. While acknowledging the physical skills of these native children, he allows the European visitors (with whom the author expects the intended child reader to identify), to compete with them successfully:

> In the management of the canoe the white boys never learn to equal the Indian lads, neither could it be expected that they could attain to the accuracy with which they use their bows and arrows; but in all trials of physical strength the Anglo-Saxon ever excels, and, surprising as it may appear to some, in shooting contests with gun or rifle the palefaces are ever able to hold their own. (Young 1896: 127)

While illustrating the skills of the Indian in the wilderness, Young makes sure to acknowledge the superiority of the "Anglo-Saxon."

Young's own religious beliefs and role as a missionary influence his portrayal of the Canadian Indian. He acknowledges "the very conflicting opinions about the red men" but considers the difference between a "savage" Indian and a "civilised" one to be a question of religion: "After studying them for many years, my opinion is that they are just about like the rest of poor humanity. They need the Gospel, and the blessed Gospel is just the thing for them" (Young 1895b 481–482). Young reveals both his sympathy and his misunderstanding here. His very use of the phrase "after studying them" implies his tendency to objectify his Indian subjects and to distance himself from them. In an issue of *The Missionary Review of the World* from the 1890s, Young writes of the experiences he and his wife shared during his time as a missionary in Manitoba. In this article, he acknowledges some of the misconceptions of Indians held by mainstream society:

> We knew the majority of white people think that Indians are thievish, dishonorable, and unreliable. We do not believe that. So we decided to trust them. We took the fastenings off all the windows, and the bolt off of the door, and the keys out of every drawer and chest, and threw them away, and . . . we have never had anything worth sixpence stolen from us by the Indians. That is our experience among the Indians, when putting them on their honor and treating them fairly. (Young 1895b: 402)

Young's statement here is somewhat problematic. Not only does he make sweeping generalisations about the attitudes and behaviour of both whites and Indians, he also undermines his own apparent statement of trust by qualifying his account with the remark "when putting them on their honor and treating them fairly." The implication is that in the absence of "fair treatment" (and one might well ask who determines this), the Indians will indeed live up to the reputation of being thievish and unreliable.

Young was a prolific writer of works for children and it is therefore important to examine the ways in which his views on Indian culture may have influenced prevailing attitudes in mainstream Canadian society. It is notable that his works did not go unchallenged by some of his contemporaries. In 1895 for instance, the Toronto publisher William Briggs,[1] who published many works for children, issued a criticism of Young's book *Indian Wigwams and Northern Camp-fires*. This work by Young, while not necessarily written exclusively for children, was advertised in such children's periodicals as *Pleasant Hours* and may therefore be assumed to have had some degree of child readership. Fellow missionary John McDougall (1842–1917) criticised Young's book. McDougall's criticism raises many doubts as to the accuracy of Young's depiction of "life among the red men" of Canada, and accuses him of pandering to existing stereotypes of Indians, rather than presenting a well-informed portrayal. McDougall himself was born in Ontario, but served for many years as a missionary in what are now the provinces of Alberta and Saskatchewan, where he used his knowledge of Indian languages to serve as a translator, and actively opposed several government policies that aimed to assimilate the plains Indians into white culture (Applied History Research Group 2003). In his criticism of Young's work, McDougall quotes directly from the text, highlighting the inconsistencies of Young's portrayal of Indian language, dress, and behaviour:

> On page 21, he says, "We know of nothing more calculated to fire an Indian's soul than one of these exciting war-dances." When could Mr. Young have possibly beheld a real war-dance, as the Indians he labored amongst had not been for some generations on the war-path, and a war-dance to them would have been an unusual and unique experience? (McDougall 1895: 6)

In his rebuttal of this particular criticism Young replied:

> No. 4 is a very absurd piece of reading. If he had taken the trouble to have noticed that the chapter was a general one, discussing the Indians as a whole, he might have saved himself from his humiliation. I also hasten to tell him that both my wife and myself have witnessed the war, and other of the wild Indian dances in all their exciting movements. (Young 1895a: 14)

Young's line of defence—that this chapter is about Indians in general—betrays one of the very faults that McDougall is criticising; the tendency to generalise and, thereby, fail to acknowledge individual differences and characteristics among indigenous people.

In his address to the Winnipeg Y.M.C.A., Reverend Bryce exemplifies this propensity for generalisation:

> While I am not among the illusionists, who regard the redman in his savage state as a hero of the Fennimore Cooper type, yet I know from many years' hearsay and experience that in intellectual ability the Indian is much above the average of savage races. He has a good eye; he learns to write easily; has a remarkably good memory as a rule, and while not particularly strong as a reasoner, he will succeed in the study of languages and the pursuit of the sciences. (Bryce 1884: 4)

Bryce's laces his assessment of what he sees as the Indian's potential with questionable anthropology, dubious science, and a large dose of generalisation. Yet this type of ambiguous characterisation, moving from admiration to condescension to outright hostility, is typical of much of the adult literature and children's fiction of the era.

Among the conflicting and often confusing portrayals of Canadian Indians in nineteenth-century children's literature, there slowly emerged a new perspective. While Canadian authors moved away from images of the violent savage and began to acknowledge the contribution of Indians to Canadian society, the vast majority of these more sympathetic portraits were still drawn from the point of view of the white coloniser. As such, the figure of the Indian continued to be one that lay on the periphery of Canadian society and identity. Yet in the late nineteenth century, Mohawk poet and performer Pauline Johnson did much to bring a new understanding and perspective to the issue of Canadian Indians and their relation to the developing sense of Canadian nationalism.

Johnson was born in Ontario in 1861 to Mohawk chief George Johnson and his English-born wife Emily. Pauline Johnson, also known by the Mohawk name Tekahionwake, was a writer and performer whose work was popular within Canada and abroad. Much of it deals with issues of Indian heritage and culture and Johnson brought a voice of authenticity to the subject that writers like Egerton Ryerson Young did not possess. While Johnson is best remembered for her poetry, she also wrote stories for children dealing with such topics as Canadian identity, Mohawk heritage, and the Canadian landscape. One of the strengths of Johnson's writing is that she manages to avoid much of the ambiguity surrounding the image of the Indian that is apparent in many children's texts. While one popular image of the Indian was that of a violent, barbaric warrior, some writers glossed over this aspect of native history, opting instead for a rosier, but equally one-sided, picture of the peaceful "noble savage." Indeed, this later trend is one that has continued in recent history, with Canadian historian Doug Davis recently remarking on the tendency of Canadian historical writing to offer what are perceived as "offense-free" versions of the past: "Apparently native people can't be shown as aggressive or warlike. Forget the fact that the Iroquois quite literally wiped out the Mohicans, enslaved the Delaware and pushed the Cherokee outside the Ohio Valley" (Sokoloff 2003). Pauline Johnson, however, sees the image of the warlike Indian as a cause for celebration rather than offence.

In an article on the Iroquois published in *The Brantford Expositor* in 1895, Johnson invokes the image of the violent Indian warrior, but reclaims it as a source of pride rather than shame:

> But in early times the dances of the domesticated Iroquois were not always the outcome of religious zeal and good-fellowship with the Great Spirit; for America knew no greater terror than when a band of eight or ten thousand Iroquois warriors chose to don their war paint, and set forth conquering and to conquer; their fierce visages, and half-naked bodies, decorated with the ominous streaks of black and red, meaning "Blood and Death," always the war colours of the Mohawks. (Johnson 1895: 25)

Johnson's depiction of the Mohawk warriors is not dissimilar to that of other writers, yet rather than condemning this past, she celebrates it and places it in the context of other nations of the world:

No, it is not a fiction. The ancestors of those calm-eyed Indian men, of those low-voiced, gentle-faced women, who on market days throng our busy little streets, were some of the bravest, most intrepid and valiant warriors known to the history of the world: men who defended their country and the "ashes of their fathers" against the inroads of a great all-conquering race; men who fought, and bled, and died to hold the western continent against an incoming eastern power, as England's sons would battle and fall to-day, were their own mother country threatened with a power that would eventually annihilate, subject—then alas! absorb their blood, their traditions, their nation, until naught promises to remain save a memory. (Johnson 1895: 26)

Johnson's article situates the history of aggression between the Iroquois and the white settler in a new context. It conflates the "savagery" of Canada's native people with the "civilised" warfare of the Europeans and forces the reader to acknowledge the extreme impact that European aggression had on the Iroquois people.

Pauline Johnson challenged many of the stereotypical portrayals of First Nations people that appeared in the literature of her era. Of the tendency toward racial stereotyping Johnson writes, "Every race in the world enjoys its own peculiar characteristics, but it scarcely follows that every individual of a nation must possess these prescribed singularities, or otherwise forfeit in the eyes of the world their nationality" (Johnson 1892). Much of the children's literature of the period portrays Indians as having a set of common characteristics, and most representations of such figures were highly stylised. In her 1892 article "A Strong Race Opinion: On the Indian Girl in Modern Fiction," Johnson points out that tribal and linguistic distinctions were virtually ignored by the non-Native population:

The term "Indian" signifies about as much as the term "European," but I cannot recall ever having read a story where the heroine was described as "a European." The Indian girl we meet in cold type, however, is rarely distressed by having to belong to any tribe, or to reflect any tribal characteristics. She is merely a wholesale sort of admixture of any band existing between the Mic Macs of Gaspé and the Kwaw-Kewlths of British Columbia, yet strange to say, that notwithstanding the numerous tribes, with their aggregate numbers reaching more than 122,000 souls in Canada alone, our Canadian authors can cull from this huge revenue of character, but one Indian girl, and stranger still that this lonely little heroine never had a prototype in breathing flesh-and-blood existence! (Johnson 1892)

Johnson's challenge of the homogeneous representation of the Indian in Canadian fiction marks a new understanding of the function of such characters in the literary landscape. With figures such as McDougall and Johnson challenging the literary representation of native Canadians, there came a new view of what this community meant both to literature and to the new concept of Canadian society as a whole. Johnson asks, "do authors who write Indian romances love the nation they endeavour . . . to describe? . . . or is the Indian introduced into literature but to lend a dash of vivid coloring to an otherwise tame and somber picture of colonial life?" (Johnson 1892). By the end of the nineteenth century, some Canadian writers like Johnson were beginning to examine the extent to which colonial and Indian life truly coloured one another.

Along with her interest in exploring her own heritage and in providing a voice for the Mohawk people, Pauline Johnson felt a need to situate these concerns in the wider context of the Canadian nation. Her works for children attempted to introduce a young readership to the intricacies of native culture. In 1907, the American juvenile periodical *The Boys' World* published Johnson's short story "Little Wolf-Willow," which tells the story of a Canadian Indian boy from the prairies and his changing relationship with the Northwest Mounted Police. The reader learns at the opening of the story that Little Wolf-Willow's father Beaver-Tail hated many things, but that "most of all he hated the Northwest Mounted Police" because "they stood for the enforcing of the white man's laws, and old Beaver-Tail hated the white man" (Johnson 1907: 1). The father sends his son away to the Indian School in Manitoba so that he may learn English and "grow up to be a keen, sharp trader like the . . . white men who were so apt to outwit the redskins in a fur-trading bargain" (1). When Little Wolf-Willow returns home after six years, his family is relieved to see that the school "had not made him into a white man" (1). The boy assures his father that he has "learned the best the white man had to give," but that he has not changed at heart (1). The father and son have a conversation, however, which reveals that not everything has remained the same:

> Old Beaver-Tail fairly chuckled, then replied between pipe puffs, "Some of our Cree boys go to school. They learn the white man's ways, and they are of no more use to their people. They cannot trap for furs, nor scout, nor hunt, nor find a prairie trail. You are wiser than that, Little Wolf-Willow. You are smarter than when you left us, but you return to us, the old people of your tribe, just the same—just the same as your father and grandfather."
>
> "Not quite the same," replied the boy cautiously, "for, father, I do not now hate the Northwest mounted police." (Johnson 1907: 1)

While the boy has fought to maintain his heritage, he develops a good relationship with the white people he works with in his role as interpreter for the Government Indian Agent.

The boy's success at maintaining his heritage while learning "the best" that school has to offer, is an idealised picture of what education could do for native populations and their role in society. According to Gerald Friesen, the establishment of the type of Indian boarding-school pictured in "Little Wolf-Willow" was really an attempt to make Indian children conform to "Canadian" cultural practices:

> The great hope of administrator and missionary alike was that education would break the hold of tradition and create a properly "Canadianized" Indian. As a result of the campaign to "civilize" and "Christianize" Indian children, schools became an issue in native-white relations as early as the 1880s. . . . The goal of white education policy was . . . to protect Indians from the worst features of white society, to prepare them for the labour market, and to "save" them for the sake of their souls. (Friesen 1992: 25)

Pauline Johnson's young hero, however, does not forget his Indian attitudes and customs while at school. Little Wolf-Willow is Canadianised not by becoming white, but by learning to move freely between the world of the Indian, and the world of established Canadian society. The author's description of Little Wolf-Willow's outward appearance reflects this connection to both Indian society and that of the white Canadians:

> He always wore a strange mixture of civilized and savage clothes—fringed buckskin "chaps," beaded moccasins, a blue flannel shirt, a scarlet silk handkerchief knotted around his throat, a wide-brimmed cowboy hat with a rattlesnake skin as a hat band, and two magnificent bracelets of ivory elks' teeth. His braided hair, his young, clean, thin dark face, his fearless riding, began to be known far and wide. (Johnson 1907: 1)

Little Wolf-Willow's appearance here is clearly a mixture of Indian and European cultures. It marks his growing relationship with the white society that exists beyond the confines of his own tribe, and is markedly different from the vision he had as a very young child of how he would one day appear: "Little Wolf-Willow's one idea of life was to grow up and be like his grandfather . . . to have nine scalps at his belt, and scars on his face; to wear a crimson-tipped eagle feather in his hair, and to give a war whoop that would . . . plant fear in the hearts of his enemies" (1). The contrast between the boy's initial vision of his future, and his subsequent reality, demonstrates a move away from the traditions of his past and a shift from what was his grandfather's reality.

The years following the upheavals caused by Confederation marked an unprecedented rate of change in lifestyle among the plains Indians, and the difference between Little Wolf-Willow's reality and that of his grandfather is typical of the period (Friesen 1992: 3). There is a sense of loss, but Johnson also presents a picture of hope for a new reality. Little Wolf-Willow is a link between past and present, tradition and development, and his character represents a bridge between Indian and white settler:

The men of the Hudson's Bay Company trusted him. The Northwest mounted police loved him. The white traders admired him. But, most of all, he stood fast in the affection of his own Indian people. They never forgot the fact that, had he wished, he could have stayed with the white people altogether, that he was equal to them in English education, but he did not choose to do so—he was one of their own for all time. (Johnson 1907: 1)

The story's hero is a figure who brings the disparate elements of society together through their affection for him.

This is clear near the story's conclusion when the Northwest Mounted Police mistake Little Wolf-Willow for a thief after his grandfather, Big Wolf-Willow, steals some cattle. To his own dismay, Corporal Manan, a friend of the boy, is sent out to arrest his young comrade, who has gone to ensure that his grandfather does not get involved in a conflict with the police. Manan, coming upon his friend who is exhausted from his long ride and nearly dead from the cold, saves him from death and returns him to his family. Upon reviving, Little Wolf-Willow explains his grandfather's actions to the corporal:

He was poor, hungry, starving. You see, Corporal, he cannot speak English, and he does not understand the white men or their laws. He says for me to tell you that the white men came and stole all our buffaloes, the millions of beautiful animals that supplied us with hides to make our tepees, furs to dress in, meat to eat, fat to keep us warm; so he thought it no harm to take two small calves when he was hungry. He asks if anyone arrested and punished the white men who took all his buffaloes, and, if not, why should he be arrested and punished for doing far less wrong than the wrong done by the white man? (Johnson 1907: 6)

When Corporal Manan, a member of the Northwest Mounted Police and a symbol of Canadian law and order, learns that he has mistakenly accused his friend and hears the eloquent defence of the grandfather's actions, he sees that the true course of justice does not lie in making an arrest. He asks Little Wolf-Willow: "can you ever forgive us all for thinking you were a cattle thief? When I think of your grandfather's story of the millions of buffaloes he has lost, and those two paltry calves he took for food, I make no arrests here. My captain must do what he thinks best" (6). Corporal Manan's behaviour earns him the admiration of his friend, but more significantly, it gains the respect of Beaver-Tail:

"And you saved me from freezing to death, and brought me home on your own horse, when you were sent out to take me to prison!" muttered the boy, turning to his soldier friend with admiration.

But old Beaver-Tail interrupted. He arose, held out his hand towards the once hated scarlet-coated figure, and spoke the first words he had ever voiced in English. They were, "Northwest Mounted Police, good man, he. Beaver-Tail's friend." (6)

With Beaver-Tail's acceptance of the white officer as an ally, Johnson is able both to offer a sympathetic portrayal of the plight of the Plains Indians, while maintaining the status of that important Canadian icon, the Mountie. Johnson's story tries to reconcile the facts of Indian displacement and loss with the image of the Northwest Mounted Police as an important tool of Canada's national growth. Little Wolf-Willow, the interpreter for the Government Indian Agent, is literally a go-between for the people of the Canadian prairies. Through his character, and through the words of his father that conclude the story, a symbol of mutual understanding is created.

Johnson's story presents a new picture of the Indian within Canadian society and culture. Unlike the stories of J.M. Oxley or Egerton Ryerson Young, which are told from the viewpoint of the white protagonist, the Indian is the central figure in Johnson's story, whose voice can be heard, and whose own perspective is shared with the reader. Rather than being simply a quiet bystander, the figure of the Indian here becomes a means of representing diversity within Canadian unity. Admittedly, as Little Wolf-Willow is himself aware, the dominant white culture largely determines the extent to which this diversity will flourish and the rules of this governing society limit the Indian's autonomy. Nevertheless, while Little Wolf-Willow does not represent a return to the independence and power his ancestors knew before coming under European rule, (something which Johnson's story acknowledges to be impossible), his character does offer reconciliation between past and present, providing a vision of increased respect and self-determination among the Indian people. What Johnson's story offers is a vision of the Indian as having a central role in Canadian society, rather than remaining in the shadow of the new nation. Johnson writes in her 1903 volume of poetry *Canadian Born*:

> Let him who is Canadian born regard these poems as written to himself—whether he be my Paleface compatriot who has given to me his right hand of good fellowship, in the years I have appealed to him by pen and platform, or whether he be that dear Red brother of whatsoever tribe or Province, it matters not—White Race and Red are one if they are but Canadian Born. (Johnson 1997)

If Pauline Johnson's tales were "deliberately designed to appeal to the expectations of a European audience" (New 2001: 8), they nevertheless offered a medium through which her vision of the role of the Indian in Canadian life could be portrayed.

Through the work of writers like Johnson, the figure of the Indian began to play a more prominent role in Canadian culture, and became more than simply the "dash of vivid coloring" in tales of colonial life that she herself feared. While the Indian remained on the periphery of Canadian society and literature at the end of the nineteenth century, native culture and history gradually became part of mainstream Canadian culture and identity. Figures such as Tecumseh, who played a crucial role in the successful routing of the Americans in the War of 1812, were celebrated in the children's history texts of Henry H. Miles and T.G. Marquis, and an awareness of the oral traditions of Canada's various tribes began to develop, albeit slowly. In 1896, for example, the family magazine *Our Home* published a series of Micmac legends, adapted from the collections compiled by Silas T. Rand (1810–1889). Rand was a Baptist minister and missionary who, in addition to his collection of oral tales, compiled a Mi'kmaq dictionary in 1888 (New 2002d). Collections such as Rand's demonstrate an interest in Indian legend, while acknowledging the different nature of Indian storytelling from the European tradition. As the editor of the magazine remarks, the legend published in *Our Home* "gives the impression that the Indian who first told it did not invent it, but dreamed it" (*Our Home* 1896a: 1). There is also evidence to show that Canadian children were considering the place of the Indian in their nation's history. In the 1893 publication *Sea, Forest and Prairie: Being Stories of Life and Adventure in Canada Past and Present, by Boys and Girls in Canada's Schools*, there are several stories written by school children from across the country that include titles such as "Indian Reminiscences," "Raid on the St. Francis Indians," "Tecumseh" and "The Extinction of a Nation." As confused and contradictory as some of the late-nineteenth century accounts of Canada's Indians may be, it is clear that educators and children's writers were turning their attention to these matters. While the oral tradition and cultural practices of the various tribes were different from those of the dominant Anglo-Canadian culture, it is apparent that they held a growing appeal for many children's writers at the beginning of the twentieth century.

One of the most popular of such writers was Ernest Thompson Seton (1860–1946). Seton was born in Durham, England and moved to Canada as a child where he began his studies in art and nature while at school in Toronto. Among the many hats he wore in his lifetime, Seton was an artist, a naturalist and a writer, who played a key role in developing and popularising the realistic animal story, publishing such tales as *The Biography of a Grizzly* and "Old Silver Grizzle: the Story of a Kindly Badger." As a naturalist, Seton also had a keen interest in Indian attitudes towards the natural world. In 1903, he published a novel for children entitled *Two Little Savages: Being the Adventures of Two Boys Who Lived as Indians and What They Learned*. This tells the story of two boys who play at being Indians, and who learn to be independent and to respect the natural world by learning Indian woodcraft skills and native attitudes towards the natural environment. In 1902, Seton also formed an organisation for young boys called "The Woodcraft Indians," which incorporated aspects of Indian culture and helped to inspire many elements of the Boy Scouts movement (Taylor 2002: 1035). Seton's work at the beginning of the twentieth century is a clear example of the ways in which Anglophone Canadian children's writers adopted and appropriated elements of Indian culture. Seton's woodcraft movement, though quickly absorbed by the Boy Scouts, played a role in shaping an image of Canadian society as one that was deeply connected to, and respectful of, the natural environment. As with Valentine Williams' use of the images of the canoe and the Indian to underscore the Canadian identity of his protagonist in *The Captain of the Club, or the Canadian Boy*, Seton's use of aspects of Indian culture helped to shape a sense of national identity that incorporated a degree of indigenous tradition. This incorporation of elements of Indian culture into mainstream Canadian identity and culture would continue throughout the twentieth century, as Canadians embraced traditional native sports such as lacrosse and canoeing, and appropriated other elements of Indian heritage, ensuring them a place in the formation of a national identity.

As writers in English-speaking Canada struggled to define a sense of Canadian identity following Confederation, they also had to come to terms with to whom this applied. Throughout the nineteenth century, children's literature that was concerned with Canada often featured portrayals of both Indians and French Canadians. Frequently portrayed as threats to the establishment of a Canadian society, the integral role that both groups played in the shaping of this society was something that writers gradually came to acknowledge. As Canadian children's literature critic Roderick McGillis observes; "We are connected to community through foreignness. We cannot but be "Other" to the communities which contain us, and when everyone is an "Other" then everyone shares an experience that might keep people together not by the bonds of community but by the choice of community" (McGillis 1997: 215). In the Canadian children's literature from the late nineteenth and early twentieth centuries, there is evidence of a growing recognition of this shared experience and active "choice of community." In this literature, the figures of both the Indian and the French Canadian function as a means of negotiating the boundary between "self" and "other," ultimately helping to construct a sense of who and what the Canadian identity should represent.

Chapter Seven
Fact or Fiction?: The Making of Canadian History

At Queenston's Heights and Lundy's Lane,
Our brave fathers, side by side,
For freedom, homes, and loved ones dear,
Firmly stood and nobly died.
And those dear rights which they maintained,
We swear to yield them never!
Our watchword evermore shall be,
The Maple Leaf forever!

(A. Muir, "The Maple Leaf Forever")

In his study *Colonial Myths: History and Narrative*, Azzedine Haddour writes that the study of history "is an active agency that makes the past pass into the present" (Haddour 2000: 1). This connection between the past and the present makes the manner in which a nation communicates its history to children, who represent both the present and the future, particularly significant. If understanding a nation's past can help determine its future, then teaching history to young citizens is of great importance. Examining early Canadian children's literature reveals the manner in which writers were exploring the nation's past, and sheds light on the ideas current in Canada during the late nineteenth and early twentieth centuries.[1]

As Canada sought to extricate itself from Britain's influence, it began to reassess its place in the changing landscape of North American and European relations. Canada shared many traits with other post-colonial societies, the most significant of which was the desire to articulate an independent voice and identity. Post-colonial critics and writers have argued that reclaiming the past is an important step in this process. As Edward Said writes:

In one instance, we assume that the better part of history in colonial territories was a function of the imperial intervention; in the other, there is an equally obstinate assumption that colonial undertakings were marginal . . . to the central activities of the great metropolitan cultures. Thus, the tendency . . . is to treat the whole of world history as viewable by a kind of Western super-subject, whose historicizing and disciplinary rigor either takes away or, in the post-colonial period, restores history to people and cultures "without" history. (Said 1994: 35)

Canada was also susceptible to such views as, prior to Confederation, many considered it to be without a history of its own. Many works of history distributed in nineteenth-century Canada, both before and after 1867, centre on events and figures from England's past, viewing Canadian history in terms of its role in building and supporting the British Empire. As part of the process of constructing a distinctly Canadian identity, however, Canadian writers gradually began to reclaim their own past.

Following Confederation, "for the first time, historians spoke primarily to their compatriots rather than a distant power" (Taylor 1989: 7). Canadian historians began to examine the past from a new perspective, and by the beginning of the twentieth century this new approach to history included a revaluation of the pre-colonial era, and a growing interest in the history of Canada's native people. Some works of historical fiction and non-fiction create a picture of an earlier, mythical Canada in which the taint of its colonial status is lessened. Citing Homi Bhabha, Canadian literature critic Margaret E. Turner observes that in new cultures there is a temptation towards history that "Bhabha describes as 'the familiar quest for an origin that will authorize a beginning'" (Turner 1995: 15). History and the "quest for an origin" are among the themes that children's writers develop in their efforts to construct a sense of Canadian unity and national identity. From textbooks on Canadian history for the classroom, to historical poems, songs and novels, there is a clear connection drawn between having a sense of national identity and being aware of national history.

The literature of the day illustrates the belief that having a strong sense of Canadian history is of great importance to the nation's future. As M. Brook Taylor observes of nineteenth-century English Canada, the purpose of historians remained constant, being "to use the past to influence the present to shape the future" (Taylor 1982: 7). Children's literature further demonstrates that writers and historians were blending fact and fiction in their efforts to construct a new historical vision of the nation. In *What is History?* British historian E.H. Carr notes that "interpretation enters into every fact of history" and that facts "speak only when the historian calls on them: it is he who decides to which facts to give the floor, and in what order or context" (11–13). The "facts" or topics selected most frequently by Canadian historians and writers of children's literature include the early days of the fur trade, Indian life in early Canada, the period of French rule and the military exploits between the French and the

English, and between the Canadians and the Americans. These tales of the past inspired a new Canadian mythology that writers hoped would help shape Canada's future.

History Textbooks and Historical Non-Fiction

Stories presented as true accounts of historical events from Canada's past appeared in history textbooks, periodicals, and as longer works of non-fiction. Both historical non-fiction and works of pure literary invention may contain some element of "fiction." As contemporary American historian Eric Foner observes, history "will be regularly rewritten, in response to new questions, new information, new methodologies, and new political, social, and cultural imperatives. But . . . the most difficult truth . . . to accept is that there often exists more than one legitimate way of recounting past events" (Foner 2002: xvii). J.W. Bengough (1851–1923) discusses the manner in which historical accounts can vary in a 1901 article that appeared in *The Canadian Boy*. Bengough was born in Toronto, and in addition to founding his own humorous weekly magazine *Grip* in 1873, he was also a poet and a cartoonist with the *Toronto Globe* and the *Montreal Star*. In this article from *The Canadian Boy*, he criticises what he sees as the traditional methods of recording Canadian history. Bengough considers it important to instil an awareness of the past in the nation's youth, and to make children feel that they have a role in their country's history.

Bengough is particularly concerned with giving boys a sense that they have an active role in their nation's history. The article opens with a criticism of existing accounts of Canada's past:

> When we think of the old days we call historic (as if we were not ourselves engaged in making history) the picture presented to our minds seems to be filled with grown up people, chiefly quite gray and venerable. Perhaps the habit affects historians as well as common folk, and that may be the reason why there is so very little mention of boys and girls in the books they write. . . . But then, of course, most of the writers who have set themselves the task of dealing with the History of the Dominion have seemed to feel it necessary to make their works as dry as possible, and no doubt think that to give space to such a lively, sportive topic as boyhood suggests, would be quite out of character. (Bengough 1901: 10)

Bengough recognises the role each generation plays in "making history" and his article addresses this interrelation between past and present, raising a number of important questions about the means by which history is constructed and recorded.

Bengough believes that by exploiting this connection between past and present, writers can make history "lively" for children. This can be done by sharing stories about children from Canada's past, which Bengough does by telling the story of young Frank Simcoe, "the son of Col. John Graves Simcoe, the first Lieutenant-Governor of Upper Canada, who came out to take charge of the affairs of the new province in the year 1791" (Bengough 1901: 10). In reality, however, Frank Simcoe is merely a device used by Bengough to gain the attention of his young reader, while he then proceeds to give an account of his father's role in Canadian history.

Other writers shared Bengough's view that Canadians needed to do more to educate children about their country's history. For example, *The Young Canadian*'s advertisement for a contest to determine the best new book on Canadian History shows that there were efforts made to promote this history and educate Canadian children about their own country, rather than about an imperial motherland most would never see: "We have no History of our country for our young Canadians—not a book that we can put into their hands, or pick up to read to them, about the land they love so well, and about the wonderful and romantic things that happened before our country was what it is" (*Young Canadian* 1891b). This advertisement reveals an awareness of the need to foster knowledge of the country's own history in young Canadians. The emphasis on what happened "before our country was what it is," demonstrates a desire to revisit the earliest stages of Canada's development, and see these as part of *Canadian*, rather than European, history. One of the criteria listed in *The Young Canadian*'s call for a new manuscript on Canadian history, is that it "must be from a Dominion and not a Provincial standpoint" (552). This further under-scores the fact that what is termed "history" is subjective, depending on the viewpoint of the teller.

There is a desire here to provide an inclusive account of Canadian history. As Taylor observes, nineteenth-century historians sought to employ history as a means of achieving national accord:

> Canadian historians now demonstrated how struggle could be directed toward progress, and . . . show the way to the future. History was for them a continuum, and their first task was to provide a credible line of descent. But they were also to bring open discord to a close, to end the partisan, racial, and other divisions of the past, and to fashion a new, unifying identity. From a history of struggle they would forge a national consensus. (Taylor 1989: 152–153)

The history written for children in Anglophone Canada follows many of the patterns that Taylor sees in Canadian historiography of the period. *The Young Canadian*'s call for a new history textbook is further evidence of what Taylor identifies as a desire to use history to help build a sense of national unity by focusing on the whole country rather than on individual provinces.

These concerns, and the importance placed on producing educational history books for children, are further demonstrated by an editorial in the August, 1897 issue of the children's periodical *Home and Youth*. This discusses the completion of a book called the *Dominion School History* and cites its "introduction into the public schools of all the provinces and territories of the Dominion, from the Atlantic to the Pacific" as an event of extreme national importance (*Home and Youth* 1). There is a clear desire here to emphasise Canadian identity and interests, rather than merely those of the individual provinces. The editorial goes on to say that "The study of the same history by all the school children of the Dominion ... will undoubtedly have the effect of strengthening Canadian sentiment" (1). The account given of the work that went into producing the *Dominion School History* further shows that the book's aim was to construct a national history, rather than to focus on items that were "purely provincial" in interest (2). Such statements reflect a desire to strengthen the union of provinces and the hope that teaching national history would help achieve a sense of unity and a shared identity.

A strong centralist perspective dominated Canadian literature in 1897 and while this editorial claims that the new children's history text will address this problem by presenting a national view, the person chosen to write this book of history was in fact one W.H.P. Clement of Toronto, Ontario. The editorial also announces that the book's joint publishers will be Copp Clarke and William Briggs of Toronto, further illustrating the continuing struggle to present a non-centralist view of the nation. While the editorial does not remark on the possibility that the choice of publisher and author might demonstrate a bias in favour of Ontario, it does note that not all the necessary efforts were made to ensure the participation of the Francophone population in adopting this important text:

> The history must be translated into French and adopted by the French-Canadian schools of Quebec province. . . . Nothing seems to have been done in this direction as yet, although prominent French-Canadian educationists declared themselves as strongly in favor of such a national history. . . . It seems a great pity that a French translation of the history was not provided for before arrangements were made for the publication of the book. English and French editions should have been ready for the school children at the same time. (*Home and Youth* 1897c: 3)

The concern expressed here reflects a desire to solidify national sentiment and strengthen the sense of national unity in Canadian children. This is in keeping with the "central tenet of National historiography that . . . real statesmanship was the ability to harmonize, to accept a pragmatic compromise rather than indulge in rigid adherence to principle" (Taylor 1989: 231). The emphasis placed on providing children with a book of history that could speak for all elements of the country is part of this recognition of the need for harmony and compromise within Canada.

Despite the allegation in the September 23, 1891 edition of *The Young Canadian* that "we have no History of our country for our young Canadians" and the attention paid to the new *Dominion School History* of 1897, there were other, earlier books of history for children produced in Canada during the nineteenth century, one of which was Henry H. Miles' *The Child's History of Canada*. Published in Montreal in 1870, this was the third number in the "New Series of Histories of Canada," and according to the title page it was designed for "the use of the Elementary Schools and of the young reader" (Miles 1870). Miles' work touches briefly upon a selection of 'key' historical events, from the time of Cartier, through the eighteenth-century expulsion of the Acadians and the victory of Wolfe at Quebec, to the defeat of the Americans in the War of 1812 and the events of 1867.

Miles' work reveals the difficulty that lies in reconciling the harsh reality of past events with idealised notions of both the nation's history, and its promise for the future. For example, in his discussion of Jacques Cartier, Miles presents the French explorer as a great man and glosses over the fact that he kidnapped several Indians and transported them back to France; "Cartier then sailed away with his captives. We cannot praise Cartier for this action, although his intention was good, and although the like was often done in those days" (Miles 1870: 2). While admitting that Cartier's actions were not praiseworthy, Miles tries to preserve the image of Cartier as a Canadian hero, excusing this act by claiming that his intentions were noble and that he acted no differently from many other men in his position. Evidently, Miles is struggling to square some ugly truths with his vision of what a Canadian hero should represent.

In addition to the difficulty of reconciling unpleasant facts of Canada's past, nineteenth-century historians also struggled to present a "national" history, rather than one that demonstrated a provincial or ethnic bias. Miles manages to achieve this to a certain extent by presenting important French historical figures as Canadian heroes, as is evident when he claims that "every lover of Canada thinks with pride and pleasure of Samuel de Champlain" (Miles 1870: 23). Indeed, a large portion of this text is devoted to the days of the French regime. Yet Miles later betrays the continuing existence of a "French *vs.* English" mindset in his discussion of the exile of the Acadians, the descendants of early French colonists in the Maritimes. England and France fought for control of Acadia during the seventeenth and early eighteenth centuries, with both sides demanding loyalty from the Acadians. After the region fell to England's control the British continued to fear that Acadian loyalty lay with France, and beginning in 1755 they expelled thousands of Acadians from the region (Morton 2001: 63–64). While acknowledging the "very sad nature" of these events (Miles 1870: 90), Miles betrays a continuing division between French and English interests by raising doubts about the accuracy of other historical accounts of the events. He writes; "Some French writers declare that no less than 7000 Acadians were removed to New England. There is, however, good reason for believing that the true number was between three and four thousand" (Miles 1870: 91). Miles here acknowledges the inherent unreliability in historical accounts, as well as the division in thought that continued between French and Anglophone Canada in the late nineteenth century.

In spite of these glimpses of discord, Miles' version of Canadian history strives to present a picture of a unified country that shares common hopes for the nation's future. He acknowledges the differences that once existed between the French and the English, but pinpoints a precise moment at which he believes reconciliation occurred:

> In June 1792, when a member was being chosen for the county of Quebec, there was almost a riot. . . . Prince Edward being there, tried to quiet the people by a speech, in which he said "let me no more hear the hateful talk about *French* and *English*. You are, all of you equally, the well beloved *Canadian* subjects of the king." These words were followed by cheers from the people, no longer on bad terms with each other. (Miles 1870: 115)

The idea of such a sudden reconciliation begs the question of how much of this history is based on fact, and how much of it is the author's own invention. It betrays a tendency to idealise the past, and by extension, the realities of the present. In this particular episode, the writer acknowledges the political tensions that existed yet tries to downplay them and to emphasise a positive outcome. As Taylor observes of Canadian historians: "In the light of later achievements, early disappointments . . . were regarded as the natural and unavoidable consequences of pioneer life" (Taylor 1989: 267). In the case of Miles' history, these tensions are to some degree seen as a natural part of Canada's early struggle on its road to nationhood. Yet in the processes of recognising the existence of such problems in the past, Miles actually admits their existence in his own time. Nevertheless, his attempt to downplay these political tensions is in keeping with a larger trend in the children's historical literature of the period: namely, the attempt by writers to acknowledge a developing sense of a unified Canadian "we," and to project this burgeoning, yet still fragile, national unity back onto the past.

The year 1893 saw the publication of Agnes Machar and T.G. Marquis' *Stories from Canadian History Based Upon "Stories of New France."* This book touches on many of the same figures and events as Miles' history of 1870 and further demonstrates the ongoing incorporation of the history of French Canada under the umbrella of "Canadian" history. Machar (1837–1927) was a Canadian-born poet and novelist for children and adults alike, and a popular contributor to Canadian, British, and American magazines, whose writing was expressly concerned with Canadian subject matter (Blenkhorn 2002). The fact that Machar is a co-author reveals that there is some proximity between historical fact and fiction in this book. Historiographer Ann Rigney acknowledges that historians "exercise some 'authorial action' in producing historical works" and argues that the historian gives the record of the past its narrative form (Rigney 1996: 35). This is key to understanding the "story-telling" that was occurring among historians and fiction-writers for children in Canada in the latter part of the nineteenth century. The narrativisation of past events was an integral means of instilling an awareness of the nation's history in Canada's young readers, a fact demonstrated by Agnes Machar's role as a contributor to Marquis' history textbook.

The titles given to each chapter of Marquis' textbook also demonstrate a tendency to create a new Canadian mythology out of this history. Chapter VI, for instance, tells the history of Daulac des Ormeaux and is entitled "A Canadian Thermopylae." Adam Dollard Des Ormeaux was a French Catholic and a soldier who, in 1660, gathered with a group of Frenchmen, Hurons, and Algonquins at the foot of Long Sault rapids on the Ottawa River to fight off an attack by several hundred Iroquois (Moogk 1988). After a more than week-long siege of their enclosure, the defenders were overwhelmed by the Iroquois, but the tale lived on in many forms as a story of the brave defence of New France (Moogk 1988).[2] In choosing the title "A Canadian Thermopylae" for this particular version of the story, Marquis attempts to place Canadian history in the context of world history, acknowledging a desire to achieve a sense of a long-standing national heritage. In 480 BC, Thermopylae was the sight of a battle between the Greeks and the Persians led by Xerxes in which the Greeks struggled to defend themselves against the invaders. While the Greeks were ultimately unsuccessful, the story of Thermopylae grew into a legend of Greek gallantry in the face of an enemy (Burn 1982: 181). By choosing to compare the two incidents (one from ancient Greece and one from pre-Confederation Canada), Marquis draws a clear comparison between Canada's history and that of the ancient world.

Chapter XI of Marquis' work again demonstrates an attempt to establish Canadian history along the same lines as that of older nations, and to create a new national folklore. This chapter tells the tale of Madeleine Verchères (1678–1747), a popular subject for Canadian writers, and is entitled the "Heroine of Castle Dangerous." Verchères, the daughter of an officer and Quebec seigneur, was made famous by the story of her defence of the family fort against raiding Iroquois when she was just fourteen years of age. The title of this chapter reads more like that of a novel than a work of non-fiction, suggesting that some blurring of fact and fancy is taking place. The description of Verchères as a heroine is a further attempt to make Canadian history both palatable to young readers, and a source of national pride. Writers searched Canada's past to build a new register of national heroes and heroines.

The story of Quebec's Madeleine Verchères is one example of the way in which children's writers were situating their examination of the history of specific regions and locales in the context of the nation as a whole. Because Canada developed in stages, with Newfoundland being the last province to join Confederation in 1949, Canadian "national" history at the end of the nineteenth century still tended largely towards the history of Ontario and Quebec. Yet there was an ever-increasing effort to examine the past in a broader context, with the result that books of local history from Ontario and elsewhere do reflect a sense of national history.

In addition to the textbooks of historians like Marquis and Miles, which attempt to provide an overview of national history, there were other works of historical non-fiction aimed at children. One example is a booklet by Jean Earle Geeson, published in Toronto in 1906. *The Old Fort at Toronto 1793–1906* gives a brief history of what is now "Fort York" in Toronto, including details of the American attack on it in 1813. In addition to providing an account of the physical structure itself, Geeson outlines the national importance of the fort, claiming it is "a spot second to no other in Canada in tragic interest," due to its role in the War of 1812 (Geeson 1906: 5). Geeson sees the events of this war as a source of pride for the nation:

> Canadians have every reason to be proud of the brave defenders of York, for the struggle for its keeping lasted eight hours, and was mainly carried on by our militia. Bodies have from time to time been dug up along the fighting line . . . showing how stoutly each step was disputed. (Geeson 1906: 9)

Geeson does not view the War of 1812 as a battle between American and British forces, but as an early example of a Canadian victory against a foe. Furthermore, the battle at Fort York is not merely seen as a part of Ontario's past, but as an event of national importance.

Geeson shows readers the important role that Toronto's local history plays in that of the nation as a whole, and argues that this history needs to be preserved and acknowledged:

> May the city which traces its earliest history to this spot treasure it as a monument of the past, and may the Government which it so nobly struggled to uphold, so protect and restore it that future generations may see from what small beginnings this great and glorious country has grown. (Geeson 1906: 16)

Geeson again emphasises the relation between the past, and the future, which is evident in many historical narratives for children from this time. For Geeson, there is glory in events from Canada's past, but there is also pride in rising from humble beginnings, and acknowledging the struggle that went into creating the nation.

The significance of these humble beginnings is emphasised in *Pen Pictures of Early Pioneer Life in Upper Canada*, published in Toronto in 1905 by William Briggs. With a title page that claims the work was written by "A 'Canuck' (of the Fifth Generation)," this book gives an account of the lifestyle and habits of the settlers of Upper Canada. The author's reference to his status as a "Fifth Generation" Canadian demonstrates that this historian takes pride in his Canadian heritage, and has a sense of identity that is rooted in Canada's past. M. Brook Taylor argues that following Confederation, historians expressed a new sense of being "wedded to place," and a loyalty to "the colonial land of their birth" that brought the responsibility of describing their home with accuracy

(Taylor 1989: 267). The author of *Pen Pictures* conveys this sense of loyalty, and the book's Dedication expresses a desire to instil a feeling of personal connection to the land and its past in the child reader; "To the Boys and Girls of Canada, and especially to those boys and girls, old and young, who are descendants of the early pioneers, this book is respectfully dedicated" ("Canuck" 1905: title page). In singling out the descendants of early pioneers, this passage also suggests that the author places those who can trace their roots back to the first settlers in a position of privilege. The past takes on a new personal significance when one can boast such a direct connection to the history of the early people of Canada.

The sense of being Canadian "by blood" emerges, and the book's introduction outlines the significance of being able to locate oneself in the history of the nation:

> The book . . . is the author's humble contribution to the history of the early days of his native province. Access to old manuscripts and records of family events retained in both his father's and mother's families for a century and more, has helped him . . . in carrying out the design which he had in view when he first commenced what, to him, was a labor of love. ("Canuck" 1905: Introduction)

The personal relationship this author has with Canada's past is noticeably different from the tone of the books by Miles and Marquis. "Canuck"'s evident satisfaction in his status as a fifth generation Canadian illustrates a very individual sense of pride in being Canadian, and particularly in being of Loyalist stock. Following the end of the American Revolutionary War in 1783, tens of thousands of people who had remained loyal to Britain during the conflict moved north from the United States to settle in the remaining British colonies. While their motivation ranged from political idealism to the tempting offer of free farmland (Morton 2001: 34–35), the story of the Loyalists endured as a symbol of Canadian fidelity and a rejection of American values. Many came to see these Loyalists as a form of Canadian nobility, and their place in Canadian history is the subject of much nineteenth-century writing.

In the collection "*Raise the Flag*," a poem by the Rev. Le Roy Hooker provides an example of the way in which some writers shared the history of the Loyalists with Canadian children. Although imbued with a strong sense of loyalty to Britain, Hooker's poem ultimately reveals the importance of these events to Canada itself and the first stanza suggests that the story has been passed down through the generations:

In the brave old Revolution days,
So by our sires 'tis told,
King's-men and Rebels, all ablaze
   With wrath and wrong,
   Strove hard and long:

And, fearsome to behold,
O'er town and wilderness afar,
O'er quaking land and sea and air,
All dark and stern the cloud of war
    In bursting thunder rolled. (Hooker 1891: 31)

After describing the victory of the Americans, the poet goes on to describe the thoughts of the defeated Loyalists, and the reasons behind their decision to leave their homes for Canadian soil:

What did they then, those loyal men,
When Britain's cause was lost?
    Did they consent,
    And dwell content
Where Crown, and Law and Parliament
Were trampled in the dust?
. . .
They would not spurn the glorious old,
    To grasp the gaudy new;
Of yesterday's rebellion born,
They held the upstart power in scorn-
    To Britain they stood true. (Hooker 1891: 32)

The poem continues with a description of the sacrifice the Loyalists made by leaving their homes for a new life in the difficult wilderness of Canada. The poet demands that his readers not forget the sacrifices and loyalty of these early Canadians:

These be thy heroes, Canada!
These men of proof, whose test
Was in the fevered pulse of strife
When foeman thrusts at foeman's life;
. . .
Stern was the test,
. . .
That proved their blood best of the best.
And when for Canada you pray,
    Implore kind Heaven
    That, like a leaven,
The hero-blood which then was given
May quicken in her veins alway:—
That from those worthy sires may spring,
    In number as the stars,

Strong-hearted sons, whose glorying
   Shall be in Right,

. . .

So, like the sun, her honored name
Shall shine to latest years the same. (Hooker 1891: 33–34)

The poem closes by emphasising the blood ties between generations of
Canadians, in the same way in which "Canuck" discusses his own personal ties
to this earlier generation. It suggests that, through this blood relation, Canadians
have become a distinct race; one that is connected to the British race, from which
the poet hopes that "strong-hearted sons" of Canada may spring. Through his
portrayal of the Loyalists as Canadian heroes, Hooker draws a direct connection
between British ancestry and the nation's bright future.

Although Hooker demonstrates a great deal of pro-British sentiment, he
focuses on the importance of the Loyalists to Canada itself. During the
nineteenth century, when there was a strong desire to strengthen a sense of
national unity, the story of the United Empire Loyalists was a natural choice for
those wishing to inspire loyalty to Canadian ideals and Canadian national
interests. While "A Canuck" draws on a personal connection to this group of
settlers in *Pen Pictures of Early Pioneer Life in Upper Canada*, Hooker's poem is
an example of the way in which the story of the Loyalists received treatment in
historical fiction, and demonstrates the ways in which fact, fiction, and the
author's imagination contribute to the making of history.

Historical Fiction

Though it is true that historical non-fiction contains a certain degree of
invention, fiction allows for an even greater range of interpretation of past events
and people. Authors can embellish their accounts of historical events through
use of description, characterisation, and dialogue. Canada's past was a rich
source of literary inspiration and some of the most popular subject matter for
children's historical fiction was the early period of settlement and exploration,
including the fur trade, the experiences of the early settlers, and the settlement
of the West. In addition to these tales, a large amount of literature dealt with
Canada's military history, from the fall of Quebec, to the War of 1812. These
historical narratives offer a range of interpretations of the events of Canada's
past. It was in this past that many of the seeds of the nineteenth century's growing
notion of "Canadian" identity were found, and it was a past that was increasingly
explored through children's fiction.

Many of these historical works of fiction centre on young protagonists and
give children an active role in their country's history, while other tales aimed at
a child readership revolve around adult characters. With subject matter ranging
from the voyages of Jacques Cartier, to the invasions by the Americans, these
works demonstrate that as the nineteenth century progressed writers in

Anglophone Canada were beginning to examine people and events of Canada's past, not just those from British history. The Preface of "*Raise the Flag" and Other Patriotic Canadian Songs and Poems*, published in Toronto in 1891, outlines the growing recognition of important national events:

> In February last a deputation consisting of a large number of influential men . . . waited upon the Minister of Education, to advocate the raising of a flag on the school houses on national anniversaries. . . . The *Empire* newspaper has also offered a large flag to the school in each county which produces the best essay on the subject of "Raising the Flag". As an encouragement to the children, who have written the best essays in each school . . . a few loyal Canadians have compiled . . . this little collection of Patriotic Songs and Poems, as the most appropriate remembrance to be given to the scholars who have written the best essays on these subjects. (Rose Publishing 1891: iii)

We are told that the "songs and poems selected . . . strike the keynote of Canadian history and sentiment" (iii). The preface also makes clear the object of the book, which is the "spreading among the children of our land those loyal and patriotic sentiments which animated our fathers and helped them to defend and hand down to us the rights and privileges which we now enjoy" (iv). This collection establishes the perceived link between teaching Canadian children their country's history, and fostering in them a sense of pride and loyalty. In this instance, fiction is the chosen mode of conveying this history.

Among the subjects discussed by the authors in this collection are Canada's military exploits, Indian life, and the early days of the fur trade. Also of interest are stories of the lives of the early settlers and in such tales, there is both a tendency to idealise this past, and an attempt to depict its difficulties. The period of early European settlement in Canada was one of much hardship as new-comers faced the difficulty of creating a life in a raw and undeveloped land. Stories about this period exhibit pride in the fact that Canada's nineteenth-century achievements are the result of hard work and dedication on the part of these early inhabitants. In the September, 1897 edition of *Home and Youth*, there is a short piece entitled "Early Days in Canada" by an author listed simply as H.M.H., which acknowledges the role of Canada's early inhabitants in developing the country:

> There are few, if any, of the present generation who can really appreciate the hardships endured by the early settlers, whose industry and enterprise have made Canada "blossom as the rose." The romance of the "back settlement" is still unwritten, but in that delightful book by Miss Lizars, "In the Days of the Canada Company," are recited many of the thrilling experiences of the brave pioneers who reclaimed the Huron tract from the wilderness. (H.M.H. 1897: 15)

The author goes on to describe an incident in Miss Lizars' book that depicts the harsh reality of Canada's early days. Kathleen Lizars (1863–1931) was a novelist and historian who was best know for the historical tales of life in Western Ontario that she wrote with her sister Robina (New 2002b: 673). H.M.H. quotes from Lizars' 1896 book that outlines the difficulties encountered by one pioneer woman and her family:[3]

> A night of terror, when her husband, with gun and watch-fires, kept a pack of wolves at bay, was one of the many adventures at The Corners. . . .
>
> Here in the succeeding years, by the light of a strip of cotton drawn to the edge of a saucer of lard, she patched garments torn in the bush and clearing, and rocked "the ten forest babies" which afterwards came to her. Here the little boy, carried so far in her arms, died, and five of the babies followed him. "But nothing daunted by poverty, death and unceasing hard work, she baked, knit, sewed . . . cut up her silk wedding gown into sun-bonnets, and saw her children capering about her in made-over relics of former days." A life of patient toil she led, duty faithfully performed, great hardships suffered. (H.M.H. 15)

This account of Canada's early days in *Home and Youth* describes some of the difficulties that settlers faced, and emphasises the hard work and sacrifice that was required for individuals, and the nation, to succeed.

While writers often acknowledged the difficulty of life in early Canada, they also saw the past as a time of adventure and opportunity. Writers saw in the harsh existence of the early settlers and fur-traders an abundant source of inspiration for tales of excitement and bravery. Their pens transformed the sometimes cruel Canadian past into a world of challenge and adventure. Writers such as Oxley, Young, Ballantyne, and Kingston transported the young reader of nineteenth-century Canada to this exciting past, developing particular ideas of masculinity in the process. Men from Canada's past were portrayed as enterprising, strong, and fearless, and represented an ideal of masculinity for boy readers to emulate. Canada's success, it was implied, was founded on the efforts of such brave men.

One such novel is *Snow-Shoes and Canoes; or, The Early Days of a Fur-Trader in the Hudson's Bay Territory* (1890) by W.H.G. Kingston. This tells the story of a group of fur traders in the area of the Red River during the early nineteenth century. Along with depictions of battles with Indians, hunting expeditions, and the joys and trials of canoeing and snow-shoeing, the novel looks to the past to project a vision of the future. After drawing a picture of life in the days of the fur-trade, Kingston concludes by presenting an image of Manitoba in the latter part of the nineteenth century, and muses on the promise it holds for the future:

> Though the Hudson's Bay Company still retain their trading-posts, the whole of this vast region now forms a part of the Canadian Dominion. A

large city, with churches and buildings of all descriptions, has sprung up close to Fort Garry on the left bank of the Red River, called Winnipeg, which contains from fifteen to twenty thousand inhabitants. . . . Many of the lakes and rivers on which formerly birch bark canoes alone were to be seen, are now navigated by steamers . . . while a band of Government surveyors have for some years past been employed in ascertaining the best course for a railway, which running entirely through the British territory, will one day form a connexion between the Atlantic and Pacific Oceans. From the above account of the country, it will be seen how great is the change which has taken place since the events I have described in the preceding pages. I was then a mere lad; I am now a grey-headed man. It was then wild in the extreme. It is still wild enough to satisfy the most romantic; but it now contains many of the elements of civilisation, and affords every opportunity of success to hardy, industrious men desirous of forming a home for themselves and their families. (Kingston 1890: 335–336)

Kingston, while finding inspiration in tales of the past, sees those events as part of a chain of progress, leading to a bright future. While his novel focuses on the events of a past time when the narrator was "a mere lad," it concludes with this picture of post-Confederation Canada, whose growth and success were due to the events and efforts of the preceding years.

Other writers found inspiration in the nation's military history. From the English defeat of the French in 1759, to the battles of the War of 1812, Canada provided its share of military heroes. The interest in tales of warfare on the part of children's writers reflects the preoccupation with military achievement and concerns of Empire in this era. Poems and songs like "The Battle of Queenston Heights" address past conflicts, and children's novelists were also writing about past military exploits. Two novelists of the age who address the subject of the defeat of the French forces in North America are J.M. Oxley and E. Everett-Green. Everett-Green's *French and English: A Story of the Struggle in America*, tells this tale from the side of a group of men who volunteer to aid the English cause, and raises the question of how much of this historical tale was based on fact. For example, when the character Humphrey resolves to fight the French he reveals a clear bias:

The old instinctive hatred of centuries between French and English, never really dead, now leaped to life in his breast. He had heard plenty of talk during his boyhood of France's boundless pretensions with regard to the great New World of the West, and how she sought, by the simple process of declaring territory to be hers, to extend her power over millions of miles of the untrodden plains and forests, which she could never hope to populate. (Everett-Green 1899: 24)

While the author is not afraid to criticise the English at times, commenting on their "internal jealousies, and . . . incompetent commanders" (108), the tale is clearly told from the perspective of the victors. Positive portrayals of French characters do occur in the book, but these figures themselves admit English superiority. For example, the English impress the young French girl Corinne who says, "I have been ashamed of my countrymen! I have felt that our foes are nobler than ourselves, and that God must surely arise and fight for them" (Everett-Green 1899: 136).

A great deal is made of the divisions between the French and the English at the time of the battle of Quebec, but the author also provides some insight into the reality of nineteenth-century Canada. To begin with, the respect accorded to certain French characters reflects the good relations one could expect among people who now share a common citizenship. Furthermore, despite the fierce loyalty to the English shown by many of the novel's characters, James Wolfe (based on the real British General who died while commanding the English forces at Quebec) muses on what he believes will be Canada's future independence from Britain:

> We shall never have a second Canada out there such as France has won— a country wholly dependent upon the one at home, looking always to her for government, help, care, money. No, no; the spirit of those who went forth from England was utterly different. They are English subjects still, but they want to rule themselves after their own way. They will never be helpless and dependent; they will be more like to shake our yoke from off their necks when they arrive at man's estate. But what matter if they do? We shall be brothers, even though the sea roll between them. The parent country has sent them forth, and must protect them till they are able to protect themselves. . . . After that we shall see. But for my part I prefer that struggling spirit of independence and desire after self-government. It can be carried too far; but it shows life, energy, youth, and strength. (Everett-Green 1899: 254–255)

Everett-Green here uses the character of General Wolfe to comment on the late-nineteenth century reality of Canada's relation to Great Britain.

The author essentially acknowledges the fact that Canada has separated from Britain, but uses this opportunity to reconcile separation with continued loyalty to the mother country. Wolfe sees the act of separation as evidence of the strength of English character and argues that independence is a sign of success and strength, and a result of the influence of English blood in Canada. He suggests that this is something the French Canadians alone could not have achieved. While ostensibly portraying the events of a much earlier time, Everett-Green's novel provides glimpses of the reality of post-Confederation Canada. As a British author, she uses this invented speech of Wolfe to see in Canadian independence evidence of an "English" spirit of "life, energy, youth, and strength," thereby reconciling the notion of an independent Canada with one that is still connected to imperial Britain.

J.M. Oxley's novel *Fife and Drum at Louisbourg* of 1899 also deals with the defeat of the French. This time, the story is told from the perspective of twin boys from Boston nicknamed Prince and Pickle. These boys, who embark on the expedition to Louisbourg as part of the fife and drums corps, share some of the attitudes toward the French displayed in Everett-Green's novel. The boys "had been brought up to regard the French as the very essence of all that was hateful in humanity, and when the attack on Louisbourg was mooted, nobody in Massachusetts was more eager than they for its successful execution" (Oxley 1899: 90–91). Yet when Prince and Pickle begin to encounter these "hateful" Frenchmen, their attitude toward them becomes somewhat uncertain. They begin to feel a degree of sympathy with the French and Prince observes, "we must seem just as strange to them, and doubtless they take us to be the greatest rascals in the world" (141). Pickle also begins to see things from the French perspective after he finds himself imprisoned in the city:

> Pickle's heart was moved to sincere pity by the discomforts the unfortunate inhabitants of the beleaguered town had to endure. . . . Gladly would Pickle have lightened their misery had it been in his power. It was not against them the colonial forces were waging war, yet they had to suffer just as if they were responsible. (Oxley 1899: 261)

Oxley's novel, like Everett-Green's, leaves the reader with an uncertain hold on what the relations between the French and English were like in the past, informing the reader as much about the late nineteenth century as it does about the historic period in which the story is set.

These two particular novels, one by a Canadian and the other by an English woman, each reflect an ongoing attempt to reconcile the nation's two main linguistic groups. Notably, both works were published in 1899, a time when the country was largely divided over the issue of conscription for the war in South Africa. With Anglophone and Francophone conflict so apparent, the earlier period of warfare between these two groups may have seemed a logical subject for children's authors to choose. Rather than merely focusing on the issue of division, however, these historical fictions each construct a version of the past that can allow for the possibility of future reconciliation between French and English Canadians. Instead of simply reliving the battles of the past, such fiction offers some hope for a unified Canadian nation.

As these novels demonstrate, there was a great degree of interest in military themes expressed in the children's literature of the day. The various battles that took place between the French and English forces during the eighteenth century were popular topics for juvenile fiction with many songs, poems, and novels written about British leaders such as James Wolfe and important French figures such as General Montcalm. The more recent events of the War of 1812 were also popular fare for writers of children's fiction. As loyalty to the Empire was still a strong force in post-Confederation Canada, tales of earlier victories of the "English" over their enemies in North America—be they French, American, or Indian—were designed in part to bolster pride in Canada's place within the British Empire. There were, however, also important lessons to be learned from these military tales about having pride in Canada itself.

In their study of the tradition of the War of 1812 narratives for children, S.R. MacGillivray and J. Lynes remark on Agnes Machar's *For King and Country* published in 1874. MacGillivray and Lynes claim that Machar's aim in relating the story of this period in Canada's past is to "inspire in a later generation of young Canadian hearts some sense of that fierce patriotism . . . that . . . animated those who defended Canada's integrity in the War of 1812" (MacGillivray and Lynes 1996: 7). Writers like Machar were reminding young readers of their nation's past to "suggest not just the progressive march toward a prosperous future, but also the price that must be paid to ensure that such a future is realized" (MacGillivray and Lynes 1996: 9). Such writers were constructing Canadian history with the aim of shaping a strong sense of national pride and loyalty in young readers following Confederation.

Although male figures such as Isaac Brock and James Wolfe earned an important status as Canadian heroes, there were also tales written about Canadian heroines. One woman who was elevated to the status of national heroine was Upper Canada's Laura Secord (1775–1868). Secord famously made a 30 km trek during the War of 1812 in order to warn the British officer James FitzGibbon that the Americans were planning to attack his position at Beaver Dams, information which she claimed to have overheard American officers discussing (McKenzie 1988). Some have speculated that FitzGibbon was already aware of these plans to attack, but regardless, two days after Secord made her journey, the American forces surrendered to FitzGibbon (McKenzie 1988). One Canadian author to celebrate this woman in verse was Charles Mair (1838–1927) whose poem "A Ballad for Brave Women" appeared in the children's poetry collection *"Raise the Flag" and Other Patriotic Canadian Songs and Poems* in 1891. Mair was a poet, a dramatist and a journalist who was deeply involved in promoting the cause of Canadian nationalism (New 2002c). His poem tells a romantic version of the story of Secord's efforts to guard Canada from American aggressors during the War of 1812, a defining moment in Canadian history:

A story worth telling, our annals afford,
'Tis the wonderful journey of Laura Secord!
Her poor crippled spouse hobbled home with the news
That Boerstler was nigh! "Not a minute to lose,
Not an instant," said Laura, "for stoppage or pause—
I must hurry and warn our brave troops at Decaws."
"What! You!" said her husband "to famish and tire!"
"Yes, me!" said brave Laura, her bosom on fire. (Mair 1891: 27)

The poet continues with several verses describing Secord's difficult journey through the forest to warn the troops. By her "woman's devotion" the day is saved, and she is accorded her place in Canadian history (Mair 1891: 30). Mair uses the elevated language of epic poetry to relate the story of Laura Secord, lending a greater sense of romance and heroism to the tale.

Not only does Mair envision Secord as a Canadian champion, but he also intends her story to serve as inspiration for young Canadian girls:

> Ah! Faithful to death were our women of yore!
> Have they fled with the past to be heard of no more?
> No, no! Though this laurelled one sleeps in the grave,
> We have maidens as true, we have matrons as brave;
> And should Canada ever be forced to the test—
> To spend for our country the blood of her best!
> When her sons lift the linstock and brandish the sword,
> Her daughters will think of brave Laura Secord! (Mair 1891: 30)

Mair's poem demonstrates that Canada's military history was something seen to inspire national pride and loyalty in both young male and young female readers. While young boys were encouraged to prepare themselves for possible battle in order to secure the nation's future, young women were also taught that they could serve their nation by being brave and loyal.

Mair's story of Laura Secord demonstrates several functions of the construction of Canadian history for young readers. In addition to making the events of the distant past more accessible to young readers, historical fiction also helped to develop a new Canadian mythology. In her evaluation of the role of myth-making in the new world, Margaret E. Turner cites the views of another critic, Colin Partridge. Partridge sees new cultures as undertaking different steps to clarify their relationship with their new surroundings:

> One of these is making myth and metaphor, which he describes as the home-made legend through which later inhabitants will view the place's origin and development: as factual history is succeeded in general consciousness by poetic or mythic history, the new culture comes to shape people's perceptions of the past. (Turner 1995: 15–16)

This claim that new cultures make myth and metaphor is supported by Canadian children's literature from the latter part of the nineteenth century, in which authors were consciously constructing what Turner calls a "poetic or mythic history." From these works emerges a sense that Canada possesses its own list of heroes and heroines, and its own unique legends.

History and Fantasy

Beyond simply blending fact and fiction, the more creative interpretations of Canada's past also employed fantasy. While many works of historical fiction centred on young characters in an attempt to engage child readers, a few writers saw fantasy as another means of interesting a young audience in Canadian history. Fantasy fiction, however, is not a very common form of Canadian children's literature from the nineteenth and early twentieth centuries, and scholars of Canadian literature have noted the country's relative lack of fantasy writing. In her study of nineteenth-century children's literature Sheila Egoff remarks that while the middle of the century saw a wealth of imaginative fiction by English writers such as Lewis Carroll, "Canadian writers stood aloof from this trend" (Egoff 1967: 244). "It is not surprising," writes Egoff "that outstanding books of fantasy were not written in Canada at this time. In fact, nothing of a richness comparable to the English productions occurred in *any* other country, least of all in a frontier society such as Canada" (244). Writing in 1882, Catharine Parr Traill claimed, "Fancy would starve for lack of marvellous food to keep her alive in the backwoods" (Ketterer 1992: 2). Despite such observations, there is evidence in the stories of the First Nations, and the folktales of French Canada (Ketterer 1992: 2), that some Canadians were writing fantasy.

Admittedly, it accounts for a small percentage, but there is some evidence that Anglophone children's literature did include elements of fantasy. William H. New has observed that: "Fantasy, an element in Canadian writing from the early days of the tale-tellers and map-makers, often appeared as documentary. Nineteenth-century animal stories, like the maps of beasts and dragons, posed as empirical truth" (New 2001: 269). One children's work that supports New's claim that fantasy can function as "documentary" is *A Wonder Web of Stories* by Margaret Charlton and Caroline Fraser. This collection of stories demonstrates the use of traditional fantasy and fairy-tale elements. Published in Montreal in 1892, it contains a story by Margaret Charlton entitled "Captain Pepper, The Valiant Knight of the Laurentians." In many ways, this story is similar to Rudyard Kipling's *Puck of Pook's Hill*, written nearly fifteen years after Charlton's tale. The two works make similar use of fantasy to explore national history. While Kipling reworks the myths and legends of England's past, Charlton's inventive tale is concerned with Canada's history. It tells the story of a boy named Fred who, while reading his book of geography and history in his garden, becomes frustrated with his lesson and decides that Quebec's Laurentian Mountains, the subject of his studies, are of no consequence. Upon declaring this, Fred is greeted by an irate little elf, who is disgusted by the boy's ignorance:

> "Bother the Laurentian Mountains!" cried the boy, getting up from the bench and throwing himself down on the grass. "Here I have been studying about them all the afternoon, and I cannot remember on which

side of the St. Lawrence they are. . . . I am not going to think about them any longer; they are not of much consequence, anyway;" and settling himself into a comfortable position, Fred closed his eyes and fell asleep. He had not slept long, when he was suddenly awakened by a shrill voice saying:

"Of not much consequence are they! that shows what a dunce you are! You stupid boy!"

Quickly raising his head, Fred looked wonderingly about him to see who was speaking, and what did he see standing by his side but a queer little figure dressed in green, with a three-cornered scarlet hat perched on his head.

"You ought to be ashamed of yourself to be such a dunce," again shrieked the little man. . . . No consequence, indeed! I would have you know, stupid boy, that they contain some of the oldest rocks in the world, and have been visited and written about by some of the most eminent men of the age. (Charlton and Fraser 1892: 106–8)

The little sprite (Captain Pepper as it turns out) is angry that Fred is ignorant of his country's history. In order to educate the boy a group of elves carry him off to the Laurentians where, very much in the spirit of Lewis Carroll's *Alice's Adventures in Wonderland*, he encounters many strange sights and figures.

At one point during these adventures, Fred meets a talking owl who helps show that the boy is not as ignorant of Canadian history as he first appears:

Then, to Fred's astonishment, he made out that the owl was saying: "Jacques Cartier, John Cabot, Sebastian Cabot, Champlain. No, Columbus; yes, that is the name: Columbus—Christopher Columbus—it was who came over in three ships."

"Oh, you are all wrong!" exclaimed Fred, unable to keep quiet any longer. "It was Cartier who came over in three ships."

"No such thing; do you mean to tell me he could separate himself into three parts. Oh, you clever boy! You wise boy! Did you take the prize in history in your class?"

"No, I did not," said Fred, getting angry at the bird's tone; "but I know it was Cartier who came over in three ships. . . ."

"I tell you what, my boy," cried the owl . . . "never again attempt to correct any of us. An owl, you know, is the bird of wisdom."

"I think you are a very stupid bird, for all you look so wise," answered Fred. (Charlton and Fraser 1892: 122–123)

Fred's encounter with this bird demonstrates that he does actually know something about his country, and over the course of his adventures his understanding of Canadian history grows and develops as he encounters the various spirits of the place.

The figure that ultimately helps Fred to understand Canada is the fairy Dew-Drop, Queen of the Air, who takes the boy on a flight to see those parts of the country of which he is ignorant:

> "You know but little of the country in which you live, my boy," said Dew-Drop, turning to Fred.
> "Yes, dear lady," answered Fred. "I have not seen much of it."
> "Then you shall see it now, you shall feast your eyes upon its beauties."
> "Is it, then, so beautiful?" asked Fred, wonderingly. The Queen of the Air smiled as she answered, "Wait and see." (Charlton and Fraser 1892: 134–5)

After seeing the riches of the country from coast to coast, Dew-Drop takes Fred across the ocean to what she tells him is, "the home of the mighty nation you have sprung from" (136). Here, with a "long, lingering look at the noble face" he gazes upon Queen Victoria (137), whom he recognises from her portrait that his family has. Upon his return home, Fred expresses his pleasure at all that he has seen:

> "I shall never, never forget what I have seen. And my country, I shall love it now as I never loved it before, it is so grand, so beautiful, so vast. Oh, I could die for it!" cried Fred, his face aglow with excitement. "And I am so glad we belong to that gracious lady we have seen." (137–138)

Charlton's story, with its stress on both Canada's beauties and England's greatness, presents a vision of the nation that includes pride in Empire. In this instance, the importance of England's role in Canada's history is emphasised.

Dew-Drop is pleased with Fred's positive response to all that he witnesses, and the tale, which begins with the boy's study of Canadian history, ends with the fairy's vision of its future:

> "Once more I rejoice. Greed and gain will yet be over-reached and conquered by the clarion tones of patriotism. 'Down with all treason towards our beloved country' shall be heard ringing throughout the land, and he, who for so long manfully strove for the glory of his country, will hear and rejoice. Oh, youth, remember that should the time ever come when thy country shall need a strong arm to defend her rights, see to it that thine is uplifted in her defence." (138)

Charlton's work begins with a lesson in history, but finishes by imparting this message to the contemporary child reader about the promise of the nation's future. Charlton's story contains many whimsical elements in the style of *Alice's Adventures in Wonderland*, including a comical King and Queen, a strange wedding party and an absurd court case. Charlton employs these elements of fantasy in the serious cause of fostering an understanding of national history and national identity which she believes includes pride in Canada's role in the Empire. While many nineteenth-century children's writers were writing more realistic historical fiction, Charlton's tale is one example of the use of fantasy to engage the reader in the subjects of Canadian geography, politics, and history, and to inspire a sense of pride and national identity.

While Charlton's tale is one of the relatively rare works of fantasy that explores the question of Canadian identity, there is another worth considering. This is the popular series of "Brownies" stories by author Palmer Cox (1840–1924). Though Palmer Cox spent much of his career in the United States, moving first to California in 1863 and then to New York in 1875, where he published his first collection of Brownie stories, he was born and raised in Granby, Quebec and returned there permanently in 1905. Cox wrote and illustrated a highly popular series of children's tales about mischievous little sprites named Brownies, inspired by Scottish legends about household spirits of the same name. Cox wrote dozens of stories about these funny little creatures and in 1894, a collection entitled *The Brownies Around the World* was published in New York. The first story in this collection is entitled "The Brownies in Canada." Cox lends particular importance to the Canadian scene by making Canada the initial stage of the Brownies' first journey outside the United States. At eighteen pages, it is also the longest of the tales in this collection, with the others being somewhere between five and ten in length (Margerum 2002). The first page of the tale includes a picture of the Canadian Brownie whose costume represents what Cox saw as some of the recognisable elements of the Canadian identity. Dressed in the heavy overcoat and wide sash that marked the familiar costume of the old *courier du bois*, the Brownie's outfit is completed by a toque and a pair of snowshoes. He also carries a flag on which is emblazoned a lacrosse stick and ball, representing Canada's national sport. Through his illustration of the Brownie, Palmer Cox encompasses the figure of the "Canadian" in a succinct visual image.

In addition to the illustrations, which include such Canadian scenes as the Bank of Montreal building and the St. Lawrence River, Palmer Cox uses his verse to describe contemporary Canada, including its cities:

Then London, Galt, and Kingston old,
In turn received the Brownies bold.
To Ottawa went all the band
To view each edifice so grand,
To Hamilton, to Goderich, too,
That overlooks Lake Huron blue,
The Brownies took a hasty run
For observation and for fun.
Through streets that are Toronto's pride
They hurried on with hasty stride,
Viewed banks, and buildings made to hold

The money which is good as gold.
Looked through each handsome court and square,
And market-place with special care. (Cox 1894: 5–6)

While drawing an attractive picture of Canada's growing cities, Cox also includes many lessons in Canadian history. The Brownie stories were very popular in the United States and this tale includes an account of Canada's former struggles with the Americans:

Once while they halted to survey
A steep and grass-grown mound of clay,
Said one, "This marks an old redoubt
Where once the British kept lookout,
When Uncle Sam and Johnny Bull
Had their last interesting pull,
Or tug of war, as records show,
Now over eighty years ago." (Cox 1894: 6)

Cox is here referring to the War of 1812, but he stops short of taking a stand on this "tug of war" over Canada between the United States and Great Britain.

On other historical matters, however, the narrator expresses a stronger opinion. As the Brownies view the beauties of the St. Lawrence and the Thousand Islands, he speculates on the history of the Indians and their struggle to maintain their land in the face of new settlers:

No wonder Indians strewed, like stones,
Along its banks the settlers' bones,
Before they'd leave a scene so fair
And turn to seek a home elsewhere.
The arm indeed might well be strong,
The hatchet heavy, arrow long,
And scalping-knife be ever keen
Defending such a lovely scene. (Cox 1894: 7)

In this short verse, though it includes some violent imagery, Cox offers a sympathetic perspective on the history of the Canadian Indians, in contrast to many of the portrayals of settler–Indian conflict by other writers.

The author's interest in Canadian history does not end here. When the Brownies reach Quebec, complete with a stop in Granby, "The birthplace of the Brownie man" (Cox 1894: 14), they make their way to Quebec City. In this episode Cox devotes a lengthy verse to explaining the events that led to the British victory in North America:

Said one, who paused to look around:
"My friends, we tread historic ground;

'Twas up this path, so rough and steep,
The British did at midnight creep,
With guns unloaded in their hands,
Obedient to the strict commands,
For fear an accidental shot
Might bring the Frenchmen to the spot.
Full in the van, with bated breath,
Brave Wolfe ascended to his death,
While Montcalm, trusting guards to keep
A careful watch, took his last sleep!
For lo! the early dawn revealed
The red coats stationed in the field;
The Plains of Abraham were bright
With troops all marshalled for the fight.
I will not here the tale intrude
About the battle that ensued
Of rallying ranks, when hope was low,
Or brilliant charges to and fro.
On history's pages read you may
How fell the heroes of that day;
And how, ere shades of night came down,
The Union Jack waved o'er the town." (Cox 1894: 16–17)

The events Cox chooses to describe in his tale, including the battle of the Plains of Abraham and the War of 1812, are events that were important not just to Canada, but to Great Britain and the United States as well. It is a national history of global significance that the author shares with his young readership.

Cox's work of fantasy helps in many ways to shape an image of Canada and includes many familiar clichés and representations of Canada popular in the nineteenth century. It is fitting, therefore, that this story closes with the familiar image of Canada as a land of the frozen north, as the Brownies engage in a snowshoe race:

While through the Canadian wilds they passed
Where snow was piled like mountains vast,
They took to snow-shoes long and stout,
With their own hands well fashioned out;
. . .
So every Brownie struggled well
His puffing comrades to excel;
But shoes would sometimes hit or hitch,
And headlong down the mountain pitch

The very ones that seemed to show
The greatest speed upon the snow.

. . .

But best of feelings governed still
The lively race o'er plain and hill. (Cox 1894: 17–18)

Palmer's whimsical tale about the Brownies' adventure in Canada is, like Margaret Charlton's tale, a rare example of the ways in which writers employed fantasy, fact, and fiction to create a particular version of Canadian history, and contribute to the sense of what it meant to be Canadian in the process. Works of fantasy and historical narratives such as these show that by the turn of the twentieth century, there was a growing awareness of the need to celebrate Canadian achievement. As Palmer Cox's reference to figures such as James Wolfe indicate, Canada was developing its own list of heroes who were being taken from different periods of its history.

Heroic Days of Yore

While Charlton and Cox demonstrate the ways in which fantasy helped shape a sense of past achievement, other works for children attained this by different means. Marquis' comparison of the story of Daulac des Ormeaux to the battle of Thermopylae in a history textbook is one example of how writers were fashioning Canadian history in the tradition of epic poetry and classical mythology. Another work that provides a different example of the ways in which Canada was beginning to form its own mythology and create its own list of heroes, is a poem by William Thomas White published in the *"Raise the Flag"* collection of poetry for children. In "The Battle of Queenston Heights," White places Isaac Brock in the same league as some of the great heroes of the classical age:

Bring forth the book of heroes' deeds, and to your listening flock,
Read reverently of Queenston Heights and the death of Isaac Brock.

Oh, there are some amongst us who spurn the patriot's name,
Who say our country has no past, no heroes known to fame.

They talk of bold Leonidas who held the pass of blood,
And how Horatius Cocles braved swollen Tiber's flood.

They never tire of dark Cortez who spared nor blood nor tears,
Nor yet of Arnold Winkelreid, who broke the Austrian spears.

Their glory is of Waterloo, that crimson-memoried fight,
Of the "thin red line" at Inkerman and Alma's bloody height.

For Canada their voice is mute, yet history's pages tell
That braver blood was never spilt than where her heroes fell.
(White 1891: 17–18)

By invoking the names of historically significant people like Cortez and battles
such as Waterloo, White places Canadian events and personages on the same
level of importance and influence as these world-famous figures. The poet
continues by describing the battle with the Americans who appear at first to be
gaining the victory. Brock, however, manages to turn the tide:

What spell so much could nerve them in that losing battle's shock,
"Courage, boys! It is the General! Onward comrades! On with Brock!"

Now forward to the battery! They lend a ready ear;
There's a hero's form to lead them and a hero's voice to cheer.

And o'er the level plain they press, and up the sloping hill,
'Mid hiss of shot and volleys' smoke his cry is "Onward!" still.

And now they pass the low ravine, they clamber o'er the wall;
The fatal death-shot strikes him; they see their leader fall.

"Push on, push on, York volunteers!" brave words—they were his last,
And like the vision of a dream the charging column passed.

. . .

One spirit moved, one thought inspired that gallant little band,
That foot of no invading foe should e'er pollute their land.
(White 1891: 19–20)

White employs the language of the epic poem to add grandeur, excitement, and
suspense to this account of the combat, and to impress upon the reader the
comradeship and unity of the "gallant little band" of soldiers willing to die to
defend Canadian soil. The poet then shifts the narrative from the report of this
past battle, to his vision of the nation's future; a future in which Canadians will
speak of Brock as a great hero:

And thou, whose sacred dust entombed on yonder summit lies,
Beneath that noble monument far-reaching toward the skies,

Thy name shall be a holy word, a trumpet-note to all,
When bravery's arm is needed and they hear their country's call.

And future sires shall take their sons at evening on their knee,
And tell the old tale over, and thus shall speak of thee—

"His is the noblest name we have in all our bright array;
He taught our youth to falter no tho' death might bar the way;

"He showed our might, he led our arms, he conquered, tho' he fell;
He gave up all he had—his life—for the land he loved so well."
(White 1891: 20)

Through the poet's image of both the past and the future, the British-born Isaac Brock becomes one of Canada's most famous champions. With a blend of invention and omission, the poet renders Brock, who did not come to Canada until 1802, as an archetypal Canadian hero.

In the same way that verse transforms Isaac Brock from a historical figure to an almost mythological hero, Madeleine Verchères (to whom Miles devotes a chapter in his history textbook) also becomes the subject of poetry in the nineteenth century. In part because she was a young girl during the events that made her famous, Madeleine Verchères was a popular figure in children's literature and W.H. Drummond clearly addresses a child audience at his poem's opening. The poem begins with a colourful vision of old Quebec:

I've told you many a tale, my child, of the
    old heroic days,
Of Indian wars and massacre, of villages ablaze
With savage torch, from Ville Marie to the
    Mission of Trois Rivieres;
But never have I told you yet of Madeleine
    Vercheres. (Drummond 1898: 6)

In Drummond's version of Verchères' history, the people of the land are gathering their autumn harvest in a peaceful, pastoral scene, unaware of the danger that surrounds them:

For news there was none of battle, from the
    forts of the Richelieu
To the gates of the ancient city, where the flag
    of King Louis flew;
All peaceful the skies hung over the seigneurie
    of Vercheres,
Like the calm that so often cometh ere the
    hurricane rends the air. (Drummond 1898: 7)

The poet's talk of the "ancient city" lends an air of significance and majesty to the Canadian scene, to which the word "ancient" is not commonly applied. This evokes the feeling that Canadian society is deeply rooted in the days of long-ago. As Madeleine Verchères bravely battles her Iroquois foe her story is cast in the style of great legends, and Nature itself seems to echo the enormity and significance of the events as they unfold:

And they say the black clouds gathered, and a
  tempest swept the sky,
And the roar of the thunder mingled with the
  forest tiger's cry,
But still the garrison fought on, while the lightning's jagged spear
Tore a hole in the night's dark curtain, and
  showed them a foeman near. (Drummond 1898: 10)

Young Madeleine's brave defence of her father's property against the attack of the Iroquois is a valiant deed and she takes her place in the growing list of Canadian heroes and heroines.

Although he celebrates the existence of brave Canadians such as Madeleine Verchères, Drummond does not idealise the past. There is a clear sense that one should be thankful that such days are over:

And this, my dear, is the story of the maiden
  Madeleine.
God grant that we in Canada may never see
  again
Such cruel wars and massacre, in waking or in
  dream,
As our fathers and mothers saw, my child, in
  the days of the old régime! (Drummond 1898: 12)

The present, it is implied, is an age of progress that has been achieved by the efforts of early Canadians such as Verchères. Despite his assertion that they were "heroic days," Drummond concludes the poem with a clear notion that Canada's present is the hard-earned result of, and a great improvement on, its past. Drummond's poem provides further evidence that towards the beginning of the twentieth century, the nation was beginning to claim its own past, and to see in its history all the potential Canada held for the future.

Exploring national history became a key part of the process of developing national unity and identity. In tales from the past, writers found a source of literary inspiration, and the tools needed to construct a Canadian identity. Historical narratives taught children about their nation's past, and groomed them for their role as contributors to its future. While ostensibly learning the facts of the past, readers were actually reading different versions of Canadian history shaped by various points of view. Many writers thought that teaching history from a national perspective would create a sense of shared bonds, thereby ensuring that the new Dominion would not crumble, and minimising inter-provincial conflict. Among the various constructions of national history, the sense of Canada as "one nation housing one people inhabiting a common land," repeatedly manifests itself (Taylor 1989: 268). This historical literature for children aims to reinforce a sense of harmony and common identity in the hopes of ensuring a successful future for the nation. Canadian society is often pictured in a condition of progress, with the past providing the seeds for present achievement and future prosperity. By helping children to understand the nation's history, writers attempted to provide a tool that their young readers could use to construct a future that fulfilled this vision of promise.

Chapter Eight
"The True North Strong and Free": Landscape and Environment

Along the line of smoky hills
The crimson forest stands,
And all the day the blue-jay calls
Throughout the autumn lands.

Now by the brook the maple leans
With all his glory spread,
And all the sumachs on the hills
Have turned their green to red.

Now by great marshes wrapt in mist,
Or past some river's mouth,
Throughout the long, still autumn day
Wild birds are flying south.

(Wilfred Campbell, "Indian Summer")

In addition to exploring the nation's history, negotiating complicated relationships with Britain and the United States, and examining issues of race and ethnicity, Canadian writers, in a quest to establish a sense of common identity following Confederation, were also discovering the influence of the natural environment on notions of national character. Canada's environment had an enormous impact on the manner in which people from both within and outside its borders viewed the country. Enveloped in a cloud of exaggeration, idealism, and misconception, Canada's landscape was a source of both pride and ridicule. Amid the many portrayals and stereotypes of the Canadian landscape, the image of Canada as a land of rugged wilderness prevailed and continues to dominate to this day. This resulted in part from the fact that, until the 1920s, Canada's population was predominately rural and its cities small in size and number. The number of urban dwellers in Canada did increase steadily from 1867 onward, whereas rural populations remained relatively constant, but in spite of this steady urbanisation, the image of Canada as a wilderness continued to prevail in art and literature.

Canadians both embraced and rejected this picture of their country. While many found pride in the vision of a nation in which only the hearty and industrious could survive, others expressed frustration with the prevailing stereotype that failed to adequately reflect Canada's natural diversity, and which downplayed the development of cities, towns, and other signs of progress and "civilisation." Amid the growing multitude of artistic and literary representations of Canada's natural environment, the physical landscape came to have an important influence on the psyche and identity of the nation. In 1849, John Ruskin wrote of architecture that we "may live without her, and worship without her, but we cannot remember without her" (Wheeler and Whiteley 1992: 216). Ruskin was writing of the relationship between national memory and civic architecture, but his observation that architecture "connects forgotten and following ages with each other, and half constitutes the identity, as it concentrates the sympathy, of nations" can be applied to Canada's relationship with the environment (Wheeler and Whiteley 1992: 221). In nineteenth-century Canada, where grand, national monuments and buildings were relatively scarce, it was the natural environment that began to concentrate the sympathy and constitute the identity of the nation.

The representation of the environment in early Canadian children's literature falls into two patterns. On the one hand, writers use the natural environment for its aesthetic and symbolic value, representing everything from moral corruption to spiritual salvation. These works celebrate and praise the beauty of the landscape, with nature pictured as a serene and rejuvenating place that can restore humanity to a more desirable state. While many works exhibit this tendency to exalt the Canadian environment, others offer a view of nature as something hostile and forbidding that one needs to tame and control. Such works reveal a belief that Canadians can conquer their natural environment, and that the commercial potential of the land will result in a glorious destiny for the nation. These stories focus on the practical or commercial aspects of the landscape and find expression in tales of fur traders, miners, woodsmen, and farmers. A particularly prevalent form of Canadian children's literature, such tales exploit the popular image of Canada as a land of wilderness while simultaneously creating a vision of a nation that is on a steady and successful civilising mission.

Frequently, these various treatments of the Canadian landscape operate simultaneously within a given work of children's literature. While many writers show their appreciation for the aesthetic value of the Canadian landscape, others are more concerned with emphasising the continuing need for Canada to be settled and developed in order to secure national economic security and independence. These prevailing literary patterns reflect the importance of the natural environment in Canadian life and the degree to which the physical landscape came to have a central role in the sense of national identity that developed following 1867.

Land of Ice and Snow? Competing Images of the Canadian Environment

As a population whose numbers are dwarfed by the sheer immensity of the land they occupy, Canadians cannot escape the dominance of nature. Some even see Canada's physical environment as one of the reasons for the country's lingering loyalty to the British Empire until the early twentieth century. Northrop Frye argues that because of its vast empty spaces, "Canada had to think of itself . . . as part of a world-circling empire, its railways filling in the gap in communication between Europe and the East, its natural resources contributing to a global technology" (Frye 1982: 43). Rather than creating a sense of isolationism on the part of Canadians, according to Frye, the challenges presented by the land contributed to a global perspective and a lingering sense of connectedness to Europe. It is certainly true that landscape and environment have always had an important impact on the Canadian psyche. For the early inhabitants who literally had to carve out a living from it—who had to battle its elements, chop down its trees, and plough its lands—it was an overwhelming and unavoidable aspect of life and gradually became an important point of identification.

The natural environment has long been an important feature in Canadian art and literature, but its function and representation have always been complicated. One of the most common misconceptions and prevalent images of the country was that it was a frozen land of ice and snow. With its considerable regional and climatic diversity, why is it that the prevailing image of Canada was, and to some extent still is, that of the "Great White North"? Certainly the abundance of literature for both children and adults alike concerning the adventures and perils of the land contributed to this perception. While Canadians penned much of this literature, British and American authors, some of whom would likely have had no firsthand knowledge of the Canadian environment, also wrote a great deal of it. One of several British children's authors who helped to shape the image of Canada as a land of ice and snow is W.H.G. Kingston, whose novel *Snow-Shoes and Canoes; or, the Early Days of a Fur-Trader in the Hudson's Bay Territory* is typical of many of the nineteenth-century wilderness adventure stories set in Canada. Published in 1890, the title of this novel alone conjures up the image of Canada as a wilderness suited to such pursuits as canoeing and that iconic winter pastime, snow-shoeing. Kingston chooses the iciest latitudes of Canada as his setting, helping to contribute to the image of Canada as an Arctic landscape:

> The winter wore on. That season occupies, as most of my readers must be aware, a large portion of the year in that region. For months together, that is to say from the middle of October to late in May, during the whole

period, the ground is covered with snow, the rivers frozen over, the trees are leafless, every drop of water exposed to the air congeals. (Kingston 1890: 100)

Kingston remark that most of his readers "must be aware" of the fact that winter lasts for a great deal of the year in Canada is an indication of just how popular and widespread the image of Canada as a snowy wasteland continued to be at the end of the nineteenth century.

Another British author who helped contribute to the icy vision of Canada was Rudyard Kipling, through works like his 1897 poem "Our Lady of the Snows":

A Nation spoke to a Nation,
    A Queen sent word to a Throne:
"Daughter am I in my mother's house,
    But mistress in my own.
The gates are mine to open,
    As the gates are mine to close,
And I set my house in order,"
    Said our Lady of the Snows. (Kipling 1897)

Although Kipling's verse is in fact about the Canadian Preferential Tariff, the poem's title and the repeated phrase "our Lady of the Snows" indicate that he imagines Canada here as a frozen wilderness.

Canadians, however, were themselves aware of the diversity of their environment and eager for a more accurate depiction of the country. Evidence of this is present in an advertising pamphlet from "The Toronto Packing Co." *circa* 1897. Much of the material in this booklet is aimed at children, as is indicated by the titles of such articles as "The Children at Tea" and "The Boy's Anthem." Anxious to promote its business and its products—prepared Canadian fruits—the company's booklet opens with a response to the prevailing perception of Canada as a land of ice and snow as expressed in Kipling's poem:

Mr. Rudyard Kipling recently wrote a poem in which he called the fair Dominion of Canada "Our Lady of the Snows." This well-meant, but ill-advised expression, has been severely criticised in the Colonial papers. One country editor concludes his remarks with a suggestion that "Kipling should be spanked with a Snowshoe." (Toronto Packing Co. *c* 1897b: 1)

Canadians, it appears, made efforts to defend and correct the image of their country that materialised in the works by foreign pens such as Kipling's. In addition to the country editor's colourful and ironic suggestion that Kipling be spanked with a snowshoe—that familiar symbol of the Canadian north—this pamphlet includes further evidence of Canadian dissatisfaction with the recurring representation of Canada as a cold and frozen land. There are two poems by Canadian poets published in this advertising booklet that respond directly to Kipling's "Our Lady of the Snows." The first of these is by J.W. Bengough and is entitled "Canada to Kipling":

> The title is pretty, I grant you,
>   And I know you meant to be kind,
> But I wish you could hit on another
>   Less risky, if you don't mind.
> Of course, as implying my "whiteness,"
>   I modestly murmur "It goes,"
> But I fear few will give that meaning
>   To "Our Lady of the Snows."
>
> You see, there's a prevalent notion—
>   Which does me a grievous wrong—
> That my climate is almost Arctic,
>   And my winters ten months long.
> Perhaps that is your idea,
>   For it's widespread, goodness knows!
> And this phrase will make it more so—
>   "Our Lady of the Snows." (Bengough c. 1897)

Bengough's direct address to such a famed British writer as Kipling is a striking example of Canada's attempt not only to establish itself as separate from Britain, but to challenge directly the motherland's misconceptions about its former colony. Bengough's short poem illustrates the manner in which those abroad perceived Canada and reveals Canadian annoyance with the frequent and persistent fallacies about their Canadian homeland.

The second poem published in this pamphlet in direct response to Kipling is by Canadian poet Arthur Weir (1864–1902). Born in Montreal, Weir worked as a journalist and as a poet, publishing three books of poetry between 1887 and 1897. Originally published in the *Montreal Star*, Weir's "Our Lady of the Snows" offers a further rebuttal to Kipling's poem:

> A poet sung of a nation in words that were kindly meant,
> And his song on ethereal pulses throughout the Empire went,
> It breathed the Imperial spirit at which the bosom glows,
> But he slurred the land that he fain had praised, as "Our
>   Lady of the Snows."
>
> She has lands unknown to summer, but she keeps them for a
>   park
> For such as find little Europe too small for ambition's mark.

She keeps them to pleasure Nansen, for a Franklin to repose,
But they lie remote from the marts and home of "Our Lady of the
Snows."

True, she has somewhere, sometime, winters when keen winds
bite,
And in the frosty heavens gleams the auroral light,
When in the drifted forest she counts the ringing blows
Of the axe that reaps a harvest for "Our Lady of the Snows."

But while the sturdy Briton still shivers in east winds,
The winter flees and the rivers no more the ice king binds,
And blossom calls upon blossom, & each its fair form shows,
In the land that is called by Kipling "Our Lady of the Snows."

She has woods of pine and maple, where England might be
lost;
She has ports that are ever open to ships that are tempest
tossed;
She has fields of wheat unbounded, where the whole horizon
glows,
And the hot sun laughs to hear her styled "Our Lady of
the Snows."

. . .

She can pluck, if she will, at Yuletide, in the balmy air,
the rose,
And the people smile when they hear her called "Our Lady
of the Snows."

The wire that brought that message on lightning under the
sea.
Had been too short to bear it to her furthest boundary.
Not by a flippant phrasing of catchword verse or prose,
Can the truth be told of the vast domain of "Our Lady of
the Snows." (Weir *c.* 1897: 2–3)

In the process of defending Canada against "flippant" and erroneous characterisation, Weir slights both England, which he claims "might be lost" in
Canada's woods, and "little Europe," which is "too small for ambition's mark."
The picture of the Briton who "still shivers in east winds," even as Canadians
bask in the warmth of spring, is a further means of portraying Canada's
perceived superiority over those nations that persist in misapprehending the
Canadian scene. Weir acknowledges the existence of the "marts and home," or
cities and towns, in Canada as he tries to correct the false impressions of his
native land as an icy wilderness.

Ironically, Weir was himself the author of several poems that did indeed celebrate Canada's winter landscape, including one entitled "Snowshoeing Song":

Hilloo, hilloo, hilloo, hilloo!
Gather, gather ye men in white;
The winds blow keenly, the moon is bright,
The sparkling snow lies firm and white:
Tie on the shoes, no time to lose,
We must be over the hill to-night.

Hilloo, hilloo, hilloo, hilloo!
Swiftly in single file we go,
The city is soon left far below:
Its countless lights like diamonds glow,
And as we climb we hear the chime
Of church bells stealing o'er the snow. (Weir 1904: 370–371)

Clearly Weir himself falls prey to the desire to celebrate his country's snow-covered hills. Yet even in "Snowshoeing Song" Weir, with his reference to the "city . . . far below" and "Its countless lights like diamonds," presents a vision of Canada as more than just a snowy wasteland. Weir acknowledges its urban component, dispelling the myth that the country remains an untouched wilderness. In his poem "Our Lady of the Snows" Weir further refutes Kipling's frosty imagery, portraying Canada as a vast and diverse land, and making reference to "the ringing blows / Of the axe that reaps a harvest," thereby demonstrating the economic potential of the Canadian landscape. Weir and Bengough, in engaging directly with the writing of Rudyard Kipling, are examples of the efforts made by Canadian writers to construct a vision of the nation that more accurately and more positively represented the reality of its diverse environment.

For the Toronto Packing Company, whose mission it is to promote Canadian fruits and vegetables, there is a vested interest in encouraging a view of Canada as a sunny and productive land. The fact that it largely aims its advertising pamphlet at children further demonstrates the belief that children could play a significant role in changing and shaping the image of, and attitudes towards, the nation. This same pamphlet contains an advertisement for a contest open to the "Young Lady or Gentleman" who writes the best response to the question "Is Canada a Land of Sunshine or Snow?" (Toronto Packing Co. c. 1897c). Other articles in this work demonstrate a clear desire to promote an image of "Sunny Canada." One such piece is a report on "Canada's Comeliest City, Sun-kissed Smiling Toronto" (Willson c. 1897: 12). After claiming that "Toronto is the most beautiful city in North America" (12), the author proceeds to give an account of the wonderful weather with which it seems the inhabitants of this city are blessed:

> The apparently eternal sunshine with which the city is bathed tempts them out of doors. . . . *Apropos* of sunshine, I should like to present Londoners with a few figures dealing with this commodity. I have been told that the total number of sunshiny days last year in London was 61. In Toronto it was 196. The number of hours of sunshine in Milan in the month of March was 293; in Toronto it was 369, rising in June to 470. . . . As to the temperature of the winter of 1896, Londoners would be surprised to hear that in January last not a fleck of snow was to be seen. The Riviera could not do better than that. (Willson *c.* 1897: 13)

This article promotes a very different view of Canada from that which Kipling presents in his poem. It is, however, related to the company's own marketing strategy, which is to bolster an image of Canada as a great supplier of fruits and other food produce. In "The Children at Tea," for instance, the merits of the "Miss Canada" brand of preserved fruit are discussed by a group of children. In an inversion of the familiar picture of life in Canada as difficult and bleak, the young girl Clarice remarks: "Is it not very kind of our Canadian friends to make everything ready for use? Ladies have not to work so hard in Canada as they do in England" ("The Children" 6). This work presents a very different image than the common picture of Canada as a land that is harsh and frozen. Rather, the stories and articles in this unique advertising pamphlet put forth a picture of Canada as an idyllic land with bountiful harvests and great beauty. These competing images of the Canadian landscape and the ongoing attempt on the part of Canadians to counter some of the misconceptions about their country all contribute to a multifaceted representation of the land and its influence on the nation's development.

'The Genius of the Place': Finding Symbolic Meaning and Aesthetic Value in the Canadian Landscape

Sunshine and snow; forest and lake; ocean and prairie; hostility and security— many such images of the Canadian landscape were put forth in art and literature following Confederation, giving rise to a multitude of symbolic representations of the natural environment. In some works of children's literature, such as the adventure tales of Egerton Ryerson Young and J.M. Oxley, Canada's environment signifies a land of opportunity for the thrill-seeker and adventurer who can test his own power in a bid to conquer the unruly wilderness. Other literature celebrates the natural beauty of the landscape, seeing it as something to cherish and preserve. On the other hand, some children's works picture the landscape as dangerous and foreboding. In several tales, the notion that the Canadian environment is one over which man can gain control is presented as a fallacy. These works picture the land itself as a force that can exert an influence over its inhabitants.

According to Frye, there is in Canada "a sense of meditative shock produced by the intrusion of the natural world into the imagination" (Frye 1982: 49). In essence, the natural world inhabits and shapes the Canadian imagination, just as much as the imagination shapes an image of the natural world. This "meditative shock" is apparent in the work of American author Jack London whose writing was popular with children from Canada, Britain, and the United States at the turn of the twentieth century. His stories of the north explore the degree of influence that the Canadian environment can have on the behaviour of those who inhabit or encounter it. London's *The Call of the Wild*, first published in 1903, tells the story of a dog named Buck who is taken suddenly from his comfortable home in the United States to be a sled dog in the Canadian Yukon. Chapter I is entitled "Into the Primitive" and sees Buck pass from "the life of a sated aristocrat" in the south (London 1903: 18), to vastly different circumstances in the Klondike. As Buck travels northward, he passes from a world of civilisation, to one of savage nature. The animal story is a popular genre of children's literature and Buck is one example of an animal protagonist who can appeal to child readers and serve as a didactic device. Buck has many anthropomorphic qualities and the reader has insight into his observations of, and reactions to, the Canadian landscape. It is on his initial journey to Canada, for instance, that Buck experiences his first beating, which has a significant effect on his outlook; "It was his introduction to the reign of primitive law. . . . The facts of life took on a fiercer aspect; and while he faced that aspect uncowed, he faced it with all the latent cunning of his nature aroused" (London 1903: 32–33). The suggestion here is that the Canadian environment helps to elicit the latent "animal" in the anthropomorphic Buck, who is made increasingly familiar with "primitive law" as he enters the frozen north.

London's account of this journey into the heart of the Canadian north helps to construct an image of Canada as a country that is clearly distinct from the American republic. Buck's first owner here is a French Canadian named Perrault, a "little weazened man who spat broken English and many strange and uncouth exclamations" (London 1903: 34). This Canadian figure speaks an unfamiliar language that Buck, who is accustomed to English, does not understand, and is distinctly different from the Americans with whom Buck is familiar. In addition to having to become used to a new type of man, Buck's first experience of the Canadian environment further confuses and bewilders him:

At the first step upon the cold surface, Buck's feet sank into a white mushy something very like mud. He sprang back with a snort. More of this white stuff was falling through the air. He shook himself, but more of it fell upon him. He sniffed it curiously, then licked some up on his tongue. It bit like fire, and the next instant was gone. This puzzled him. He tried it again, with the same result. The onlookers laughed uproariously, and he felt ashamed, he knew not why, for it was his first snow. (London 1903: 39)

Buck's encounter with the Canadian environment (represented in this case as the one of ice and snow celebrated by Kipling) evokes a range of emotions including wonder, curiosity, and the shame experienced by a newcomer whose foreignness is ridiculed. Buck's first day in Canada is filled with experiences similar to the shock he feels at encountering "his first snow." This new environment is vastly different from the southern land he has left behind and he quickly learns that it is full of danger and savagery:

> He had been suddenly jerked from the heart of civilization and flung into the heart of things primordial. No lazy, sun-kissed life was this, with nothing to do but loaf and be bored. . . . All was confusion and action, and every moment life and limb were in peril. There was imperative need to be constantly alert; for these dogs and men . . . were savages, all of them, who knew no law but the law of club and fang. (London 1903: 43)

London establishes a dichotomy between the civilised United States and the "primordial" land of Canada. Both the men and the dogs in Canada are "savages" in what Buck initially perceives as a brutal land, far removed from civilisation.

The Canadian north, it appears, is a potentially corruptive force. His exposure to the "sad and lonely North" changes Buck physically (57), but London further constructs an image of this environment as one that can influence moral character:

> A dainty eater, he found that his mates, finishing first, robbed him of his unfinished ration. . . . To remedy this, he . . . was not above taking what did not belong to him. . . . This first theft marked Buck as fit to survive in the hostile Northland environment. It marked his adaptability, his capacity to adjust himself to changing conditions, the lack of which would have meant swift and terrible death. It marked, further, the decay or going to pieces of his moral nature, a vain thing and a handicap in the ruthless struggle for existence . . . in the Northland, under the law of club and fang, whoso took such things into account was a fool, and in so far as he observed them he would fail to prosper. (London 1903: 58–60)

Echoing the nineteenth-century evolutionary discourse sparked by such figures as Lamarck, Spence, and Darwin, this passage highlights Buck's need to change his behaviour or otherwise face destruction. In this view of nature, morality is a weakness that can jeopardise one's survival. Through the changes undergone by Buck, London presents an aggressive picture of evolution in which the environment, in this case the Canadian one, can alter the character of those who enter it: "Civilized, he could have died for a moral consideration . . . but the completeness of his decivilization was now evidenced by his ability to flee from the defence of a moral consideration and to save his hide" (London 1903: 60). Moral considerations, it appears, are a luxury of the civilised world. In presenting this view, London's children's story lends power to the vision of the Canadian environment as a potentially corruptive force that can bring out the lust for blood in both man and beast: "All that stirring of old instincts which at state periods drives men out from the sounding cities to forest and plain to kill things . . . the blood lust, the joy to kill—all this was Buck's" (London 1903: 90). This is Tennyson's nature "red in tooth and claw," in which man and beast are reduced to their basic instincts.

Yet even as Jack London portrays Canada as lacking the refinement that one can apparently find in the United States, he suggests that this may in itself be a virtue. While Buck's story helps to shape an image of Canada as a wild and mysterious land, it also suggests that the Canadian environment is one that demands hard work and perseverance from its inhabitants. The North may be a tough and brutal place, but it was living in the south that allowed Buck to be lazy and indolent, or to "loaf and be bored." Canadians, it appears, and anyone wishing to survive in the North, can be neither lazy nor complacent. A certain degree of vigour is not only required, but is also inspired, by the environment. For Buck, the primal nature of the Canadian setting awakens something vital within him and he rediscovers instincts of which he was previously unaware. These instincts are essential for survival in an environment where the false trappings of civilisation are out of place. There is no room for the life of a "sated aristocrat" here; all must rely on hard work and perseverance in order to survive.

Although London depicts the Canadian landscape, and those who will survive in it, as "uncivilised," he does not portray civilisation itself as an exclusively positive force. Rather, it too is a corruptive influence. While the primitive law of the north may be savage, it is at least honest, whereas civilisation represents a level of decadence and falsity in the novel. Those who refuse to acknowledge the rules of natural law will fail to survive. In London's story, it is the Americans who purchase Buck's team of dogs whose attempt to conquer the land ultimately destroys them:

> Hal was a youngster of nineteen or twenty, with a big Colt's revolver and a hunting-knife strapped about him on a belt that fairly bristled with cartridges. The belt was the most salient thing about him. It advertised his callowness—a callowness sheer and unutterable. Both men were manifestly out of place, and why such as they should adventure the North is part of the mystery of things that passes understanding. (London 1903: 126)

There is a clear sense in this passage that the Americans are not in their own element and "manifestly out of place" in the Canadian environment. They quickly succumb to the trials they face, revealing their apparent refinement and civilization to be only a façade; "all the amenities and gentleness of the Southland had fallen away from the three people. Shorn of its glamour and romance, Arctic travel became to them a reality too harsh for their manhood and womanhood"

(London 1903: 141). Whereas Buck recognises the demands of the environment, this group fails to acknowledge the power of their surroundings and they quickly fall victim to their own greed and arrogance. They lack respect for the supremacy of the landscape and are incapable of adjusting to this new environment. This failure to adapt spells their demise and the voyage of these Americans ends in disaster as they plunge through the spring ice.

In London's work, Canada, frequently described as a "new" or "young" country in literature of the period, is simultaneously a land that is ancient and "primordial." In the words of Margaret Atwood, "to enter the wilderness is to go backwards in time" (Atwood 1995: 49), and this is Buck's experience. Finding himself in the Canadian wilderness, he remembers "the youth of the breed" (London 1903: 62), and when on "the still cold nights, he pointed his nose at a star and howled long and wolflike, it was his ancestors, dead and dust, pointing nose at star and howling down through the centuries and through him" (62). The chorus of cries from the huskies further links the arctic scene to an ancient and more primitive age: "It was an old song, old as the breed itself—one of the first songs of the younger world in a day when songs were sad" (London 1903: 84). The land is here shown to have a deep connection to the past, and the Canadian landscape London describes arouses "the strain of the primitive" (166), and can leave one "bewildered and spirit-broken by the strange savage environment" (136). Ultimately, it is a land where only the fittest survive, and where "civilised" influences are lost in the face of this struggle: "Mercy did not exist in the primordial life. It was misunderstood for fear, and such misunderstandings made for death. Kill or be killed, eat or be eaten, was the law; and . . . mandate, down out of the depths of Time" (167). The Canadian Arctic reduces the behaviour of both man and beast to its most fundamental level—survival. In London's tale, the Canadian environment symbolises the threat of degeneration, where a lack of civilisation can reduce humanity to its most base level. At the same time, however, London's Canadian north is a place that strips away the falsity, greed, and arrogance of the civilised world. It is a complex and often contradictory representation but, ultimately, London's tale is one that demands respect for the natural environment. In order to survive it and conquer it, one must work within its own set of ancient, natural laws.

London's work presents an image of the Canadian environment that Atwood calls "the malevolent north in Canadian literature." According to Atwood, "popular literature, established early that the North was uncanny, awe-inspiring in an almost religious way, hostile to white men, but alluring; that it would lead you on and do you in; that it would drive you crazy, and, finally, would claim you for its own" (Atwood 1995: 19). While many children's writers celebrate the glories of the Canadian landscape, there is also a sense in much of this work that one must remain wary and on guard in the wilderness. An early example of children's literature that embraces both a desire to conquer the Canadian environment, but also a sense of fear or helplessness in the face of it, is the British novel *The Forest Home; or, Life in the Canadian Wilds* by "Bruin" *circa* 1875.

While this is predominantly a light-hearted tale, the Macdonalds face innumerable dangers and mishaps in their new home where, "in those days, living so near a forest, no one knew what might happen" ("Bruin" *c.* 1875: 5). This description expresses a sense of mystery and dread and suggests that the Canadian wilderness is a place where there is something to fear from the unknown. The otherwise stalwart Mrs. Macdonald confesses that she feels nervous and uneasy when left alone with only the forest surrounding her, and young Ned reports to her that his uncle has his own frightening visions of the potential danger which lurks nearby saying, "he's always in an awful way when he hears you've had to be in the house alone for an hour or two. I believe he suspects half the wolves in the forest of wanting to gobble you up" (7). The family's servant Betsy, meanwhile, repeats her familiar refrain that she will "never feel safe here again" (17). Over the course of the novel, the Canadian landscape poses numerous threats to the settlers in the way of bears, wolves, snakes, and frigid waters. While Jack London's work constructs an image of the Canadian environment that comes to symbolise the frailty of society's ethical and moral codes, "Bruin" employs the landscape to evoke mystery, danger, and adventure.

At the same time as foreign writers such as "Bruin" and London were helping to influence the significance attached to the Canadian landscape, local authors were also contributing to the picture of their environment as a formidable fact of life. Part of the process of developing a true sense of Canadian identity in the nineteenth and early twentieth centuries rested with laying claim to these darker aspects of the nation. In the *"Raise the Flag"* collection of poetry for children "The United Empire Loyalists" further contributes to this image of the Canadian wilderness as a place of darkness and loss. In describing the painful sacrifice made by those who chose to leave their homes in the United States out of loyalty to Great Britain, the poet describes the harsh Canadian wilderness that these migrants faced as they left their established homes:

> They looked their last, and got them out
>   Into the wilderness,
> The stern old wilderness,
>   All dark and rude
>   And unsubdued;
> The savage wilderness,
>   Where wild beasts howled,
>   And Indians prowled. (Hooker 1891: 32–33)

Here the Canadian environment is a physical threat, where one is at risk from prowling Indians and wild beasts. It is a place where the pleasures of civilisation are hard to come by and survival is a struggle:

> The lonely wilderness
> Where social joys must be forgot,

And budding childhood grow untaught;
Where hopeless hunger might assail
Should autumn's promised fruitage fail;
Where sickness, unrestrained by skill,
Might slay their dear ones at its will;
    Where they must lay
    Their dead away,
Without the man of God to say
The sad sweet words, how dear to men,
Of resurrection hope! (Hooker 1891: 33)

Hooker pictures the Canadian environment as a spiritual wilderness that cannot offer the comforts of an established Christian tradition. Yet while the Canadian wilderness serves to symbolise sacrifice, danger and hardship in this poem, the poet goes on to develop the image of this land as one that requires a noble race to populate it.

The Loyalists, the reader is told, are willing to make the sacrifices that the land requires. From a land of despair and savagery, the Canadian wilderness comes to symbolise loyalty, freedom, justice and security:

'Twas British wilderness!
    Where they might sing,
    God save the King!
And live protected by his laws,
And loyally uphold his cause!
    'Twas welcome wilderness!
    Though dark and rude
    And unsubdued
    Though wild beast howled
    And Indians prowled;
For there their sturdy hands,
By hated treasons undefiled,
Might win from the Canadian wild
A home on British lands! (Hooker 1891: 33)

In the course of this poem, the two predominant symbolic representations of the Canadian wilderness—threatening land and place of security—are manifest.

For those familiar with a literary tradition that celebrated the beauty of the picturesque over that of the sublime, there could be no true beauty or salvation in the kind of wild landscape found in Canada. Ruskin, for example, was one critic who felt that the "New Continent" lacked a human tradition, which weakened the beauty and power of its natural surroundings (Wheeler and Whiteley 1992: 216). Yet many Canadian writers did see the "aboriginal forest" as having its own kind of beauty and power. As "The United Empire Loyalists" demonstrates, despite the presence of various malevolent aspects of the Canadian environment in children's literature, there is another side to this picture, including what Margaret Atwood describes as the urge "to see wilderness as salvation" (Atwood 1995: 4). Writers began to explore both the natural beauty and the commercial resources of Canada in the nineteenth century. In *The Captain of the Club*, for instance, the English boy Percy and his Canadian friends are all struck by the beauty of a winter day:

> The boys stood looking at the beauty of the scene for a long time. "It's no wondah to me the Canadians love this country," said Percy at length. "In the whole bweadth of England theah's nothing to compaah to this."
>
> This was a compliment to their native land, and the boys stood each of them fully two inches higher for it.
>
> "Yes," said Jack, and his face glowed with the fire of the young patriot, "you may well say that, Percy. We are proud of Canada. She is a beautiful land, and nature must have been in a gentle humor in laying out the grand lakes and rivers, and the noble forests that surround us." (Williams 1889: 125)

Here the Canadian landscape is a source of pride and a unique element of Canada's national identity that sets it apart from England. Canada's natural surroundings are not simply valuable commodities but are something one can appreciate in their own right. They also have an effect on the very structure of Canadian society, determining patterns of settlement across the country, contributing to provincial and regional diversity, and even influencing the organisation of the federal government.

In addition to the pleasure gleaned from contemplating its sheer natural beauty, the Canadian landscape was a symbol of hope and new beginnings for countless people who uprooted themselves from their ancestral traditions to establish a new life in the young country. The wilderness, which held the potential for prosperity and freedom, was quite literally a beacon of salvation for those seeking to better their lot in life. Northrop Frye refers to the duality of the image of Canada as a land of both salvation and destruction when he writes:

> [M]any nineteenth-century writers in Canada . . . spoke in what could be called . . . the rhetoric of a divided voice. Up above was vigor and optimism and buoyancy and all the other qualities of life in a new land with lots of natural resources to exploit; and underneath were lonely, bitter, brooding visions of cruelty without and despair within. (Frye 1982: 37)

These contrasting visions of the Canadian environment, which symbolised everything from cruelty and despair to promise and salvation, were all voiced in the children's literature of the late nineteenth century. While foreign writers helped contribute to this complex imagery, Canadian writers themselves were coming to terms with the environment and its role in shaping the nation and their own sense of national identity. Ultimately, it was Canada's natural environment that increasingly led the nation to realise just how distinct it was from its European motherland, and from its continental neighbours.

(Mis)adventures in the Wilderness: the Environment as a Playground and a Symbol of National Progress

In 1867, one of the most obvious features that distinguished the new Canadian nation from the British model on which it was founded was the sheer size of its wilderness. It clearly captured the imagination of many foreign authors and there is evidence that many Canadian writers were themselves overwhelmed by their surroundings, the vastness of which "creates something curiously self-alienating" (Frye 1982: 49). Perhaps it was the desire to overcome this sense of alienation and to achieve a sense of belonging to the land that motivated Canadian children's writers to frequently explore a wilderness that was both elusive and omnipresent. In the field of late nineteenth-century children's literature, one of the most popular types of stories set in Canada was the wilderness adventure. With plots involving characters who encounter fun and danger in the outdoors, aspects of this genre permeate almost every category of Canadian children's literature to some degree with many songs, poems, short stories, novels, and works of non-fiction celebrating the natural world. Often very regional in nature, this literature includes tales of Arctic adventure, stories of the Western plains, and most frequently, tales of the northern "bush" or the ubiquitous "backwoods." Its figures run the gamut from French fur traders to East Coast fishermen. A quick glance through any bibliography of children's literature from early Canada will reveal a wealth of titles demonstrating the overwhelming popularity of this genre, including such works as "A Summer Ride in Labrador" (1876), "An Adventure with Wolves: A Canadian Story" (1880) and "An Adventure in a Canadian Swamp" (1882) (Moyles 1995). Some of the better known writers of Canadian-themed adventure stories include Egerton Ryerson Young, R.M. Ballantyne and J.M. Oxley, but many lesser known poets, novelists, and short story writers recognised the potential of Canada's wilderness for providing a setting for adventure stories. There were also non-fiction accounts of life in the Canadian wilderness aimed at children, including John McDougall's autobiographical *Forest, Lake, And Prairie*, which is a recollection of the twenty years he spent living and working as a missionary in Western Canada during the middle of the nineteenth century.

One of the most popular forms of the children's wilderness tale was the animal story, of which London's *The Call of the Wild* is an example. In addition to Canada's physical environment, the animals that share this space have also played a significant role in the development of the country's national identity. To begin with, the nation owes its development in large part to the beaver, whose fur was such a popular commodity in Europe that it sparked the North American fur trade, ultimately leading to the development of the North American continent.[1] In spite of relentless accounts of hunting and animal slaughter in works of both fiction and non-fiction, nineteenth-century children's writers were beginning to take a more benign and sympathetic look at Canada's wildlife, as evidenced in the animal stories of E.T. Seton and Charles G.D. Roberts.

Roberts [1860–1943] was a professor, journalist, novelist, and poet but was most famous for his role in helping to develop the genre of the animal story. Inspired by his own experiences in the Canadian environment, Roberts wrote more than 250 such stories in his time and was a staple in the children's journals and school readers until the middle of the twentieth century. He also authored a book on Canadian history and was a strong promoter of a national literature for Canada, inspiring and supporting many Canadian poets and authors (Boone 2002: 979–980). Roberts' poetry and animal stories contribute to the image of Canada as a land of natural beauty and diversity and foster the view that the landscape is a point of national identification. Roberts also sees the potential for progress and prosperity in the environment. In "The First Ploughing," published in an Ontario school reader, the poet uses the perspective of a crow to observe the promise of this development, which is heralded by the arrival of spring:

> Call the crow from the pine-tree top
> When the April air is still.
> He calls to the farmer hitching his team
> In the farmyard under the hill.
> "Come up," he cries, "come out and come up,
> For the high field's ripe to till.
> Don't wait for word from the dandelion
> Or leave from the daffodil."
>
> . . .
>
> Then dips the coulter and drives the share,
> And the furrows faintly steam.
> The crow drifts furtively down from the pine
> To follow the clanking team.
> The flycatcher tumbles, the high-hole darts
> In the young noon's yellow gleam;
> And wholesome sweet the smell of the sod
> Upturned from its winter's dream. (Roberts 1909: 95–96)

While celebrating nature, Roberts' poem also helps to reflect the development of Canadian society (here represented by the farmer's work) by illustrating that the country is more than simply a wilderness. Roberts' literature celebrates the place of nature in Canadian life.

The celebration of Canada's environment and wildlife in the work of writers such as Seton and Roberts also exhibits an awareness of the frailty of this world. Frye argues that the continuing efforts to cultivate and utilise Canada's natural resources, including the trapping of animals and the felling of trees, have resulted in a sense of guilt in Canadian literature, and that in tales "where people are killed in log jams or on glaciers, there is a lurking sense not only of the indifference of nature to man, but almost of its exasperation with this parasite of humanity that has settled on it" (53). While there may be a sense of remorse over the exploitation of the environment in Canadian literature, there is still an enormous body of children's literature that celebrates the attempt to conquer the wilderness. Although writers such as Seton and Roberts showed an appreciation of the beauty, diversity, and vulnerability of Canada's landscape, stories of hunting and fishing continued to be popular and prolific.

Throughout the nineteenth century, young Canadians consumed countless stories and poems centred on outdoor pursuits such as canoeing, hunting, and fishing. These include "Canadian Camping Song" by Sir James D. Edgar, a lawyer, Liberal MP and onetime speaker of the House of Commons, which celebrates the Canadian landscape as an outdoor playground:

> A white tent pitched by a glassy lake,
> Well under a shady tree,
> Or by rippling rills from the grand old hills,
> Is the summer home for me.
> I fear no blaze of the noontide rays,
> For the woodland glades are mine,
> The fragrant air, and that perfume rare,—
> The odour of forest pine. (Edgar 1909: 91)

Edgar, who expresses a sense of belonging to the environment when he declares, "the woodland glades are mine," dispels the frosty image of Canada, favouring a picture of its summertime beauties. He continues by emphasising the image of the Canadian environment as a playground:

> A cooling plunge at the break of day,
> A paddle, a row, or sail;
> With always a fish for a midday dish,
> And plenty of Adam's ale;
> With rod or gun, or in hammock swung,
> We glide through the pleasant days;
> When darkness falls on our canvas walls,
> We kindle the camp-fire's blaze. (Edgar 1909: 92)

Edgar's poem is a celebration of the fun and adventure offered by the wilderness, employing the familiar images of swimming, canoeing, and sailing. Works such as Edgar's acknowledge some of the beauties of the land and its commercial and recreational uses, but they also present a picture of environmental exploitation. Even "Canadian Camping Song," in keeping with the pattern of the wilderness adventure genre, celebrates the culture of "rod or gun."

Countless birds and animals meet their demise in the pages of juvenile literature in an apparent effort to stress that man can conquer the land, no matter how forbidding. Pursuits like hunting and trapping form the backdrop of many adventure tales set in Canada, which tend to be for a male readership. In these works the land is something to battle, often denoting a young male protagonist's entry into manhood. In the majority of these tales, Canada's wild surroundings are completely devoid of women and envisioned as an ideal locale for "manly" and dangerous pursuits. The wilderness is a place where, despite hardships, mankind will ultimately succeed in its mission to civilise and dominate the natural environment. Many of these tales, therefore, are also tales of Canada's commercial potential and, consequently, chronicle the nation's social and economic development. These wilderness tales include accounts of the fur, lumber, and mining trades of early Canada.

J.M. Oxley's *The Young Woodsman*, set in a lumber camp near the Ottawa River, exhibits an awareness of the relation between the wilderness' commercial potential and the development of the nation. The narrator perceives the exploitation of the environment as having both positive and negative implications, but above all sees it as a central part of the nation's history and a key component of its future development:

> The march of civilization on a great continent means loss as well as gain. The opening up of the country for settlement, the increase and spread of population, the making of the wilderness to blossom as the rose, compel the gradual retreat and disappearance of interesting features that can never be replaced. The buffalo, the beaver, and the elk have gone; the bear, the Indian, and the forest in which they are both most at home, are fast following. (Oxley 1895: 9–10)

This passage acknowledges the degradation of the environment caused by development in Canada, particularly the disappearance of unique species, habitat, and traditional ways of life. Oxley conflates the image of the Indian with woodland creatures such as the bear and the beaver and sees all of these elements of the Canadian scene as features that are inevitably fading. The Indian, "uncivilised" way of life is, like the buffalo and the endless forest, a symbol of the past and has no place in Oxley's vision of the future.

Oxley expresses some concern about this, but he also accepts the need for development in the name of progress and civilisation. The history of the country is congruent with the landscape's history of loss and gain:

> Along the northern border of settlement in Canada there are flourish-
> ing villages and thriving hamlets today where but a few years ago the

verdurous billows of the primeval forest rolled in unbroken grandeur. The history of any one of these villages is the history of all. An open space beside the bank of a stream or the margin of a lake presented itself to the keen eye of the woodranger traversing the trackless waste of forest as a fine site for a lumber camp. In course of time the lumber camp grew into a depot from which other camps, set still further back in the depths of the "limits," are supplied. Then the depot develops into a settlement surrounded by farms; the settlement gathers itself into a village with shops, schools, churches, and hotels; and so the process of growth goes on, the forest ever retreating as the dwellings of man multiply. (Oxley 1895: 10)

Oxley treats the Canadian environment as representative of the development of the nation. The "forest ever retreating" expresses both a sense of man's triumph over nature, and a feeling of regret and loss. Canada's forest is both an element of "unbroken grandeur" and a "trackless waste," and this opposing imagery highlights the complex relation between man and his environment in a new country. The description of the "verdurous billows of the primeval forest" does not simply present an image of the country as a wilderness, but rather helps to shape the author's picture of a country that is in a state of progress and development. The "history" of these "villages and thriving hamlets" is emblematic of the history of the nation: the gradual shaping of a society out of the wilderness.

In addition to representing the historical and economic development of Canada, the lumber camp pictured in Oxley's text is a microcosm of the nation's diverse society. Despite their cultural and ethnic differences, the woodsmen are bound together by their craft. For this group of Canadians, personal identity is closely tied to the natural environment and the role each man plays in helping to utilise this environment for national growth. This profession attracts the young protagonist because his soul is filled "with a longing for adventure and enterprise that no ordinary everyday career could satisfy" (Oxley 1895: 16). Although diverse, these Canadians share certain characteristics such as physical strength, endurance, and a desire for adventure, which complement the tough environment from which they earn their living. While in its very essence the lumber trade is a form of exploitation of the landscape, the woodsmen are not simply in conflict with the environment. Rather, they are figured as an integral part of the natural surroundings, and share a bond with the Canadian environs. As Oxley writes: "A shantyman is never so completely in his element as when the snow lies two feet deep upon the earth's brown breast. An open winter is his bane, Jack Frost his best friend" (73). Central to the depiction of these Canadian workers is the sense that they are in harmony with their environment.

Even with Oxley's picture of Canadians in a symbiotic relationship with nature, however, the degree to which men in the lumber camp are in their element in the wilderness varies. The figure who stands out as most "admirably suited" for the demands of life in a lumber camp is Foreman Johnston (60). He has the strength of body and character needed to thrive in this environment:

> His grave, reserved manner rendered impossible that familiarity which is so apt to breed contempt, while his thorough mastery of all the secrets of woodcraft, his great physical strength, and his absolute fearlessness in the face of any peril, combined to make him a fit master for the strangely-assorted . . . men now under his control. (Oxley 1895: 60)

Johnston deals capably with the demands of the physical environment and those of the human society in which he finds himself. As one of the few characters not distinguished as "French," "Scottish," "Indian" or so forth, he is by default a representation of the quintessential "Canadian." As a clear Canadian figure, the fact that he is the one best suited to the demands of the woodman's life strengthens the image of Canadians as a distinct population whose suitability to the natural environment forms a central part of their identity.

As a young woodsman, Frank has many experiences in the Canadian environment including being chased by a bear, being nearly eaten by wolves, and witnessing the danger and excitement of the spring log run. His adventures serve as a backdrop to the story of his personal development. This juxtaposition of adventure tale and coming-of-age story is also found in the work of Oxley's contemporaries, including Egerton Ryerson Young's *Three Boys in the Wild North Land: Summer*, which traces the experiences of three young male protagonists as they search for adventure in the Canadian wilderness. The experiences of these boys, who have come to northern Canada from England, Scotland, and Ireland to spend a summer with some men from the Hudson's Bay Company, revolve around hunting, fishing, and canoeing. In the novel, the image of Canada as a wild country presents a striking contrast to the European homes the boys have left behind:

> Great indeed was the change which they saw between the populous cities of the home land and this quiet, lonely region upon whose shores they had now landed. . . . The only signs of habitation were the few civilized dwellings, called in courtesy the fort, where dwelt and traded the officers and their families and servants of the great fur-trading company. (Young 1887: 15)

Echoing the writing of such contemporaries as George Gissing and Thomas Hardy, who were concerned with what they saw taking place in the growing cities and urban slums of England, Young sees the open wilderness as offering some advantages over the crowded cities of Europe his characters are happy to leave for a time.[2] Having come out with the express purpose of "wild adventure and exciting sport," the boys are "simply delighted with the absence of the multitude to whom they had been so accustomed" (17). The comparative emptiness of Canada is, apparently, a great benefit in itself.

While highlighting some of the harsh realities of life in Canada's wilderness, Young also expresses a view of the superiority of this life. Clearly, for instance, the European boys have come to Canada in search of recreation and activity because they cannot find these at home. While the novel is a rather protracted account of their subsequent exploitation of this land in a series of hunting, shooting, and fishing expeditions, the boys develop a respect for Canada's advantages. The trappings of their old life are out of place, and inappropriate, in this new land: "At first they found the use of the soft, pliable moccasin very strange, after the heavy boots of civilization, and for a while complained of soreness in the soles of their feet. These, however, soon hardened and then they much preferred the soft Indian shoes to all other" (Young 1887: 57–58). In ways they had not imagined, the environment exerts its power and influence over the boys. They soon learn that this "lonely region" has its own advantages, one of which Young suggests is that the isolation faced by its inhabitants increases the friendliness of the people: "In all new lands there is an open-hearted hospitality that is very delightful, and this was emphatically so in the vast lonely region of the Hudson Bay Territory, where the white men in those days were so few and so widely scattered apart" (11). In addition to this hospitality, the young visitors are pleased with the other experiences Canada provides, which their homeland cannot offer.

While the new society may lack some of the material benefits of Europe, Young expresses the view that Canada's natural environment offers its own rewards, such as the sight of the Northern Lights: "Thus in the beauties of the night visions, and in other sights peculiar to the North, there were compensations for some of the privations incident to being so remote from the blessings of civilization" (142). Young's novel gives further examples of the fact that he was promoting the beauties of their own landscape to young Canadian readers:

> The Dominion of Canada has in it more fresh-water lakes than any other country in the world. Some of them are equal, if not superior, in the clearness and purity of the water, in the distinctness of the reflections cast upon their limpid surface by surrounding hill or forest, and in the wild, weird beauty of their environments, to any of the world's old favourite ones that have been long praised in song and story. They are slowly being discovered and prized, for some of them are as a poet's dream and a painter's vision. (Young 1887: 237)

This posits that Canada compares favourably to other nations and there is evident appreciation of the aesthetic value of this environment in addition to its commercial potential. Young recognises that Canada's "wild, weird beauty" can take its place among the splendours of the earth, but while he reflects on the landscape's aesthetic qualities, he is also aware of its lucrative potential. At one point in the story the boys are told a legend about a cave of silver which, the narrator suggests, has its roots in reality; "By and by, when it is needed, it will be found and utilized, as will the vast resources of other mineral wealth which this great new country has in reserve when the supplies in older lands begin to be exhausted" (Young 1887: 111). This story sees Canada as a supplier of products for other nations, but also as a nation whose future is bright, and to whom others will one day need to turn for vital natural resources. The nation is thereby constructed as a place that will play an important role in the world's industrial and economic development.

The works of Egerton Ryerson Young and J.M. Oxley develop an image of Canada's natural environment as a place of adventure and excitement, as well as a land full of potential for economic and social development. They belong to a genre of literature that envisions the remoter regions of the country as a boundless arena for thrilling experiences. In order for there to be conquest of the environment, however, there must be battle; and if man is victor, it follows that to some extent the environment is an enemy to struggle with and overcome. In Young's *Three Boys in the Wild North Land*, the land itself can create chaos, and impede the process of civilisation. This is reflected in the discipline with which Mr. Ross, an important man in the Hudson's Bay Company and the person who houses the boys during their trip, runs his life:

> Every day had its duties and amusements. Mr. Ross, although the best of masters, was almost a martinet in his affairs, both in the home circle and among those in his employ. This strict disciplinary method is absolutely essential for comfort and success in such a land. If there is a lax method of living and conducting business, soon everything is in confusion and wretchedness. (Young 1887: 183)

The society Mr. Ross has created in this part of the world is apparently under constant threat in a land where one must struggle to preserve order. The achievement of civilisation is a continual struggle with the unruly wilderness.

Many Canadian children's writers promoted the view that a hearty and industrious race of people could succeed in this struggle. Their writing celebrates the natural beauty, power, and potential of Canada's landscape, which was not simply something to battle, but something to rejoice in. One poem that captures this attitude toward the landscape is aptly entitled "Here's to the Land" by William Wye Smith (1827–1917). Smith came to Canada from Scotland at the age of ten. After working as a journalist and teacher and publishing his first book of poetry in 1850, he became a minister (Smith 2003). "Here's to the Land" was included in a Public School poetry book in 1909 and celebrates both the natural beauty and the lucrative potential of the Canadian environment:

> Here's to the Land of the rock and the pine:
> Here's to the Land of the raft and the river!

Here's to the Land where the sunbeams shine,
    And the night that is bright with the North-light's
quiver!

Here's to the Land of the axe and the hoe!
    Here's to the hearties that give them their glory;—
With stroke upon stroke, and with blow upon blow,
    The might of the forest has passed into story!

Here's to the Land with its blanket of snow,—
    To the hero and hunter the welcomest pillow!
Here's to the Land where the stormy winds blow
    Three days ere the mountains can talk to the billow!

In these first three stanzas, Smith evokes some of the beauties of the wilderness including such elements as the Northern Lights and winter snow. He also shapes an image of the people who inhabit this land, picturing those that wield "the axe and the hoe" as hearty people, who have conquered the legendary "might of the forest" and are so at home in their northern environment that they welcome a blanket of snow as their pillow.

The poem goes on to convey other images of a land that is being cultivated and civilised by its inhabitants:

Here's to the buckwheats that smoke on her board;
    Here's to the maple that sweetens their story;
Here's to the scythe that we swing like a sword;
    And here's to the fields where we gather our glory!

Here's to her hills of the moose and the deer;
    Here's to her forests, her fields, and her flowers;
Here's to her homes of unchangeable cheer,
    And the maid 'neath the shade of her own native
        bowers! (Smith 2003: 46)

The last stanza of Smith's poem feminises the Canadian landscape. The nation becomes something of a mother figure as "her" forests, fields, and flowers are celebrated, and the picture of the smoking buckwheats creates an image of domesticity. While many Canadian wilderness tales centre exclusively on male characters, the landscape itself is frequently feminised, resulting in a feeling that Canada is a Motherland for its native inhabitants. From the maple that has been harnessed for its syrup to the fields from which a harvest is reaped, the Canadian landscape is pictured as one that can be dominated, but also as one that has nurturing qualities for its citizens. Furthermore, it is a landscape in which the Canadian people are truly at home in their "own native bowers."

In the July 1897, edition of *Home and Youth*, the poem "The Glories of Canada" further expresses the landscape's duality as a thing of wild beauty and a sign of potential for economic growth. While the poet praises its natural splendour, he also sees the land's potential for trade and industry and, consequently, national progress:

> The grand old woods of Canada!
> How cool and dim below
> The shade of their sweet rustling leaves!
> Swift-changing webs the sunlight weaves
> Where ferns and mosses grow.
>
> The giant trees of Canada!
> Dark pine and birch drooped low;
> The stately elm, the maple tall,
> The sturdy beech, I love them all
> And well their forms I know.
>
> The forest wealth of Canada!
> The choppers' blows resound
> Thro' the crisp air, while cold and still
> The snow's deep cloak o'er vale and hill,
> Lies white upon the ground.
>
> The sparkling streams of Canada!
> That 'neath cold shadows pass,
> That wind, where sleek-fed cattle sleep,
> Thro' verdant meadows, ankle-deep
> In clover bloom and grass.
>
> The crystal streams of Canada!
> Deep in whose murmuring tide,
> From pebbly caverns, dimly seen
> 'Neath leafy shades of living green,
> Grey trout and salmon glide.
>
> The beauteous lakes of Canada!
> With loving eyes I see
> Their waters, stretched in endless chain
> By fair St. Lawrence to the main,
> As ocean, wild and free.
>
> Where white sails gleam o'er Huron's wake,
> Or fade with dying day.
> Fond memories in my heart awake,
> Of home's dear dwelling by the lake,
> Like sunshine passed away.
>
> The prairies vast of Canada!
> Where sun sinks to the earth,

In setting, whispering warm good-night
To myriad flowers, whose blushes bright
Will hail the morrow's birth.

The prairie wealth of Canada!
Whose dark, abundant soil,
Unfurrowed yet, awaits the plow:
Who sows shall have true promise now
Of rich reward for toil.

What tho' the winter wind blows keen
When daylight darkly wanes!
A strong, true heart is hard to chill;
When seen afar, the home light still,
Shines bright across the plains.

The robust life of Canada
In cheery homes I see!
Tho' gold nor jewels fill the hand,
'Tis Nature's self has blessed the land,
Abundant, fair and free. (*Home and Youth* 1897b: 17)

Canada, this poet tells the child reader, is a land "blessed" by nature. The "giant trees of Canada" are admired both for their beauty and for the "forest wealth" they provide. Even the romantic picture of the winter wind blowing across the vast and imposing prairies is accompanied by the mercenary promise of "rich reward for toil" for those who can exploit its natural endowments.

Numerous children's poems and stories popular in the nineteenth and early twentieth centuries are essentially tales of the wilderness. While many of these envision this as a place of fun and adventure, some writers express concern over the loss of this pristine wilderness, seeing its existence as an essential part of the Canadian experience. At the same time, however, writers recognise the need to cultivate this landscape in order for the Canadian nation to grow and develop. These works help to construct a national identity in which the environment's natural resources come to represent all of Canada's future potential. While some lament the loss of the wilderness, others celebrate this as evidence of the steady progress of Canadian civilisation.

Many elements of the Canadian landscape were truly distinct from both Britain and America, and were an important factor in the shaping of a uniquely Canadian sense of identity. On the one hand, the environment was seen to have a spirit of its own and was pictured as a vast territory full of mystery, adventure, and symbolic meaning, whose economic rewards were not easy to come by. On the other, the environment was viewed in pragmatic terms and seen as full of possibilities for economic development and exploitation. These two major perceptions of the environment—the conquerable versus the unconquerable—

were both accurate to some degree and were both expressed in the children's literature of the day.

The influence of these stories about the Canadian landscape on young Canadians is evident in the 1893 collection of tales written by Canadian school children entitled *Sea, Forest and Prairie: Being Stories of Life and Adventure in Canada Past and Present.* In addition to the title of the collection itself, which emphasises the role of the natural environment in the Canadian experience, the short stories by girls and boys are further evidence of the prevalence of wilderness tales among literature for the young. With titles such as "In the Snow," "Left on the Prairie in a Blizzard," and "Two Nights in the Bush," the stories in this collection demonstrate the influence of the environment and the impact of the popular wilderness adventure tale on young readers. The multitude of images associated with the Canadian environment and incorporated in literature further reflects the impact that landscape had on the national psyche. While at times these representations are contradictory, their combined influence helped to construct a sense of the Canadian identity as one that is inextricably bound up with the natural world. Whether viewed as hostile or rejuvenating, this environment was promoted in the children's literature of the day as a unique feature of the nation. In order to survive in the face of overwhelming natural elements, Canadians, it was argued, must be a people fundamentally suited to the demands of this environment. As such, the images of the Canadian environment in children's literature helped to construct a vision of a Canadian race that is industrious, productive, brave, and, perhaps most importantly, willing to adapt and to accept change. Aided in large part by the children's writing from the late nineteenth and early twentieth centuries, the natural environment came to be envisioned as an integral part of the Canadian national identity.

Conclusion

It would be difficult to argue that any nation, no matter how ancient, has a single, fixed identity to which all of its citizens subscribe. Nations are complex and ever-changing entities that are not always easily defined. Yet this fact has not precluded a continuing effort to establish and lay claim to national identities, regardless of how imperfect or inadequate they may be. Many of the criteria often used to define a group of people who inhabit a particular territory as a nation, including common ancestry, language, or culture, are insufficient. In the case of nineteenth-century Canada, for instance, much of the population could not claim common descent or language, yet there were stirrings of a national consciousness. Instead, the "nation" appears to be an organising principle that seeks to order society around a set of core values and beliefs.

Laying claim to a national identity can be an important means of promoting these ideals and of fostering a sense of community and common purpose. Given the inherent arbitrariness and instability of nations, a sense of common identity can help achieve a feeling of coherence and unity in an otherwise diverse body of people. National bonds can also be formed through the development of a common culture. Benedict Anderson acknowledges the process of actively constructing national identities and the various mechanisms employed in this quest:

> [s]o often in the "nation-building" policies of the new states one sees both a genuine, popular nationalist enthusiasm and a systematic, even Machiavellian, instilling of nationalist ideology through mass media, the educational system, administrative regulations, and so forth. . . . One can thus think of many of these nations as projects the achievement of which is still in progress. (Anderson 1983: 113–114)

173

Anderson acknowledges both the natural, organic growth of nationalist sentiment and the "systematic" process by which national spirit is fostered. One important addition to the list of tools that aid the spread of both "genuine" and "systematic" nationalist ideology is literature. Literature is, after all, an important means by which individuals and communities express and share the ideas and values they hold dear.

While Anderson is referring to a modern process of nation-building, the scenario he describes is similar to the reality of Canada in the years following Confederation. In the days before modern media and communication technologies, literature and the educational system were the two most powerful means by which this process could be aided, both consciously and unconsciously. By citing the role of the educational system in the process of nation-building Anderson underscores the importance placed on instilling national loyalty and ideology in children. Literature itself is an important educational device and, given the impressionable nature of young children, children's literature is a particularly powerful tool for inscribing a set of ideals or beliefs in readers. As such, this literature is an important means by which a sense of belonging to a larger national community can be achieved. As children's literature scholar Margaret Meek observes:

> If we agree that literature offers and encourages a continuing scrutiny of "who we think we are", we have to emphasise the part that children's literature plays in the development of children's understanding of both belonging (being one of us) and differentiation (being other). In the outside world, children adopt adult attitudes that their books either confirm or challenge. (Meek 2001: x)

Children's literature played a role in this process of developing an understanding of belonging and differentiation among young Canadians in the crucial decades following Confederation. The overt imperialism of the era has caused many scholars to overlook these efforts to articulate Canada's uniqueness, but there is a wealth of material that demonstrates just how widespread this process of self-definition was. Anglophone writers both consciously and inadvertently helped to shape the debates surrounding the nation's sense of identity that emerged following 1867. The multi-faceted and sometimes competing ideologies presented in this children's literature all contributed to the construction of new notions of what it meant to be Canadian. It was a complex identity shaped by the views of Canadians, Americans, and Europeans alike.

In her discussion of the use of the child figure in Canadian writing, literary critic Margery Fee writes that for nineteenth-century Canadian children's writer Charles G.D. Roberts "the link between the child and the nation . . . was a natural, even stereotyped one" (Fee 1980: 46). According to Fee, this assumption that there is a "connection between child and nation" continues to be used by writers "to make a nationalist point" (46). Outlining the important symbolism embodied in the figure of the child since the time of Rousseau,[1] Fee draws a connection between the child in literature and the issue of Canadian national identity:

> [A]fter Rousseau the child was commonly used as a symbol of nature, imagination, sensibility and innocence, and frequently, by the best writers, as a "symbol of the greatest significance for the subjective investigation of the Self". Although many Canadian writers used the child in precisely these ways, it is hardly surprising that many more of them link an image so suitable to a discussion of individual identity with that great Canadian obsession, the search for national identity. Certainly Rousseau felt that if one's goal was to inculcate patriotism one began with the child. (Fee 1980: 46)

While Fee is concerned with the image of the child in literature, her argument can be applied to children's literature itself. Early Canadian writers clearly saw a link between children and the relative "infancy" of the nation and many endorsed the view that the best way to inspire patriotism was to begin by instilling it in children. There was an active link between children, literature, and the search for national identity in post-Confederation Canada.

The process of self-definition can also be one of exclusion and as such, nationalism has come under fierce criticism. Many of the constructions of early Canadian identity are competing and contradictory, reflecting a complex process of inclusion and exclusion. For some early Anglophone writers, loyalty to the Empire was a cornerstone of the Canadian identity. For others, annexation with the United States was viewed as the ideal path for the nation to follow. Yet another view held that Canada's identity was bound up with the image of a strong and independent nation, ruled neither by Britain nor by the interests of the United States. Together, these oft-competing strains formed part of a steady search for an identity that would suit the needs of an ever-changing and developing new country.

While some of the early expressions of national identity in Anglophone Canada had a racial or ethnic basis, others recognised the inherent need for a spirit that would help unify a country founded on a biracial, bilingual system. Amid the struggles to articulate a sense of what being Canadian meant, writers were searching for an identity that could incorporate this type of diversity and avoid some of the negative consequences associated with nationalism. In his essay "Canadian Nationalism" from 1911, John Boyd writes:

> If nationalism meant a campaign for the dominance of any race or creed to the detriment of other races or creeds in the Dominion; if nationalism meant an appeal to racial, religious or sectional prejudice of any kind; if nationalism meant exclusive privileges for any section ... then I do not believe that such nationalism could be countenanced. ... But if

nationalism means . . . the search for a common ground for all Canadians, the development of all Canadian forces, mental, moral and material; if nationalism means the union of all Canadians, whether French speaking or English speaking, for the upbuilding of our common country and the development of its vast resources; if nationalism means the fullest freedom for all races and for all creeds and respect for the guaranteed rights of all minorities; if nationalism means the honest administration of public affairs and the punishment of betrayers of the public trust; if nationalism means that we should jealously guard the autonomy won for us by the struggles of our forefathers, if nationalism means pride in the name Canadian, the greatness of our country and the glorious destiny that awaits it; if nationalism, I say, means all these, then, sir, I fail to see how the declaration, the support or the triumph of such principles can cause alarm to any patriotic Canadian or be a menace to our free institutions. (Boyd 1911: 8–9)

Boyd articulates a view of a Canadian nationalism based not on language or race, but on common ideals and values.

In the children's literature read by Canadian children between Confederation and the early years of the twentieth century, one can see differing opinions as to what some of these national values are. For some writers, these ideals are bound up with notions of race and ethnicity. Boyd for instance, though not a children's writer, highlights the complexity of these issues. While he argues for an inclusive form of nationalism he also writes:

We see a foreign element . . . pouring into our country by the thousands, lowering the wage value of our working classes and sowing on the free soil of this country the seeds of crime and disease, of irreligion and of the destructive doctrines of revolutionary Europe. If this continues it is only a question of time when we, English speaking and French speaking Canadians, will be at the mercy of the foreign element. . . . Is it not time, sir, that instead of quarrelling amongst ourselves and wasting our energies on minor differences we should unite our forces and stand shoulder to shoulder to guard that birthright for which our forefathers fought and died? We shall welcome all people of good will to our broad Dominion but they must understand that freedom is not license and that they must conform to our free institutions and our national ideals. (Boyd 1911: 11)

While Boyd pleads for Canada to move on from the bitter and costly divisions between French and English Canadians, his notion of racial harmony and inclusiveness still appears limited to members of these two groups.

While some writing promotes the view of Canadians as a hearty northern race founded upon Anglo-Saxon stock, much of it exhibits an awareness of the true diversity of the country. The two clearest representations of this diversity are the figures of the French Canadian and the Indian. The often conflicting portrayal of these characters reflects the ongoing process of negotiating issues of race, language, religion, and culture in post-Confederation Canada. It is perhaps this process of negotiation, of reconciling notions of race and national identity, which most clearly articulates the means by which national identity can be constructed and developed in accordance with changing needs and attitudes.

While the question of what kind of future may result from these changes is one of central concern, the past is also recognised as an important locator of national character. The fascination with Canada's past was shared by British and American authors whose interpretations of Canadian history helped to colour the nation's own view of itself. By choosing Canadian history as a subject and by claiming this past as their own, Canadian children's writers engage directly in the process of answering the questions; "Who are we?" "Where do we come from?" and, by extension, "Where are we going?" By examining the past, by creating their own blend of historical fact and fiction, these writers engage in the process of envisioning Canada as a country with a unique history of which to be proud. What is more, they see the events of the past as part of a long journey of progress.

Throughout the process of attempting to articulate a sense of national identity, these children's writers exhibit a set of some commonly-held notions of what Canada and its inhabitants represent. The most obvious of these is the role of the natural environment. Whether seen as daunting or uplifting, as friend or foe, it is an inescapable aspect of the Canadian reality and a signifier of Canada's uniqueness. It also comes to embody traits held to be part of the Canadian character including strength, resourcefulness, and perseverance. There is a prevailing image of Canada as a land of natural beauty and rich resources waiting to be developed, and a place that represents freedom, opportunity, and independence.

Of course, such an ideal view of a nation is difficult to live up to. Freedom is tempered by government policy, diversity is not uniformly embraced, and certain linguistic and ethnic groups are excluded from the mainstream. The concepts of national identity put forth in the Anglophone children's literature examined here contain their share of both the very positive and the deeply negative. Regardless of this mix of elements, this process of coming to terms with what makes Canada unique reveals that this period was a time of widespread belief in the nation's potential. Yet the aim of much of this children's literature was not just to celebrate this potential, but to ensure it would be fulfilled. While rejoicing in Canada's glories, this literature also demonstrates an implicit understanding that this potential is under threat. Following Confederation, internal divisions, geographical barriers, the threat of domination by Britain, and the fear of annexation by the United States all endangered Canada's development. It is for these reasons that many writers felt a need to foster a spirit of national unity and loyalty and undertook to define what it actually meant to be Canadian. The power of literature to influence young readers was not lost on writers anxious to promote their own view of the national dream, and was furthered even by those who were not consciously trying to promote a specific agenda.

The study of the relationship between children's literature and issues of nationalism and national identity in Canada is one that is worthy of further study. Contrary to what some critics have argued, the decades following Confederation were not simply ones in which Anglophone Canada bowed to the call of Empire. While there is a strong imperialistic tone to much of the country's children's literature, these were important years for fostering a spirit of independence and self-definition. The process of helping to construct and influence a sense of national identity did not end, however, in the early twentieth century. One important question to address, for instance, if we are to have a true picture of the development of nationalist sentiment and ideology in Canada, is the degree of influence the First World War had on this process. How did children's literature in Canada deal with the events of this conflict? What impact did debates over conscription and the resulting friction between Francophone and Anglophone Canadians have on the representation of the Canadian identity in Anglophone literature for children? Did Canada's participation in the war alter the perception of it as a nation of peace? These and other questions need to be answered in order to take full measure of the role played by children's literature in shaping Canadian national identity.

The Canadian identity is not static nor is it easily defined, yet it is clear that the process of attempting to articulate it has its roots in the nation's earliest days. The stirrings of a national consciousness and the desire to foster a sense of common unity and purpose were an important part of the cultural life of early Canada. Canada's national identity remains one fraught with complexities, contradictions, and uncertainties and the decades following Confederation sowed the seeds of some of these tensions. While direct ties to Britain have decreased steadily since the start of the twentieth century, other issues that were of concern in that era remain. There is a continuing struggle to find a balance between the country's two main linguistic groups, there is ongoing adjustment to the ever-changing cultural face of the nation, and there is a lingering fear of absorption by the United States, be it economic, geographic, or cultural. These struggles are not, as some would argue, a sign of the nation's failure to fulfil its potential but are rather an inherent part of Canada's distinctiveness. They represent a continuation of some of the national ambitions that were being encouraged in those who laid the ground for modern Canadian society: namely, the children of the late nineteenth and early twentieth centuries.

Notes

Introduction

1   The Canada First Movement, active between 1868 and 1874, aimed to promote national spirit and greater independence for Canada including a much larger role in the decision-making process of the Empire. Two important figures associated with this movement were Goldwin Smith and Charles Mair. For further reading on W.A. Foster and the Canada First Movement see A.G. Bailey's *Culture and Nationality*, pages 153–176.

2   I gathered the majority of this material from archival sources. Special collections now house many early works of Canadiana that are no longer in print. Canada's largest collection of children's literature is in the Osborne Collection of Early Children's Books at the Toronto Public Library. Its Canadiana Collection includes a selection of early children's books in English whose subject matter relates to Canada, or whose writers and publishers have an association with Canada. Another major source of material for this study is the Canadian Institute for Historical Microreproductions, which includes over 75,000 catalogued items published before 1901 on microfiche, including Canadian leaflets, books, pamphlets, posters, and magazines. Wherever possible I have provided detail as to the authorship or publication history of my chosen texts, but it has not always been possible to provide the details for the more obscure texts. While the popularity of these works varied, and some may be more familiar to today's public than others, they represent a comprehensive sampling of the children's literature that helped to shape Canada's early sense of national identity.

Chapter 1

1   For evidence of the extent to which children's literature was published in Canada prior to Confederation, see Bernard Amtmann's *Early Canadian Children's Books 1763–1840. A Bibliographical Investigation into the Nature and Extent of Early Canadian Children's Books and Books for Young People*

and Amtmann's *A Bibliography of Canadian Children's Books and Books for Young People 1841–1867.*

2 Henty and Kingston are two prolific children's writers among many British authors who wrote on Canadian topics during the nineteenth and early twentieth centuries. Among his many works set in North America, G.A. Henty published the popular *With Wolfe in Canada,* which outlines the glorious victory of British forces over the French in North America. W.H.G. Kingston published several stories concerning Canada, including *Rob Nixon, the Old White Trapper: A Tale of Central British North America.*

3 The continuing movement of population from Canada to the United States in the early twentieth century was of concern to many who thought it might lead to eventual political annexation. See Chapter 4 for a further discussion of this question of the perceived American threat.

Chapter 2

1 In protest of Canada's purchase of territory from the Hudson's Bay Company in order to begin settlement of the West, the Métis of the Red River settlement formed a provisional government, led by Louis Riel, and succeeded in securing some rights and protection through the Manitoba Act, which saw the creation of the new province of Manitoba in 1870. Riel, however, was exiled for his part in the murder of Thomas Scott, a Protestant Canadian and an opponent of Riel's provisional government who was executed by firing squad. After new grievances arose between the Métis population and the federal government in 1884, Riel returned to Canada and led a new uprising. Riel was hanged for high treason on 16 November 1885, a decision which still sparks controversy. For an insightful examination of Riel and his legacy, see J.M. Bumsted (1993) "The West and Louis Riel."

Chapter 3

1 In 1900, Britain accounted for 85 per cent of the foreign capital in Canada, and as late as 1920 the majority of such investment was still held by the United Kingdom (Pomfret 1981: 62). The United States and Great Britain have traditionally dominated foreign ownership of Canadian industry. In the twentieth century, however, Britain's dominance gave way to the U.S. While in 1900 Britain represented 85 per cent of foreign capital and the U.S. just 14 per cent, by 1960 these figures had done almost a complete reverse, with the U.K. representing only 15 per cent of foreign capital in Canada and the United States an overwhelming 75 per cent (Pomfret 1981: 62).

2 As McCormack illustrates, Canadian attitudes towards English immigrants were not wholly positive, and were particularly negative during times of economic crisis when 'No English Need Apply' notices were posted and

Canadians resented the thought of these new arrivals taking precious jobs. There was also a strong feeling that Canada should not become the "dumping ground" for the social problems of English cities and their pauper populations. In 1908 70 per cent of the people deported from Canada were returned to the British Isles (McCormack 1993: 335).

3 No information is available on Williams, who is not to be confused with Valentine Williams (1883–1946), the author of detective fiction. This may be a pseudonym, as a fifteenth edition of this novel was published under the names of Barbara Williams and Rev. John Talbot Smith. While Smith was a known Catholic clergyman and editor, I have not been able to find any further information on his connection to this text, or any details on either Barbara or Valentine Williams.

Chapter 4

1 For a thorough examination of the development of the book trade in Canada and the importance of nineteenth-century copyright laws, see George L. Parker's *The Beginnings of the Book Trade in Canada.*

2 For a more detailed discussion of MacTavish's Story, see Galway, Elizabeth (2005) "'A Young Canadian's Manly Stand'; Canadian Nationalism and Anti-American Sentiment in Margaret MacTavish's Short Story." Short Story: *Tripping Across the 49th Parallel.* 13: 1: 45–59.

Chapter 5

1 For the purposes of this discussion I use the term "Indian" in accordance with its usage in the literature of the nineteenth and early twentieth centuries.

2 While Laurier's election indicates a certain level of respect for and acceptance of French Canadians, some have argued that this election in fact inspired greater antagonism among some English Canadians. Writing in 1902 Byron Nicholson speculates that discord among the two groups "appears to be largely traceable . . . to the fact that ever since the federal elections of 1896 Canada has had a French-Canadian as Prime Minister, which is not very grateful to a certain class of people who are proud . . . of their British origin" (Nicholson: 2).

3 Legal recognition of the term "Canadian citizenship" did not occur until The Canadian Citizenship Act of 1946. Prior to that time, Canadians were British subjects. Canada became the first Commonwealth country to establish its own citizenship that was separate from that of Britain (CIC 2003). Prefontaine's use of the term in this passage, however, indicates that there was a sense of Canadian citizenship at the turn of the twentieth century, even though the term would not be legally recognised until after the Second World War.

Chapter 6

1   William Briggs (1836–1922) was a major figure in the field of children's literature publishing in nineteenth-century Canada, and he published many of the works examined in this study. An ordained Methodist minister, Briggs was born in Ireland and came to Canada in 1859. In 1879, he was appointed as Book Steward at the Methodist Book and Publishing House, and quickly became an astute and forward-thinking bookman, transforming the publishing house into "the largest printing and publishing house in Canada by the early 1890s" (Parker 1985: 209). Until 1894, the books published by this denominational publisher consisted of "biographies of missionaries, local histories, some volumes of poetry, and uplifting fiction" (Parker 1985: 236). Then Briggs made two decisions "which characterized the new directions of Canadian publishing" (Parker 1985: 236). He "persuaded the Methodist Church to let him expand the trade book division by publishing more history and fiction" and he "turned the firm into the Canadian agency of many New York and London houses" which included the Religious Tract Society, Thomas Nelson and Blackie (Parker 1985: 236). From this point onward Briggs' Toronto-based publishing business was responsible for supplying the bulk of children's literature to young Canadian readers.

Chapter 7

1   For an extended version of some discussions in this chapter see Galway, Elizabeth. "Fact, Fiction, and the Tradition of Historical Narratives in Nineteenth-Century Canadian Children's Literature." *Canadian Children's Literature* 27:2 (2001): 20–32. Material from this article has been included here with the permission of *CCL*.

2   The story of Dollard Des Ormeaux has received much literary treatment. Scholars continue to question various accounts of these events, including the portrayal of this Frenchmen and his allies as saviours of New France, which was an image discredited by historians in the 1920s and 1930s (Kennedy). A work that examines the many variations of this story is Patrice Groulx's *Pièges de la Mémoire: Dollard des Ormeaux, les Amérindiens et Nous* (Wien).

3   This article refers to Lizars' 1896 publication, *In the Days of the Canada Company, 1825–1850*, which tells the life of William "Tiger" Dunlop (New "Lizars"). Dunlop, a Scottish army surgeon, was sent to Upper Canada during the War of 1812, where he eventually became a member of the legislature and became a well known figure, publishing several autobiographical accounts of his experiences in India and in Canada during the War of 1812 (New "Dunlop").

Chapter 8

1   For a detailed account of the far-reaching influence of the fur trade on Canada's development, see Harold Innis' *The Fur Trade in Canada: An Introduction To Canadian Economic History.*

2   George Gissing (1857–1903) was concerned with the condition of the working poor in London, the subject of several of his novels. In *The Nether World* (1889), Gissing explores the effect of crowded and polluted conditions on urban workers raised in what he terms "The putrid soil of that nether world" (8). Gissing's concerns and Thomas Hardy's fears about the disappearance of England's pastoral tradition, are echoed in Egerton Ryerson Young's portrayal of the Canadian wilderness as a place for rejuvenation and freedom from Britain's urban conditions.

Conclusion

1   Jean Jacques Rousseau (1712–1778) is widely regarded as having a great influence on changing attitudes towards children and childhood education. Rousseau's 1762 work *Émile* explores the notion of the child as an embodiment of naturalness and simplicity with the potential to achieve, by means of the correct educational method, great wisdom and understanding (Townsend 1976: 40–41).

Selected Bibliography

Primary Sources

Anon. (1911) *Present Conditions in Canada: Remain British Speak English.* Quebec: n.p.

Ballantyne, R.M. (1856) *Snowflakes and Sunbeams; or, The Young Fur Traders. A Tale of the Far North.* London: Nelson. Reprinted as *The Young Fur Traders.* London: Octopus, 1979.

Bender, Prosper (1886) "The Disintegration of Canada." [no title]. Boston: February: 144–52.

Bengough, J.W. (1901) "A Boy of Early Canada." *Canadian Boy* May: 10–11.

—— "Canada to Kipling." *The Toronto Packing Co.* Advertisement. [*c.* 1897]: 1.

Bourinot, Sir John (1900) "Literature and Art in Canada." *The Anglo-American Magazine.* February: 99–110.

Boyd, John (1911) *Canadian Nationalism.* Montreal: n.p.

"Bruin." (*c.* 1875) *The Forest Home; or, Life in the Canadian Wilds.* London: "Our Young Folks" Shilling Story Books, James Henderson.

Bryce, Reverend Dr. (1884) *"Our Indians." Delivered Before the Y.M.C.A., Winnipeg, December 1st, 1884.* Winnipeg: Manitoba Free Press.

Burpee, Lawrence J. (1901) *Canadian Novels and Novelists.* N.p.: n.p..

Cameron, Rev. Charles J., ed. (1893) *Sea, Forest and Prairie: Being Stories of Life and Adventure in Canada Past and Present, By Boys and Girls in Canada's Schools.* Montreal: Dougall and Son.

Campbell, Wilfred (1909) "Indian Summer." *Public School Poetry Book Part II.* Eds J.F. White and W.J. Sykes. Morang's Literature Series. Toronto: Morang: 33.

Canada Boy (1901) "Yes, We Are Succeeding." *Canadian Boy* May: 38.

—— (1902a) "In Memoriam." *Canadian Boy* Aug.: 47.

—— (1902b) "Play the Game." *Canadian Boy* Aug.: 43.

—— (1902c) "Why Go to the United States?" *Canadian Boy* Aug.: 34.

"Canuck" (1905) *Pen Pictures of Early Pioneer Life in Upper Canada.* Toronto: William Briggs.

Carroll, Lewis (1865) *Alice's Adventures in Wonderland and Through the Looking Glass.* Oxford: Oxford World's Classics, Oxford University Press.

Charlton, Margaret Ridley and Caroline Augusta Fraser (1892) *A Wonder Web of Stories.* Montreal: F.E. Grafton & Sons.

Cockin, H.C. (1891) "This Fair Canadian Land." *"Raise the Flag" and Other Patriotic Canadian Songs and Poems.* Toronto: Rose Publishing: 9.

Cox, Palmer (1894) "The Brownies in Canada." *The Brownies Around the World.* New York: Century Co.: 1–18.

Crockewit, John H. (1906) "Life in the Canadian North-West." *The Boy's Own Annual.* London: "Boy's Own Paper" Office: 496.

De Mille, James (1874) *The Lily and the Cross: A Tale of Acadia.* Boston: Lee and Shepard.

Denison, Muriel (1937) *Susannah of the Yukon.* New York: Dodd.

Drummond, William Henry (1898) "Madeleine Verchères." *"Phil-o-rum's Canoe" and "Madeleine Verchères."* New York: G.P. Putnam's Sons: 6–12.

Edgar, Sir James D. (1909) "Canadian Camping Song." *Public School Poetry Book Part II.* Eds J.F. White and W.J. Sykes. Morang's Literature Series. Toronto: Morang: 91–2.

Everett-Green, E. (1899) *French and English: A Story of the Struggle in America.* London: Nelson.

Foster, W.A. (1871) *Canada First; or, Our New Nationality; An Address.* Toronto: Adam, Stevenson & Co.

Geeson, Jean Earle (1906) *The Old Fort at Toronto 1793–1906.* Toronto.

Geikie, John C., ed. (1865) *Life in the Woods: A Boy's Narrative of the Adventures of a Settler's Family in Canada.* 1864. Boston: Crosby and Ainsworth.

Gissing, George (1889) *The Nether World.* Oxford: Oxford World's Classics, Oxford University Press, 1992.

Godfrey, H.H. (1897) "The Land of the Maple." *Home and Youth* August: 8–9.

Half Hours in the Wide West Over Mountains, Rivers, and Prairies (1883) The Half Hour Library of Travel, Nature and Science for Young Readers. London: Isbister.

Harper's Young People (1879–1899) New York.

Henty, G.A. [1887?] *With Wolfe in Canada.* Glasgow: Blackie.

H.M.H. (1897) "Early Days in Canada." *Home and Youth* Sept.: 15.

Home and Youth (1897a) "Canada's Greatness." *Home and Youth* Sept.: 1–2.

—— (1897b) "The Glories of Canada." *Home and Youth* July: 17.

—— (1897c) "The Point of the Pen; The Dominion School History." *Home and Youth* Aug.: 1–3.

Hooker, Le Roy (1891) "The United Empire Loyalists." *"Raise the Flag" and Other Patriotic Canadian Songs and Poems.* Toronto: Rose Publishing: 31–4.

Hughes, James L. (1893) "Canada to England." *Pleasant Hours* 1 July: 104.

Hughes, Thomas (1857) *Tom Brown's Schooldays.* London: Puffin, Penguin Books, 1994.

Huntingdon, Aimee (1891) "Brothers Awake!" *"Raise the Flag" and Other Patriotic Canadian Songs and Poems.* Toronto: Rose Publishing: 21.

Johnson, E. Pauline (Tekahionwake) (1892) "A Strong Race Opinion: On the Indian Girl in Modern Fiction." *Toronto Sunday [Globe]* 11 May: 1.

—— (1895) "The Six Nations." *Buckskin and Broadcloth: A Celebration of E. Pauline Johnson–Tekahionwake 1861–1913.* Sheila M.F. Johnston. Toronto: Natural Heritage, 1997: 24–6.

—— (1904) "The Song My Paddle Sings." *A Treasury of Canadian Verse.* 2nd ed. Ed. Theodore H. Rand. Toronto: Henry Frowde: 155–6.

—— (1907) "Little Wolf-Willow." *Boys' World* 7 Dec.: 1–6.

Johnston, Sheila M. F. (1997) "Canadian Born." *Buckskin and Broadcloth: A Celebration of E. Pauline Johnson–Tekahionwake 1861–1913.* Toronto: Natural Heritage: 164.

Kingston, W.H.G. (1890) *Snow-Shoes and Canoes; or, The Early Days of a Fur-Trader in the Hudson's Bay Territory.* London: Sampson Low, Marston & Co..

Kipling, Rudyard (1897) "Our Lady of the Snows." *Whitewolf Site Index.* 12 June 2003 http://whitewolf.newcastle.edu.au/words/authors/K/KiplingRudyard/verse/p1/ourladysnows.html.

—— (1906) *Puck of Pook's Hill.* London: Popular Classics, Penguin Books, 1994.

London, Jack (1903) *The Call of the Wild.* New York: Grosset & Dunlap.

Long, William J. (1899) *Ways of Wood Folk.* First Series. Boston: Ginn.

McCarthy, D'Alton (1889) *D'Alton McCarthy's Great Speech; Delivered in Ottawa, December 12th, 1889.* Toronto: Equal Rights Association.

McClung, Nellie L. (1908) *Sowing Seeds in Danny.* Toronto: Ryerson Press, 1929.

McDougall, John (n.d.) *Forest, Lake, and Prairie. Twenty Years of Frontier Life in Western Canada—1842–62.* Toronto: Ryerson Press.

—— (1895) *"Indian Wigwams and Northern Camp-fires." A Criticism.* Toronto: William Briggs.

McGee, Thomas D'Arcy (1858) Preface. *Canadian Ballads, and Occasional Verses.* Montreal: John Lovell.

—— (1893) "Jacques Cartier." *Pleasant Hours* 1 July: 102.

Machar, Agnes Maule (1874) *For King and Country.* Toronto: Adam, Stevenson.

MacTavish, Margaret (1902) "A Young Canadian's Manly Stand: A True Story." *Canadian Boy* Aug.: 9–10.

Mair, Charles (1891) "A Ballad for Brave Women." *"Raise the Flag" and Other Patriotic Canadian Songs and Poems.* Toronto: Rose Publishing: 27–30.

Marquis, T.G., ed. (1893) *Stories from Canadian History Based Upon "Stories of New France."* Miss Machar and T.G. Marquis. Toronto: Copp Clark.

Miles, Henry H. (1870) *The Child's History of Canada.* Montreal: Dawson Brothers.

Moberly, T.E. (1891) "Destiny." *"Raise the Flag" and Other Patriotic Canadian Songs and Poems.* Toronto: Rose Publishing: 22.

Montgomery, L.M. (1908) *Anne of Green Gables.* Toronto: Scholastic, 2001.

Moodie, Susannah (1852) *Roughing it in the Bush, or, Life in Canada.* Toronto: McClelland, 1989.

Morrison, Llewellyn A. (1909) "A Chat with a Moose." *The Empire Annual For Boys*. London: Unwin Brothers: 211–15.

Muir, Alex (1891) "The Maple Leaf Forever." *"Raise the Flag" and Other Patriotic Canadian Songs and Poems*. Toronto: Rose Publishing: 12.

Nelson, E.G. (1891) "My Own Canadian Home." *"Raise the Flag" and Other Patriotic Canadian Songs and Poems*. Toronto: Rose Publishing: 23–4.

Nicholson, Byron (1902) *The French-Canadian: A Sketch of His More Prominent Characteristics*. Toronto: Bryant Press.

Odlum, E. (1901) "Letters Describing Western Canada." *Canadian Boy* May: 37.

Our Home (1896a) "Micmac Wonder Men." *Our Home* Dec.: 1–3.

—— (1896b) "Moving On." *Our Home* Aug.: 1–2.

—— (1896c) "The Story of "Twok"." *Our Home* Sept.: 45.

—— (1897) "They Like "Our Home"." *Our Home* March: 7.

Oxley, J. Macdonald (1895) *The Young Woodsman, or Life in the Forests of Canada*. New York: Nelson.

—— (1899) *Fife and Drum at Louisbourg*. Toronto: Musson.

—— [1903?] *In Paths of Peril: A Boy's Adventures in Nova Scotia*. Toronto: Musson.

Pickthall, Marjorie L.C. (1907a) "All Together." *Boys' World* 22 June: 1–8.

—— (1907b) "The Day of Victory." *Boys' World* 18 May: 1.

Prefontaine, R. (1901) "French and English Boys in Canada." *Canadian Boy* May: 16.

Rathborne, St. George (1912) *Canoe Mates in Canada or Three Boys Afloat on the Saskatchewan*. Chicago: M.A. Donahue & Co.

Revoil, Benedict (1887) *In the Bush and On the Trail. Adventures in the Forests of North America: A Book for Boys*. London: Nelson.

Roberts, Charles G.D. (1909) "The First Ploughing." *The Ontario Readers Fourth Book, Authorized by the Minister of Education*. Toronto: T. Eaton: 95–6.

Rose, James A. (1880) *A Boy's Vacation on the Great Lakes*. Providence: E.L. Freeman.

Rose Publishing (1891) Preface. *"Raise the Flag" and Other Patriotic Canadian Songs and Poems*. Toronto: Rose Publishing: iii–iv.

Seton, Ernest Thompson (1949) *The Best of Ernest Thompson Seton*. Ed. W. Kay Robinson. London: Hodder & Stoughton.

—— (1900) *The Biography of a Grizzly*. Toronto: Copp Clark.

—— (1903) *Two Little Savages: Being the Adventures of Two Boys Who Lived as Indians and What They Learned*. New York: Doubleday.

Siegfried, André (1907) *The Race Question in Canada*. London: Eveleigh Nash.

Smith, William Wye (1909) "Here's to the Land." *Public School Poetry Book Part II*. Eds J.F. White and W.J. Sykes. Morang's Literature Series. Toronto: Morang: 46.

Strang, Margaret (1902) "The Hero of Camp Roberts." *Canadian Boy* Aug.: 3–8.

The Times (1886) *Canada at the Colonial and Indian Exhibition*. Reprinted from the *The Times*. London.

Toronto Boy, A. (1880) *Canada First. An Appeal to All Canadians*. Toronto: Hunter, Rose.

Toronto Packing Co. [*c.* 1897a] "Is Canada A Land of Sunshine or Snow?" Advertisement: cover page.

—— [*c.* 1897b] "Miss Canada." Advertisement: 1.

—— [*c.* 1897c] "Prize Competitions." Advertisement: 16.

—— [*c.* 1897d] "The Children at Tea." Advertisement: 5–7.

Tracy, Frank Basil (1908) *The Tercentenary History of Canada: From Champlain to Laurier MDCVIII–MCMVIII*. Volume 3. Toronto: P.F. Collier.

Traill, Catharine Parr (1836) *The Backwoods of Canada: Being Letters from the Wife of an Emigrant Officer, Illustrative of the Domestic Economy of British America*. Toronto: Canadian Collection, Prospero, 2000.

—— (1852) *Canadian Crusoes. A Tale of the Rice Lake Plains*. Ed. Agnes Strickland. London: Arthur Hall, Virtue, & Co.

Walker, Jesse, Judge (1845) *Queenston, A Tale of the Niagara Frontier*. Buffalo: Steele's Press.

Weir, Arthur [*c.* 1897] "Our Lady of the Snows." *The Toronto Packing Co.* Advertisement: 2 3.

—— (1904) "Snowshoeing Song." *A Treasury of Canadian Verse*. 2nd ed. Ed. Theodore H. Rand. Toronto: Henry Frowde: 370–372.

White, William Thomas (1891) "The Battle of Queenston Heights." *"Raise the Flag" and Other Patriotic Canadian Songs and Poems*. Toronto: Rose Publishing: 17–20.

Williams, Valentine (1889) *The Captain of the Club; or, The Canadian Boy*. New York: Kenedy.

Willson, Beckles [c. 1897] "Canada's Comeliest City, Sun-Kissed Smiling Toronto." *The Toronto Packing Co.* Advertisement: 12–13.
—— [c. 1910] *Canada.* Romance of Empire Series. London: Caxton.
Young Canadian (1891a) "The Census." *Young Canadian.* 23 Sept.: 553.
—— (1891b) "$500.00." *Young Canadian* 23 Sept.: 552.
—— (1891c) "Its Aim." *Young Canadian* 23 Sept.: 552.
—— (1891d) "Its Features." *Young Canadian* 23 Sept.: 552.
—— (1891e) "The Secret of Success for Our Boys." *Young Canadian* 23 Sept.: 553.
Young, Egerton Ryerson (1895a) ""A Criticism" Reviewed by the Author, and the "Wigwams" Defended." *"Indian Wigwams and Northern Camp-fires." A Criticism.* John McDougall. Toronto: William Briggs: 13–22.
—— [1895b] "Life Among the Red Men of America." *The Missionary Review of the World.* [Toronto]: July.
—— (1896) *Three Boys in the Wild North Land: Summer.* New York: Abingdon, 1896.
Young, T.F. Preface (1887) *"Canada", and Other Poems.* Toronto: Hunter, Rose: iii.

Secondary Sources

Amtmann, Bernard (1976) *Early Canadian Children's Books 1763–1840. A Bibliographical Investigation into the Nature and Extent of Early Canadian Children's Books and Books for Young People.* Montreal: Amtmann, 1976.
—— (1977) *A Bibliography of Canadian Children's Books and Books for Young People 1841–1867/ Livres de l'Enfance & Livres de la Jeunesse au Canada 1841–1867.* Montreal: Amtmann.
Anderson, Benedict (1983) *Imagined Communities: Reflections on the Origin and Spread of Nationalism.* Rev. edn. London: Verso, 1995.
Applied History Research Group (2003) The University of Calgary. *Multimedia History Tutorials: Calgary and Southern Alberta.* 13 May 2003 http://www.ucalgary.ca/applied_history/tutor/calgary/mcdougall.html.
Arbuthnot, May Hill and Zena Sutherland (1972) Preface. *Children and Books.* 1947. 4th edn. Glenview: Scott, Foresman.
Armstrong, Christopher (1993) "Provincial Rights and Dominion-Provincial Relations." *Interpreting Canada's Past: Volume 2, Post-Confederation.* Ed. J.M. Bumsted. 2nd edn. Toronto: Oxford University Press: 43–63.
Arnason, David, ed. (1976) *Nineteenth Century Canadian Stories.* Toronto: Macmillan.
Atwood, Margaret (1995) *Strange Things: The Malevolent North in Canadian Literature.* Clarendon Lectures in English Literature 1991. Oxford: Clarendon.
Avery, Donald H. (1995) *Reluctant Host: Canada's Response to Immigrant Workers, 1896–1994.* Toronto: McClelland.
Baden-Powell, Lord (1939) *Scouting for Boys: A Handbook for Instruction in Good Citizenship Through Woodcraft.* Special Canadian edition. [Ottawa?]: [Boy Scouts Association?].
Bailey, Alfred Goldsworthy (1972) *Culture and Nationality: Essays by A.G. Bailey.* Toronto: McClelland.
Ballstadt, Carl, ed. (1975) *The Search for English-Canadian Literature: An Anthology of Critical Articles from the Nineteenth and Early Twentieth Centuries.* Toronto: University of Toronto Press.
Banks, Margaret A. (2001) *Sir John George Bourinot, Victorian Canadian: His Life, Times, and Legacy.* Montreal & Kingston, Queen's University Press.
Baucom, Ian (1999) *Out of Place: Englishness, Empire, and the Locations of Identity.* Princeton: Princeton University Press.
Beddoe, John (1912) *The Anthropological History of Europe: Being the Rhind Lectures for 1891.* Rev. edn. London: Paisley.
Berger, Carl (1969) "Imperialism and Nationalism, 1884–1914: A Conflict in Canadian Thought." *Readings in Canadian History: Post-Confederation.* Eds R. Douglas Francis and Donald B. Smith. 3rd ed. Toronto: Holt, 1990: 168–75. Rpt. of Introduction. *Imperialism and Nationalism, 1884–1912: A Conflict in Canadian Thought.* Ed. Carl Berger. Toronto: Copp Clark: 1–5.
Berton, Pierre (1974) "The Pacific Scandal." *The National Dream. The Last Spike.* Toronto: McClelland: 44–96.
Blenkhorn, Deborah (2002) "Machar, Agnes Maule." *Encyclopedia of Literature in Canada.* Ed. W.H. New. Toronto: University of Toronto Press: 690.

Bochinski, Hazel (2003) "The History of Thoroughbred Racing in Manitoba, Canada." *Second Running: Horse Racing History*. 24 June 2003 http://www.secondrunning.com/ Manitoba. htm.

Boone, Laurel (2002) "Roberts, Sir Charles G.D." *Encyclopedia of Literature in Canada*. Ed. W.H. New. Toronto: University of Toronto Press: 978–80.

Bratton, J.S. (1981)*The Impact of Victorian Children's Fiction*. London: Croom Helm, 1981.

—— (1989) "British Imperialism and the Reproduction of Femininity in Girls' Fiction, 1900–1930." *Imperialism and Juvenile Literature*. Ed. Jeffrey Richards. Manchester: Manchester University Press: 195–215.

Bumsted, J.M. (1993) "The West and Louis Riel." *Interpreting Canada's Past: Volume Two, Post-Confederation*. Ed. J.M. Bumsted. 2nd edn. Toronto: Oxford University Press: 64–74.

Burn, A.R. (1982) *The Pelican History of Greece*. Rev. edn. Markham: Pelican, Penguin Books.

Burns, Robin (1988) "McGee, Thomas D'Arcy." *The Canadian Encyclopedia*. 2nd edn.

Canadian Encyclopedia (2003) "My Own Canadian Home." 6 March 2003 http://www.th-marschall.de/music_history/december/texte/ 17.html.

Canadian Musical Heritage Society (2003) *Historical Anthology of Canadian Music*. 9 May 2003 http://collections.ic.gc.ca/cdnmus/compinfo/godfrey.html.

Careless, J.M.S. (1953) *Canada: A Story of Challenge*. British Commonwealth Series, Book II. Cambridge: Cambridge University Press.

Carleton County Home Page (2003) 6 March 2003 http://www.rootsweb.com/~nbcarlet/news-page45.htm.

Carr, E.H. (1981) *What is History? The George Macaulay Trevelyan Lectures Delivered in the University of Cambridge January–March 1961*. Markham: Penguin.

Citizenship and Immigration Canada (CIC) (2003) *Forging Our Legacy: Canadian Citizenship and Immigration 1900–1977*. 25 April 2003 http://www.cic.gc.ca/english/department/legacy/chap-5.html.

CBC Television (2003) *The National Transcripts* 12 March 2003 http://tv.cbc.ca/national/trans/T000917.html.

Currie, A.W. (1960) *Canadian Economic Development*. 1942. 4th edn. Toronto: Thomas Nelson.

Davin, Anna (1978) "Imperialism and Motherhood." *History Workshop Journal* 5: 9–65.

Dean, Misao (1990) "'You May Imagine My Feelings': Reading Sara Jeannette Duncan's Challenge to Narrative." *Re(dis)covering Our Foremothers: Nineteenth-Century Canadian Women Writers*. Ed. Lorraine McMullen. Ottawa: University of Ottawa Press: 187–97.

Diakiw, Jerry (1997) "Children's Literature and Canadian National Identity: A Revisionist Perspective." *Canadian Children's Literature* 87: 36–49.

Dixon, Bob (1977) *Catching Them Young 2: Political Ideas in Children's Fiction*. Pluto Press.

Doyle, James (1983) *North of America: Images of Canada in the Literature of the United States, 1775–1900*. Toronto: ECW Press.

—— (1990) "Canadian Women Writers and the American Literary Milieu of the 1890s." *Re(dis)covering Our Foremothers: Nineteenth-Century Canadian Women Writers*. Ed. Lorraine McMullen. Ottawa: University of Ottawa Press: 30–6.

Easterbrook, W.T. and Hugh G.J. Aitken (1956) *Canadian Economic History*. Toronto: Macmillan.

Egoff, Sheila A. (1967) *The Republic of Childhood: A Critical Guide to Canadian Children's Literature in English*. Toronto: Oxford University Press.

—— (1992a) "Canadian Girl's Annual." *Canadian Children's Books 1799–1939*. Special Collections and University Archives Division, University of British Columbia Library. 16 Feb. 2003 http://www.library.ubc.ca/edlib/egoffbib/ 1916.html.

—— (1992b) "Miles." *Canadian Children's Books 1799–1939*. Special Collections and University Archives Division, University of British Columbia Library. 22 April 2003 http:// www.library. ubc.ca/edlib/egoffbib/1870.html.

—— (1992c) "Young Canada." *Canadian Children's Books 1799–1939*. Special Collections and University Archives Division, U of British Columbia Library. 16 Feb. 2003 http:// www. library.ubc.ca/edlib/egoffbib/1896.html.

Egoff, Sheila and Judith Saltman (1990) *The New Republic of Childhood: A Critical Guide to Canadian Children's Literature in English*. Toronto: Oxford University Press.

Fee, Margery (1980) "Romantic Nationalism and the Child in Canadian Writing." *Canadian Children's Literature* 18/19: 46–61.

Foner, Eric (2002) Preface. *Who Owns History? Rethinking the Past in a Changing World*. New York: Hill and Wang.

Francis, R. Douglas (1993) "Changing Images of the West." *A Passion for Identity: An Introduction to Canadian Studies.* 2nd edn. Eds David Taras, Beverly Rasporich, and Eli Mandel. Scarborough: Nelson: 440–55.

Fraser, Blair (1967) *The Search for Identity: Canada, 1945–1967.* Toronto: Doubleday.

Frayne, June, Jennifer Laidley and Henry Hadeed, eds. (1975) *Print for Young Canadians: A Bibliographical Catalogue of Canadian Fiction for Children, From 1825–1920.* Toronto: Dumont.

Friesen, Gerald (1992) "Prairie Indians, 1840–1900: The End of Autonomy." *The Challenge of Modernity: A Reader on Post-Confederation Canada.* Ed. Ian McKay. Toronto: McGraw: 3–26.

Frye, Northrop (1982) *Divisions on a Ground: Essays on Canadian Culture.* Ed. James Polk. Toronto: Anansi.

Galway, Elizabeth (2001) "Fact, Fiction, and the Tradition of Historical Narratives in Nineteenth-Century Canadian Children's Literature." *Canadian Children's Literature* 27:2: 20–32.

—— (2004) "Poetical Patriotism: Canadian Children's Poetry and Nationalist Discourse in the Late Victorian Period." *Victorians Institute Journal: Poetry and the Colonies* 32: 37–62.

—— (2005) "'A Young Canadian's Manly Stand'; Canadian Nationalism and Anti-American Sentiment in Margaret MacTavish's Short Story." *Short Story: Tripping Across the 49th Parallel.* 13:1: 47–59.

Gammel, Irene and Elizabeth Epperly (1999) "L.M. Montgomery and the Shaping of Canadian Culture." *L.M. Montgomery and Canadian Culture.* Eds Irene Gammel and Elizabeth Epperly. Toronto: University of Toronto Press: 3–13.

Gerson, Carole (1980) "*The Snow Drop* and *The Maple Leaf:* Canada's First Periodicals for Children." *Canadian Children's Literature* 18/19: 10–23.

—— (1989) *A Purer Taste: The Writing and Reading of Fiction in English in Nineteenth-Century Canada.* Toronto: University of Toronto Press.

Groulx, Patrice (1998) *Pièges de la Mémoire: Dollard des Ormeaux, les Amérindiens et Nous.* Hull: Éditions Vents d'Ouest.

Haddour, Azzedine (2000) Introduction. *Colonial Myths: History and Narrative.* Manchester: Manchester University Press: 1–3.

Hannabuss, Stuart (1989) "Ballantyne's Message of Empire." *Imperialism and Juvenile Literature.* Ed. Jeffrey Richards. Manchester: Manchester University Press: 53–71.

Harvey, Kenneth J. (2000) "Who is Reading Canadian?" *National Post* 1 July: B12.

Hofstadter, Richard (1960) *Social Darwinism in American Thought.* Rev. edn. Boston: Beacon Press, 1960.

Johnston, Sheila M.F. (1997) *Buckskin and Broadcloth: A Celebration of E. Pauline Johnson–Tekahionwake 1861–1913.* Toronto: Natural Heritage.

Keith, W.J. (1990) "Third World America: Some Preliminary Considerations." *Studies on Canadian Literature: Introductory and Critical Essays.* Ed. Arnold E. Davidson. New York: MLA: 5–17.

Kennedy, Margaret (2003) "Lampman and the Canadian Thermopylae "At the Long Sault: May, 1660." *Research Web Site of the Faculty of Arts, University of Western Ontario: The Canadian Poetry Press.* 20 May 2003 http://www.arts.uwo.ca/canpoetry/cpjrn/vol101/ kennedy.htm.

Ketterer, David (1992) *Canadian Science Fiction and Fantasy.* Bloomington: Indiana University Press.

Kohn, Hans (1955) *Nationalism: Its Meaning and History.* Toronto: Van Nostrand-Anvil.

LaPierre, Laurier L. (1996) *Sir Wilfrid Laurier and the Romance of Canada.* Toronto: Stoddart.

"Lawrence Burpee and William Wallace" (2003) *Libraries Today.* University of Guelph. 11 July 2003 http://www.uoguelph.ca/~lbruce/photos/Burpewal.htm.

Lesnik-Oberstein, Karin (1999) "Essentials: What is Children's Literature? What is Childhood?" *Understanding Children's Literature: Key Essays from the International Companion Encyclopedia of Children's Literature.* Ed. Peter Hunt. London: Routledge: 15–29.

Levitt, J. (1970) "Henri Bourassa on Imperialism and Bi-culturalism, 1900–1918." *Readings in Canadian History: Post-Confederation.* Ed. R. Douglas Francis and Donald B. Smith. 3rd edn. Toronto: Holt, 1990. 175–89. Rpt. of Introduction. *Henri Bourassa on Imperialism and Bi-culturalism, 1900–1918.* Toronto: Copp Clark.

"McClung" (1988) *Time Links.* 8 December 2002 http://timelinks.merlin.mb.ca/referenc/dbooo3.htm.

McCormack, Ross (1993) "Immigration and Ethnicity." *Interpreting Canada's Past: Volume Two, Post-Confederation.* Ed. J.M. Bumsted. 2nd edn. Toronto: Oxford University Press: 331–51. Rpt. of "Cloth Caps and Jobs: The Ethnicity of English Immigrants in Canada 1900–1914." *Ethnicity, Power and Politics in Canada.* Ed. Jorgen Dahlie and Tissa Fernando. Toronto: 1981: 38–55.

McGillis, Roderick (1997) "Self, Other, and Other Self: Recognizing the Other in Children's Literature." *The Lion and the Unicorn* 21:2: 215–28.

MacGillivray, S.R. and J. Lynes (1996) "Paradise Ever Becoming: War of 1812 Narratives for Young Readers." *Canadian Children's Literature* 84: 6–16.

McKenzie, Ruth (1988) "Secord, Laura." *Canadian Encyclopedia.* 2nd edn. Edmonton: Hurtig: 1972.

MacLulich, T.D. (1988) *Between Europe and America: The Canadian Tradition in Fiction.* Oakville: ECW Press.

Malchow, H.L. (1996) "The Half-Breed as Gothic Unnatural." *The Victorians and Race.* Ed. Shearer West. Aldershot: Scolar: 101–11.

Mangan, J.A. (1989) "Noble Specimens of Manhood: Schoolboy Literature and the Creation of a Colonial Chivalric Code." *Imperialism and Juvenile Literature.* Ed. Jeffrey Richards. Manchester: Manchester University Press: 173–194.

Margerum, Eileen (2002) "The Brownies are on the Way." E-mail to the author. 21 March.

Meek, Margaret (2001) Preface. *Children's Literature and National Identity.* Stoke on Trent: Trentham: vii–xvii.

Moogk, Peter N. (1988) "Dollard Des Ormeaux, Adam." *Canadian Encyclopedia.* 2nd edn. Edmonton: Hurtig: 610.

Morgan, Wayne (2003) "Palmer Cox and His Brownies." *International Book Collectors Association.* 3 June 2003 http://www.rarebooks.org/fall98child.htm.

Morton, Desmond (2001) *A Short History of Canada.* 5th edn. Toronto: McClelland.

Moyles, R.G. (1995) "Young Canada: an index to Canadian materials in major British and American juvenile periodicals 1870–1950." *Canadian Children's Literature* 21:2: 6–64.

Moyles, R.G. and Doug Owram (1988) *Imperial Dreams and Colonial Realities: British Views of Canada, 1880–1914.* Toronto: University of Toronto Press.

New, W.H. *A History of Canadian Literature.* Montreal: McGill University Press.

—— (2002a) "Dunlop, William ('Tiger')." *Encyclopedia of Literature in Canada.* Ed. W.H. New. Toronto: University of Toronto Press: 323.

—— (2002b) "Lizars, Kathleen." *Encyclopedia of Literature in Canada.* Ed. W.H. New. Toronto: University of Toronto Press: 673.

—— (2002c) "Mair, Charles." *Encyclopedia of Literature in Canada.* Ed. W.H. New. Toronto: University of Toronto Press: 703.

—— (2002d) "Rand, Silas T." *Encyclopedia of Literature in Canada.* Ed. W.H. New. Toronto: University of Toronto Press: 936.

Page, Robert J.D. (1972) *Imperialism and Canada, 1895–1903.* Canadian History through the Press Series. Toronto: Holt.

"Palmer Cox" (2003) *Grand Lodge of British Columbia and Yukon.* 3 June 2003 http://www.freemasonry.bcy.ca/Brownies/cox_bio.html.

Parker, George L. (1985) *The Beginnings of the Book Trade in Canada.* Toronto: University of Toronto Press.

Partridge, Colin (1982) *The Making of New Cultures: A Literary Perspective.* Amsterdam: Rodopi.

Pearlstein, Steven (2000) "O Canada! A National Swan Song?" *Washington Post* 5 September: A01.

Perren, Susan (2001) "Forward Into Our Past." *Globe and Mail* 25 Aug.: D10—D13.

Pierce, Lorne (1924) *Fifty Years of Public Service: A Life of James L. Hughes.* Toronto: Oxford University Press.

Pomfret, Richard (1981) *The Economic Development of Canada.* Toronto: Methuen.

Prentice, Alison L. and Susan E. Houston, eds (1975) *Family, School and Society in Nineteenth-Century Canada.* Toronto: Oxford University Press.

Raffan, James and Bert Horwood, eds (1988) Introduction. *Canexus: The Canoe in Canadian Culture.* Toronto: Betelgeuse: 1–3.

Richards, Jeffrey, ed. (1989) *Imperialism and Juvenile Literature.* Manchester: Manchester University Press.

Rigney, Ann (1996) "Semantic Slides: History and the Concept of Fiction." *Konferenser 37: History Making: The Intellectual and Social Formation of a Discipline. Proceedings of an International Conference, Uppsala, September 1994.* Eds Rolf Torstendahl and Irmline Veit-Brause. Stockholm: KVHAA: 31–46.

Roberts, Kenneth G. (1988) "Lilly Dipping it Ain't." *Canexus: The Canoe in Canadian Culture.* Eds James Raffan and Bert Horwoods. Toronto: Betelgeuse: 107–121.

Rose, Jacqueline (1994) *The Case of Peter Pan or The Impossibility of Children's Fiction.* Rev. edn. London: Macmillan.

Rutherford, Paul (1982) *A Victorian Authority: The Daily Press in Late Nineteenth-Century Canada.* Toronto: University of Toronto Press.

Said, Edward W. (1994) *Culture and Imperialism.* New York: Vintage, Random House.

Salat, M. F. (1993) *The Canadian Novel: A Search for Identity.* New Delhi: B.R. Publishing.

Skelding, Hilary (2001) "Redefining the Angel in the House: Evelyn Everett-Green and the Historical Novel for Girls." *Women's Writing* 8: 119–38.

Smith, W.W. (2003) "The Poems of William Wye Smith." *The Brick Row Book Shop Inc.* 24 June 2003 http://www.brickrow.com/cgi-bin/br455.cgi/16021.

Sokoloff, Heather (2003) "History Textbook Tells Buried Military Past." *National Post* 12 May: A2.

Stevenson, Laura Alice (1967) "The Image of Canada in Canadian Children's Literature." Diss: University of Western Ontario.

Stott, Jon C. and Raymond E. Jones, eds (1988) *Canadian Books for Children: A Guide to Authors and Illustrators.* Toronto: Harcourt.

Strauss, Marina (2001) "U.S. Demands Trample Canadian Kids' Lit." *Globe and Mail* 1 June: M1.

Tausky, Thomas E. (2001) "Nationalism." *Encyclopedia of Literature in Canada.* W.H. New, ed. Toronto: University of Toronto Press: 795–800.

Taylor, M. Brook (1989) *Promoters, Patriots, and Partisans: Historiography in Nineteenth-Century English Canada.* Toronto: University of Toronto Press.

Taylor, Peter A. (2002) "Seton, Ernest Thompson." *Encyclopedia of Literature in Canada.* Ed. W.H. New. Toronto: University of Toronto Press: 1034–6.

Townsend, John Rowe (1976) *Written for Children: An Outline of English-language Children's Literature.* Markham: Penguin.

Trumpener, Katie (1997) *Bardic Nationalism: The Romantic Novel and The British Empire.* Princeton: Princeton University Press.

Turner, Margaret E. (1995) *Imagining Culture: New World Narrative and the Writing of Canada.* Montreal: McGill-Queen's University Press.

Vann, J. Don and Rosemary T. VanArsdel, eds (1996) *Periodicals of Queen Victoria's Empire: An Exploration.* Toronto: University of Toronto Press.

Walden, Keith (1992) "The Great March of the Mounted Police in Popular Literature, 1873–1973." *The Challenge of Modernity: A Reader on Post-Confederation Canada.* Ed. Ian McKay. Toronto: McGraw-Hill: 102–21.

Walker, Colin (2003) *A Virtual Boy Scout Museum: Boy Scout Stuff 1910–1919.* 17 Feb. 2003 http://www.boyscoutstuff.com/boyscout.html.

Warner, Marina (1994) *Managing Monsters: Six Myths of Our Time.* The 1994 Reith Lectures. London: Vintage.

Waterston, Elizabeth (1992) *Children's Literature in Canada.* Twayne's World Authors Series Children's Literature. Toronto: Macmillan.

Westfall, William (1993) "On the Concept of Region in Canadian History and Literature." *A Passion for Identity: An Introduction to Canadian Studies.* 2nd edn. Eds David Taras, Beverly Rasporich, and Eli Mandel. Scarborough: Nelson: 335–44.

Wheeler, Michael and Nigel Whiteley, eds (1992) *The Lamp of Memory: Ruskin, Tradition and Architecture.* Manchester: Manchester University Press, 1992.

Wien, Thomas (2003) Rev. of *Pièges de la Mémoire: Dollard des Ormeaux, les Amérindiens et Nous,* by Patrice Groulx. *Canadian Historical Review* Sept. 2000. 20 May 2003 http:// www.utp journals.com/product/chr/813/1memoire.html.

Wise, S.F. (1993) "The Ontario Political Culture: A Study in Complexities." *A Passion for Identity: An Introduction to Canadian Studies.* 2nd edn. Eds David Taras, Beverly Rasporich, and Eli Mandel. Scarborough: Nelson: 407–18.

Index

Acadians 120
adventure literature 19, 147, 152, 160–1;
    American authors of 25; as coming of
    age tales 165; English characters in 15,
    21–2; hunting in 163; masculinity in
    8–9
Alaska 12, 30, 54–5, 76
"All Together" 27
American periodicals 10, 19, 28, 121
American publishers 10, 24, 27, 67–8
American readership 28, 68
Anderson, Benedict 4, 173–4
Anglo-American Magazine, The 4, 19
animal stories 25, 29–30, 113–14, 134,
    153, 161
Anne of Green Gables 9, 36
annexation by the United States 28, 66,
    72, 177, 180; American views on 24,
    32; Canadians in favour of 175;
    impact of ties to Britain on 50;
    settlement of the West and 38;
Arctic 30–1, 34, 147–9, 155–6, 160
Atwood, Margaret 156, 159

Baden-Powell, Lord 69
"Ballad for Brave Women, A" 132–3
Ballantyne, R. M. 9, 21–3, 82, 128, 160
"Battle of Queenston Heights, The"
    140–2
Beddoe, John 83–5
Bender, Prosper 24
Bengough, J.W. 117–18, 149, 151
Berger, Carl 46–7
Boer War 12, 46–8, 56, 86, 92, 93
Bourassa, Henri 46, 54
Bourinot, Sir John George 4, 19
Boy Scout Movement 69, 113–14

Boyd, John 93, 175–6
Boy's Own Paper, The 14, 18–19, 32
Boy's Vacation on the Great Lakes, A
    29–30
Boys of the Empire 49
Boys' World, The 26–8, 109
Brantford Expositor, The 107
Bratton, J.S. 8
Briggs, William 105, 119, 123, 182
British North America Act, 1, 54, 68
Brock, Isaac 132, 140–2
"Brothers Awake!" 50
Brownies 137–40
Brownies Around the World, The 137
"Bruin" 15–19, 100, 157
Bryce, Reverend Dr. 101–2, 106
Butler's Rangers 98

Call of the Wild, The 30–1, 153–6, 160
Cameron, Rev. Charles J. 42
Campbell, Wilfred 145
Canada, and Other Poems 2
Canada Day *see* Dominion Day
Canada First. An Appeal to All Canadians
    55–6
Canada First movement 3, 179
*Canada First; or, Our New Nationality,
    An Address* 3
"Canada to England" 52–3
"Canada to Kipling" 149
Canadian Ballads, and Occasional Verses
    91
Canadian Born 112
*Canadian Boy: A Journal of Incident,
    Story and Self-Help, The* 40, 44, 48–9,
    92, 94
"Canadian Camping Song" 162–3

Canadian Crusoes: A Tale of the Rice Lake Plains 22
Canadian Girl's Annual, The 44
"Canadian Nationalism" 175–6
canoe 31–2, 68–72, 114, 128–9
Canoe Mates in Canada or Three Boys Afloat on the Saskatchewan 31–2
Canuck 31–2, 92
"Canuck" 98, 123–4, 126
Captain of the Club; or, The Canadian Boy, The 57, 60, 68, 69, 114, 159
"Captain Pepper, The Valiant Knight of the Laurentians" 134–6
Cartier, Jacques 88, 90–1, 120, 126–7, 135
Catholicism *see* religion
census 72–3
centralist perspective 33, 35–6, 41, 119
Charlton, Margaret 134–7, 140
"Chat with a Moose, A" 19
Child's History of Canada, The 88–9, 120
Chisholme, David 3
Christie, A.J. 3
Chums 14
citizenship 69, 90, 92, 181
civic nationalism 11
class: British class structure 15–17, 22, 57, 60, 63; educated class 4; working class 61, 176; middle class readership 7–8; and race 101–2, 103–4
Colonial and Indian Exhibition 21
colonists 9–10, 43, 82, 120
copyright law 67, 181
Cox, Palmer 137–40
Crockewit, John H. 18

daily press 76
"Day of Victory, The" 27
De Mille, James 36–7
Denison, Muriel 9
"Destiny" 46–7
"Disintegration of Canada, The" 24
Dollard des Ormeaux 122, 140, 182
Dominion Day 1, 27–8, 38, 52, 90–1, 168
Dominion School History 118–20
Doyle, James 10, 25–6, 30–32
Drummond, W.H. 142–3
Duncan, Sarah Jeannette 67
Dunlop, William 182

"Early Days in Canada" 127–8
Easterbrook, W.T. 66, 72
Edgar, James 162–3

education: books used in 8, 60, 71–2, 88, 119–20, 167; and children's literature 5–6; and Indian culture 112–13; Indian School 109–11; and nation-building 53, 127, 173–4; Public schools 6–7, 52, 68, 86–7; Separate schools 68
Egoff, Sheila 15, 44, 89, 95–6, 102–3, 134
Empire Annual for Boys, The 19
Epperly, Elizabeth 36–7
Everett-Green, E. 22, 80–2, 96–98, 129–31

fantasy 134, 137, 139–40
Fife and Drum at Louisbourg 36, 131s
"First Ploughing, The" 161
First World War 2, 53, 178
Forest Home; or, Life in the Canadian Wilds, The 15–19, 99, 156
Fort York 123
Foster, W.A. 3–4, 179
Francis, R. Douglas 38
Fraser, Blair 43
Fraser, Caroline 134–5
French and English: A Story of the Struggle in America 96, 129
"French and English Boys in Canada" 92–3
French and English relations: Boer War and 47–8; French Canadian views on 91–3; French views on 13; in historical fiction 11, 23, 80–2, 90–1, 129–32; in history textbooks 89, 119–21; negative depictions of 24, 87–8, 96; positive depictions of 82, 86, 91–2;
Frye, Northrop 34–5, 147, 153, 159–60, 162
Fur Country, The 14

Gammel, Irene 36–7
Geeson, Jean Earle 123
Geikie, John Cunningham 15
Gender 7, 11
"Glories of Canada, The" 38–9, 168–9
Godfrey, H.H. 91

Haggard, Rider 6
Half Hours in the Wide West Over Mountains, Rivers, and Prairies 20–1
Hannabuss, Stuart 9
Henty, G.A. 19, 80–1, 86, 180
"Here's to the Land" 167–8

"Hero of Camp Roberts, The" 45–6, 48
Home and Youth 38–9, 51, 91, 118–17, 127–8, 168–70
Hooker, Le Roy 124–6, 157–9
Hughes, James L. 52–3
Hughes, Thomas 69, 83
Huntingdon, Aimee 50–1

immigration 38, 41–2, 51, 73, 79
In Paths of Peril: A Boy's Adventures in Nova Scotia 36
In the Bush and On the Trail. Adventures in the Forests of North America: A Book for Boys 14
"Indian Summer" 145
Indian Wigwams and Northern Camp-fires 105
Indigenous population: unions between Europeans and 84–5, 97, 100–1, 103–4; Indian girl in fiction 108–9

Johnson, Pauline 28, 70–2, 95, 107–13
July 1 see Dominion Day

Kingston, W.H.G. 19, 21, 128–9, 147–8, 180
Kipling, Rudyard 6, 14, 134, 148–52
Klondike 30, 55, 153

"Land of the Maple, The" 91–2
Laurier, Sir Wilfrid 11–12, 46, 48, 76, 86, 181
Life in the Woods: A Boy's Narrative of the Adventures of a Settler's Family in Canada 15
Lily and the Cross: A Tale of Acadia, The 36
"Little Wolf-Willow" 28, 109–12
Lizars, Kathleen 127–8, 182
London, Jack, 30–1, 153–7, 160
Long, William J. 29
Louisbourg 36, 80, 131

Machar, Agnes 90, 121–2, 132
MacLulich, T.D. 2, 13, 41–2
MacTavish, Margaret 74–5, 181
Mair, Charles 132–3, 179
Malchow, H.L. 85, 97, 104
Manitoba School Crisis 7
"Maple Leaf Forever, The" 115
Marquis, T.G. 90, 113, 122–4, 140
masculinity 8–9, 85, 128

McCarthy, D'Alton 87–8
McClung, Nellie 37
McDougall, John 105–6, 108, 160
McGee, Thomas D'Arcy 90–1
McGillis, Roderick 114
Métis 38, 180
Miles, Henry H. 88–90, 113, 120–1, 124, 142
missionaries 103, 105, 110, 160
Missionary Review of the World, The 105
Montcalm 89, 98, 131, 139
Montgomery, L.M. 9, 36–7
Montreal 33, 36, 47–8, 79, 91–2, 94
Morrison, Llewellyn A. 19
Mountie see Royal Canadian Mounted Police
Moyles, Gordon 6, 14–15, 19–20, 29, 32, 40, 160
Muir, A. 115
"My Own Canadian Home" 61–3
mythology 122, 133, 140
Nelson, E.G. 61–3
Nicholson, Byron 90, 181
Northwest Mounted Police see Royal Canadian Mounted Police

Odlum, Professor E. 40–1
Old Fort at Toronto 1793–1906, The 123
Our Home 29, 40, 42, 113
"Our Lady of the Snows" (Rudyard Kipling) 14, 148–9
"Our Lady of the Snows" (Arthur Weir) 149–51
Owram, Doug 14–15, 32
Oxley, J.M. 36–7, 83–6, 100–1, 131, 163–5

Pen Pictures of Early Life in Upper Canada 98, 123–4, 126
Pickthall, Marjorie L.C. 26–8
Plains of Abraham 80, 139
"Play the Game" 49
Pleasant Hours 52–3, 91, 105
politicians 1–2, 33, 38, 40, 45–6, 53–4, 92
population numbers see census
pre-Confederation children's literature 179–80
Prefontaine, R. 79, 92–4, 181
propaganda 3, 60, 92
Public schools see education
Public School Cadet movement 53

Queenston, A Tale of the Niagara Frontier 25–6

Race Question in Canada, The 13
racism 10, 16, 22, 83, 94, 108, 175
railway 11, 18, 40, 70, 129
"Raise the Flag" and Other Patriotic Canadian Songs and Poems 124, 127, 132, 140, 157
Rand, Silas T. 113
Rathborne, St. George 31
religion 7, 89, 101, 105, 177; Catholicism 68, 80, 82, 87–8
Revoil, Benedict 14
Riel, Louis 12, 38, 180
Roberts, Charles G.D. 161–2, 174
Rose, James A. 29–30
Rousseau, Jean Jacques 175, 183
Royal Canadian Mounted Police 39–40, 109, 111–12

Said, Edward 97–100, 115–16, 138–9, 148
Saltman, Judith 15, 95–6
Sea, Forest and Prairie: Being Stories of Life and Adventure in Canada Past and Present, by Boys and Girls in Canada's Schools 113, 171
Secord, Laura 132–3
Seton, Ernest Thompson 95, 113–4, 161–2
Siegfried, André 13
Smith, William Wye 167
Snowflakes and Sunbeams: A Tale of the Far North 22
Snow-Shoes and Canoes; or, The Early Days of a Fur-Trader in the Hudson's Bay Territory 128
"Snowshoeing Song" 151
"Song My Paddle Sings, The" 70–1
Sowing Seeds in Danny 37
sports 32, 69–70, 113–14, 137, 165–6; *see also* canoe
Stories from Canadian History Based Upon "Stories of New France" 90, 121–3
Strang, Margaret 45, 48
"Strong Race Opinion: On the Indian Girl in Modern Fiction, A" 108

Taylor, M. Brook 116–18, 121, 123–4, 143–4

"This Fair Canadian Land" 75–6
Three Boys in the Wild North Land: Summer 102–3, 165, 167
Times, The 21–2
Tom Brown's Schooldays 69, 83
Toronto Packing Company 148, 151
Traill, Catharine Parr 8, 22, 134
Treaty of Washington 55–6
Trumpener, Katie 23
Two Little Savages: Being the Adventures of Two Boys Who Lived as Indians and What They Learned 113
Twok 29

United Empire Loyalists 98, 124–6, 157–8

Verchères, Madeleine 122, 142–4
Verne, Jules 14
Victoria Day 27

Walden, Keith 39
Walker, Jesse 25–6, 49
war: attitudes towards 58
War of 1812 25–6, 113, 123, 132–3, 138–9, 182
Ways of Wood Folk 29
Weir, Arthur 149–51
Westfall, William 34, 37
White, William Thomas 140–2
"Why Go to the United States?" 73
Williams, Valentine 57–61, 68–72, 159, 181
Winter Amid the Ice, A 14
Wise, S.F. 35–6
With Wolfe in Canada 180
Wolfe, James 81, 89, 130–2, 139–40, 180
Wonder Web of Stories, A 134
Woodcraft Movement 114

Young Canada: An Illustrated Magazine for the Young 44–5
Young Canadian, The 54, 60–1, 72–3
"Young Canadian's Manly Stand, A" 74
Young, Egerton Ryerson 10, 102–7, 165–7, 183
Young, Thomas Frederick 2
Young Woodsman, or Life in the Forests of Canada, The 82, 84, 100, 163–5
Yukon 30, 33, 55, 153

eBooks - at www.eBookstore.tandf.co.uk

A library at your fingertips!

eBooks are electronic versions of print books. You can store them onto your PC/laptop or browse them online.

They have advantages for anyone needing rapid access to a wide variety of published, copyright information.

eBooks can help your research by enabling you to bookmark chapters, annotate and use instant searches to find specific words or phrases. Several eBook files would fit on even a small laptop or PDA.

NEW: Save money by eSubscribing: cheap, online acess to any eBook for as long as you need it.

Annual subscription packages

We now offer special low cost bulk subscriptions to packages of eBooks in certain subject areas. These are available to libraries or to individuals.

For more information please contact webmaster.ebooks@tandf.co.uk

We're continually developing the eBook concept, so keep up to date by visiting the website.

www.eBookstore.tandf.co.uk